STILL WATERS

A Book of
Daily Devotional Meditations

by

James Alexander Stewart
D. D.

LAMPLIGHTER PUBLICATIONS
P. O. Box 1708 ● Alexandria, La. 71301

**Address all inquiries about
the Ministry of Dr. James
Stewart and Gospel Projects to:
GOSPEL PROJECTS
159 Davenport Road
Asheville, N. C. 28806**

PREFACE

It is with great joy that I send forth this book of Daily Devotions. They are especially chosen or written for missionaries and native Christians in foreign lands, to encourage and strengthen them in their witness for their blessed Lord.

As I have meditated, myself on each of these writings, my heart has been strangely warmed and drawn closer to God.

Mrs. Stewart and I feel that for a well-balanced Christian life, our spiritual food must have the ingredients of worship, challenge, comfort, inspiration, correction and Bible exposition. Sometimes we need a word of comfort. At other times we need a word of correction.

We would suggest earnestly that these devotional readings do not take the place of a definite, systematic, deep study of the Word itself.

Except each reader prayerfully ponders and meditates over the Scripture reference and comments for each day, he will receive no real deep blessing to his own soul. Even in the busy hustle of the modern atomic age, every one of us must fight to have what Samuel Chadwick called "the breathing spaces for the soul".

If, at the first reading, you find no blessing in the particular portion, please go back and read it quietly and prayerfully over again. We are sure that in this way God will speak intimately to your soul. As General William Booth said, "We must take time every day to pray the glory of God upon our soul or else we will become backsliders".

Your servant in our Soon-coming Lord,

James A. Stewart
Asheville N.C.

ACKNOWLEDGMENTS

Acknowledgment is gratefully given to the following for permission to use their material:

John Ritchie Publishers, Kilmarnock, Scotland — FROM EGYPT TO CANAAN by John Ritchie.

Loizeaux Brothers, Inc, New York 10, N. Y. — THE CONTINUAL BURNT OFFERING by H. A. Ironside.

Marshall, Morgan & Scott, London — MY UTMOST FOR HIS HIGHEST by Oswald Chambers.

Zondervan Publishing House, Grand Rapids, Mich. for the writings of F. J. Huegel.

Bible Truth Depot, Swengel, Pa. for the writings of A. W. Pink.

The Alliance Witness, New York 36, N.Y. for the writings of A. W. Tozer.

McCall Barbour Publishers, George IV Bridge, Edinburgh, Scotland for the poems of J. Danson Smith.

The writings of Samuel Logan Brengle are published by the Salvation Army Publishing House.

The Overcomer magazine of England for the writings of J. Penn-Lewis.

The writings of the various men and women of God in this book may be procured by ordering from your own local Christian Book Store. As some of the writings have come to us in clippings it has not always been possible for us to trace the source of from what book it was extracted. For this we beg indulgence.

J. A. S.

January 1

THY GOD REIGNETH. — Isaiah 52: 7

THOU STANDEST ON THE THRESHOLD

Thou standest on the threshold of days which are
*   unknown;*
Thou standest at the gateway of paths unmapped,
*   unshewn;*
But God Himself is with thee—thy Saviour, Keeper,
*   Friend;*
And He will not forsake thee, nor leave thee to life's
*   end.*

Thou standest, and thou askest — "What have the days
*   in store?"*
He answereth thee "Blessing! yea, blessing more and
*   more."*
What form that blessing taketh thou mayest not yet
*   know,*
But, blessing upon blessing, He waiteth to bestow.

Thou waitest — and He waiteth: He waiteth now to
*   bless;*
To link His sovereign greatness to human helplessness;
To shew, through all life's journey, His tireless care for
*   thee;*
To fill thy incompleteness with His sufficiency.

Thou pausest on the threshold — enfolded lies the year;
But, with God's arms beneath thee, there is no cause
*   for fear;*
Through shadowed days or sunlit — whate'er the year
*   may bring,*
This fact may be thy comfort — God reigns in every-
*   thing.*

— *J. Danson Smith*

Bless the Lord, O my soul!

9

January 2

TAKE NO THOUGHT FOR THE MORROW.
— Math. 6: 34

That means, "Be not anxious regarding the morrow".
*In the first place, we do not know whether we shall
see the morrow.* If we see the morrow, our Heavenly
Father is just the same as to love, as to power, as to readiness to help us as ever He was; He is not changed on
the coming day, and therefore as He has been mindful
of us to-day, He will be mindful of us to-morrow. If the
morrow come, well, with it, our Father is in existence.
His love is not changed; His power is the same as ever
it was.

*Therefore, under no circumstances whatever should
the children of God be anxious.* They may be very earnest in prayer, they may greatly exercise faith, but under
no circumstances should they be anxious, for this anxiety
invariably indicates a want of real trust in God, for real
trust in God allows no anxiety.

In prospect of the future we should hold it fast, "I
have a Father in Heaven who loves me with an eternal,
unchanging love. He has given me already the greatest
proof of His love — the only begotten Son. And if He
has supplied my necessities when young and able to work,
most assuredly will He do so when I am advanced in
years and unable to work. He will not forsake me." The
peace that comes thus to the soul cannot be described. It
must be known from experience in order to be able to
enter into it.

"Sufficient unto the day is the evil thereof." *God
does not give grace for next week, but for the day;* not
for the day after to-morrow, but for the day; not even
for the coming day, but for the day. We have to live by
the day, and to look to the Lord by the day, and we
shall be helped by the day.

Oh! how great the importance to keep this before us.
Our business is to live for God to-day. Live by the day,

10

live by the day, live by the day, and God will be with you. Living thus brings peace beyond description, while not living so brings wretchedness and misery for the whole life.

— *George Muller*

January 3

THEREFORE IF ANY MAN BE IN CHRIST, HE IS A NEW CREATURE. — II Cor. 5: 17

When a convicted sinner truly repents of his sin and receives Christ as his Lord and Saviour, a revolutionary change takes place in his heart and life. He is raised from the dead. He passes from death unto life, by the quickening power of the Holy Ghost, through the supernatural Word. He is delivered from the authority of darkness and is transplanted into the Kingdom of God's dear Son. He is made fit to become partaker of the inheritance of the saints in light. He is now a child of God, having been supernaturally born again by the Spirit into God's Family. Having been incorporated into Christ, he is a new creation. *As a new creature in Christ he experiences the holy aspirations after God, for he has a propensity for holiness.* All things have become new. He has a new set of appetites, and now he walks in newness of life. Because he has a new-found Saviour, he has a new Name, a new Family, a new Father, a new Book, a new Song, a new Guide, and a new King. As he is now walking in the new narrow way, he is walking in newness of life in a new direction. According to Ephesians, the second chapter, the whole course of his life has been directed into a new channel: "And you hath He quickened, who were dead in trespasses and sins, wherein *in times past ye walked according to the course of this world ... according to the prince of the power of the air,* the spirit that now worketh in the children of disobedience" (vv. 1, 2). The believer is no more a stranger

.

11

and a foreigner, but a fellow-citizen with the saints in the household of God, through the Spirit. Truly, "old things have passed away, and all things have become new"!

— *James A. Stewart*

Oh Loving Father! I thank Thee for these holy aspirations after Thyself. Amen!

January 4

THOU, OH GOD, HAST PROVED US: THOU HAST TRIED US, AS SILVER IS TRIED. — Psalm. 66:10

Our Father who seeks to perfect His saints in holiness knows the value of the refiner's fire. It is with the most precious metals that the assayer takes most pains, and subjects them to hot fires, because only such fires melt the metal, and only molten metal releases its alloy, or takes perfectly its new form in the mould. The old refiner never left his crucible, but sat down by it, lest there should be one excessive degree of heat to mar the metal, and so soon as, skimming from the surface the last of the dross, he saw his own face reflected, he put out the fire.

— *A. T. Pierson*

THE REFINER'S FIRE

He sat by a fire of seven-fold heat,
As He watched by the precious ore,
And closer He bent with a searching gaze
As He heated it more and more.

He knew He had ore that could stand the test,
And He wanted the finest gold
To mold as a crown for the King to wear,
Set with gems with a price untold.

12

So He laid our gold in the burning fire,
Though we fain would have said Him "Nay",
And He watched the dross that we had not seen,
And it melted and passed away.

And the gold grew brighter and yet more bright;
But our eyes were so dim with tears,
We saw but the fire — not the Master's hand —
And questioned with anxious fears.

Yet our gold shone out with a richer glow,
As it mirrored a Form above
That bent o'er the fire, though unseen by us,
With a look of ineffable love.

Can we think that it pleased His loving heart
To cause us a moment's pain?
Ah, no! but He saw through the present cross
The bliss of eternal gain.

So He waited there with a watchful eye,
With a love that is strong and sure,
And His gold did not suffer a bit more heat
Than was needed to make it pure.

— *Selected*

January 5

WERE NOT OUR HEARTS BURNING IN US
WHILE HE WAS TALKING TO US ON THE WAY,
MAKING CLEAR TO US THE HOLY WRITINGS.
— Luke 24: 32, Basic English N. T.

The Emmaus experience can be ours today. Notice that
this heart-glow came though the exposition of the Old
Testament writings by the risen Redeemer Himself. I
believe the desperate need of the hour is for Bible study.
Hymn singing will warm your heart, but the blessing

will not last unless the Spirit of God unfolds before your wondering gaze the beauty of our Lord. When we have a delightful view of the Majestic Redeemer, then our hearts will burst forth into singing.

— *James A. Stewart*

Oh, what a Bible-reading have we here,
Not barren theory — musty, dry and drear —
But Christ, the "altogether lovely", full in view,
Himself the preacher, text and sermon too.

HALLELUJAH! What a SAVIOUR!

January 6

GO YE, SACRIFICE TO YOUR GOD IN THE LAND. — Exodus 8: 25

This looks very gracious, it is a considerable stretch on Pharaoh's part. It thinly veils the treachery of the devil. The aim of this piece of strategy is to destroy the very object of the people's redemption, and their testimony to the true God. But Moses detected the plot, and immediately resisted it with the plain word of Jehovah — "We will go *three day's journey* into the wilderness, and sacrifice to our God *as He shall command us*" (Exod. viii. 27).

The word of God was definite, it could not, therefore, be compromised. The distance out of Egypt, where the altar of Jehovah was to stand, was measured by Jehovah Himself, and Moses could have no hand in lowering the standard. He presents Jehovah's claims in full, in the face of the enemy.

Here then is one of the wiles of the devil. If he cannot, as a roaring lion, hinder the deliverance of a sinner by open opposition, he will endeavour as a subtle serpent to keep him sacrificing in the land. And has he not succeeded? Satan has no objection to any man adopting

14

a religion that keeps him as a decent worldling, "sacrificing in the land." Oh no, he will even give such his patronage and applause. The world will speak well of him; he will be caressed and admired by all. Wordly religion embraces everything, and condemns nothing but wholeheartedness for Christ. It is conducted *"in the land"* on the principles of the world's charity, and being of the world, the world loves well its own. But let the call of God to march "three day's journey" into the wilderness be insisted on — that is, the full length of the Cross, and, what followed on "the third day", the resurrection of Christ, to lead the believer — and Satan will move hell to hinder that. *He hates an out-and-out separation to God.* Full well he knows, that he who apprehends that he is dead and risen with Christ, bids farewell to him, his empire, his service, and his land for ever.

Professing Christian, have you taken "the three day's journey out of Egypt?" Are you separate from the world? Remember, you cannot bear a true testimony for God, or worship Him in truth, and at the same time have fellowship with worldlings, either in their sinful pleasures, or in their religion. "Ye *cannot* serve God and Mammon."

The call of God is clear — "Come out from among them and be ye separate, saith the Lord" (2 Cor. 6: 17).
— *John Ritchie*

January 7

And he arose, and did eat and drink, and went in the strength of that meat forty days and forty nights unto Horeb the Mount of God. And he came thither unto a cave, and lodged there; and, behold, the word of the Lord came unto him, and He said unto him, What doest thou here, Elijah? — I Kings 19: 8—9
There is many a chosen servant of God today sitting in a cave of self-pity and despondence, hugging his grievances to his bosom, when he should be carrying on mighty exploits for God in the front line of the battle.

15

HE NEEDS YOU!

My dear fellow-Christian, sitting lonely in your cave today, has the still small voice of the Spirit spoken to you, urging you to come out and take your stand once again before the Lord on the Mount? Then hasten to obey. He wants to refit you for the battle; to renew your vision. He will give you a new outlook and renew your commission. He will bring you into a new fellowship with Himself, and reveal to you the thousands of other saints who, like yourself, have been walking the lonely pathway of fatih and obedience. He is able to banish your fears and to make the crooked paths straight. *He desperately needs you to take your place once again in the thick of the battle.*

— *Ruth Stewart*

Go, labor on; spend, and be spent, —
Thy joy to do the Father's will;
It is the way the Master went,
Should not the servant tread it still?

Go, labor on; 'tis not for nought;
Thy earthly loss is heavenly gain;
Men heed thee, love thee, praise thee not;
The Master praises, — what are men?

Toil on, and in thy toil rejoice;
For toil comes rest, for exile home;
Soon shalt thou hear the Bridegroom's voice,
The midnight peal, Behold, I come!

— *H. Bonar*

January 8

AND THEY WERE ALL FILLED. — Acts. 2: 4

Pentecost was the initial day of a new order. It was a sample opening page of a new book entitled, "The Acts of the Holy Ghost", or "The Autobiography of the Holy

16

Spirit." It was a new beginning — the commencement of a new spiritual life, a new relationship, a new fellowship, a new authority, and a new power. "Not yet" was changed to "This it that" (John 7, 39; Acts 2, 16). This new life created a new fellowship of men, a new race incorporated into Christ (I Cor. 12, 13; II Cor. 5, 17; I Peter 2, 9). Mantled with unction, they went everywhere preaching the Word. Theirs was a spontaneous evangelism. They did not need to conduct clinics or conventions concerning the task of evangelism. Methinks they held no large conferences to stir the believers to evangelize the lost. Oh, no! such a notion never entered their heads. *Saturated with the Spirit, filled with the love of Christ, bubbling over with their new-found joy, they crusaded for Christ. It was as natural as breathing to them.* "We cannot but speak the things which we have seen and heard." It was spiritual combustion! So great was their enthusiasm and aggressiveness that the enemy hurriedly called a council meeting with the theme, "How can we stop this Gospel epidemic?" ("that it spread no further" Acts 4, 15—17). The more they were persecuted and insulted, the more dynamic they became. Soon they were accused of being "these that have turned the world upside down" (Acts 17, 6). *Glory! they abode in the Pentecostal fervor, preached the Pentecostal Gospel, lived the Pentecostal life, and garnered a Pentecostal harvest!*

— *James A. Stewart*

January 9

AS THOU HAST SENT ME INTO THE WORLD, EVEN SO HAVE I ALSO SENT THEM INTO THE WORLD. — John 17: 18

Wonderful statement is this, anticipatory of what He says in 20: 21: "as my Father hath sent me, so send I you." How evident that Christ *has* given us *His* place — *His* place of acceptance on high, His place of witness here below! But those who witness here below have a special character: it is as those belonging *to Heaven* that we are called upon to bear testimony in the world. Christ did not belong to the world, He was the Heavenly One come down to earth; so we, as identified with Him, as partakers of the heavenly calling, are now commissioned to represent Him here below. What a proof that we *are not* "of the world!" *It is only as first "chosen out of the world", that we can be "sent into the world!"* That this is not limited to the apostles is clear from 1 John 4: 17, which is speaking of *all* believers — "as *he* is, *so* are we in this world."

— *Arthur Pink*

Wonderful condescension! Oh that I might be a true ambassador of Christ today.

January 10

BUT OF HIM ARE YE IN CHRIST JESUS, WHO OF GOD IS MADE UNTO US WISDOM, AND RIGHTEOUSNESS, AND SANCTIFICATION, AND REDEMPTION. — 1 Cor. 1: 30

As we see in 1 Corinthians 1: 30, the Lord Jesus is not only the believer's Justifier but also his Sanctifier:
The unregenerated man needs not only pardon from the guilt of his sin, but cleansing from the defilement of it. The guilty sinner is redeemed that he might become holy. Bishop Ryle has warned us, "Boast not of Christ's work for you unless you can show unto us the Spirit's work in you."

C. H. Spurgeon has stated clearly, with his usual scriptural sanity: "Dear Friend, salvation would be a sadly incomplete affair, if it did not deal with the whole part of our ruined estate. We want to be purified as well as pardoned. Justification without sanctification would not be salvation at all. It would call the leper clean, and leave him to die of his disease; it would forgive the

18

rebellion, and allow the rebel to remain an enemy of his King. It would remove the consequence but overlook the cause, and this would leave an endless and hopeless task before us. It would stop the stream for a time, but leave an open fountain of defilement which would sooner or later break forth with increased power."

What strange kind of salvation does the seeking sinner desire who cares not for holiness?

What strange kind of salvation does the seeking sinner desire who has no inclination to separate himself from sin and the world?

What strange kind of salvation does the seeking sinner desire who rebels against the lordship of Christ?

What strange kind of salvation does the seeking sinner desire who does not intend to become a bond-slave of Jesus Christ?

— James A. Stewart

Oh dear Reader! do you long to be more holy?

January 11

WITHOUT SHEDDING OF BLOOD IS NO REMISSION. — Heb. 9:22

The importance of the death of Christ in His earthly story is indicated by the proportion of space given to it there. If we remember that the Passion Week is a period of seven or eight days in the thirty-five years of our Lord's life on earth, we shall be able better to appreciate the emphasis in the Gospels on His death and resurrection. This week occupies eight of Matthew's twenty-eight chapters, nearly one-third of the whole. It occupies three of Mark's sixteen chapters, about one-fifth of the whole. It occupies five-and-a-half of Luke's twenty-four chapters, nearly one-fifth of the whole. And it occupies nine of John's twenty-one chapters nearly one-half of the whole. That is, of the eighty-nine chapters in the Gospels, twenty-five and a half are about the last week of Jesus' life; more than one-third of the entire record is given to one week in a life of nearly thirty-five years! The significance of this is that the dominating factor and feature of Christ's earthly life was not His entrance into the world; not His sinless character; not His wonderful teaching; not His miraculous works, and not His peerless example, but *His death and resurrection.* The incarnation and the perfect life without the death and the resurrection would be our greatest condemnation; because 'without shedding of blood there is no remission'

— *W. Graham Scroggie*

Oh dear friend! are you trusting the merit of the sacrificial work of Christ *alone* for your salvation?

January 12

BE FILLED WITH THE SPIRIT. — Eph. 5: 18

Potentially, every believer is filled with the Holy Ghost at the threshold of his new life in Christ but only a few seem to know and appropriate this blessing at the time. The Holy Spirit is the executive member of the Godhead to apply the redemptive blessings of Christ to the individual believer. It is only as the believer allows the Holy Spirit to take full possession of his life that he will be able to utilize and enjoy all the provisions which are his for his Christian life. Alas, as the result of not being filled with the Spirit there are many poverty-stricken saints being deprived of untold riches in Christ which the indwelling Spirit would minister to them, were He but permitted to fill them. The illimitable resources and immeasurable power which are potentially theirs in Christ lie idle and unused, waiting to be realized in the life by the infilling and controlling presence of the Spirit of Christ.

God's power toward us is declared in the letter to the Ephesians to be none other than that transcending might of God by which Christ was raised from the dead, exalted and enthroned at the Father's right hand. As the deliverance out of Egypt was a token of God's power on behalf of His covenant people, so Christ's resurrection exemplifies the exceeding greatness of the divine potency which is available in the Holy Spirit for the life and work of the Christian: "the exceeding greatness of His power to us-ward who believe, according to the working of His mighty power, which He wrought in Christ when He raised Him from the dead, and set Him at His own right hand in the heavenly places" (Eph. 1: 19—21). Think of all the possibilities and potentialities of the Spirit-filled life! How sad that many of God's dear people are willing to sell their birthright privilege for a mess of pottage!

Oh that God would send revival by the mighty power of His Spirit and deliver us from second-rate Christianity!

Bow now dear reader, and claim your inheritance.

— *James A. Stewart*

January 13

THE FRUIT OF THE SPIRIT IS LOVE. — Gal. 5: 22

I ask with these passages open before us, "Are we holy and yet not kindly affectioned? Is it possible to be holy and yet not prayerful? Is it possible to claim holiness and yet not to be forgiving? If corrupt communications proceed out of one's mouth, is it possible then to be holy? If bitterness, if anger, if malice is present, is it possible to be holy? If I am a young person—and I say this for the few who are here—is it possible to claim holiness and yet not be rightly related with parents, inconsiderate to them, disobedient to them?"

I find nothing in the whole of Scripture—I confess this for myself—so utterly pulverizing and so thoroughly crushing as the reading of 1 Cor. 13. That reduces one infinitely more than the Law, as it seems to me. Just because it has become so familiar, let me read it to you in a modern translation, William Pitfield's, not perhaps that this is better than the old. I love the dignity of the archaic phrases of the Authorized Version, but let us lift

21

this passage out of the archaic setting into the language of the twentieth century.

"Love patiently persits, is tender; love is not envious, is not pompous, not ill-mannered, not irritable; makes no personal demands; does not impute evil motives; has no taste for anything impure, but a responsive delight in all that is genuine. Love shelters all things; is always trustful, always sanguine, always composed. Love can never at any time lose its colour, nor fade away."

I was meditating on this very chapter when a letter came from China from a young doctor to whom God had spoken through a senior missionary, on this chapter. In this letter he writes, "I have been taught to put Jesus Christ, who is incarnate love, in this chapter." Let me read it to you again with that revision.

"Jesus Christ patiently persists, is tender; Jesus Christ is not envious, is not pompous, not ill-mannered, not irritable. He makes no personal demands; He does not impute evil motives, has no taste for anything impure. He has a responsive delight in all that is genuine. Jesus Christ shelters all things; is always trustful, always sanguine, always composed. Jesus Christ can never at any time lose His colour, nor fade away."

— *Fred Mitchell*

January 14

YE SORROW NOT, EVEN AS OTHERS.

— I. Thess. 4:13

I would not have you grieve for me today
Nor weep beside my vacant chair,
Could you but know my daily portion here
You would not, could not, wish me there.

I know now why He said "Ear hath not heard"
I have no words, no alphabet
Or even if I had, I dare not tell
Because you could not bear it yet.

22

So only this — — I am the same, tho changed,
Like Him! A joy more rich and strong
Than I had dreamed any heart could hold
And all my life is one glad song.

Sometimes when you are talking to our Lord
He turns and speaks to me — — Dear Heart
In that rare moment you and I are just
The distance of a word apart.

And so, my beloved ones, do not grieve for me
Around the family board today
Instead, rejoice, for we are one in Him
And so I am not far away.

— *Martha Snell Nicholson*

January 15

NOT AS THOUGH I HAD ALREADY ATTAINED,
EITHER WERE ALREADY PERFECT: BUT I FOL-
LOW AFTER, IF THAT I MAY APPREHEND THAT
FOR WHICH ALSO I AM APPREHENDED OF
CHRIST JESUS. — Phil. 3: 12.

My soul! take the apostle for an example in thy medi-
tation. Here he freely and fully confesseth himself, after
all his attainments in the life of grace, to be far short of
what he longed to attain. And observe the aim of the
apostle: all his pursuit, and all his desire was, like an
arrow shot at a mark, to apprehend Christ, as Christ had
first apprehended him: to grasp Jesus, as the Lord Jesus
had held, and did hold him. *Happy desire! happy pur-*
suit! and blessed mark of grace! For let the Lord have
given out to the soul ever so largely, there is more to give
out, more to be received, more to be enjoyed. And the
Holy Ghost, who is leading a child of God out of himself, more and more, to lead him more and more to the
enjoyment of Jesus, is sweetly training that precious soul,

and advancing him to the highest lessons in the school of grace. Paul felt this, when he cried out, "Not that I have already attained, either were already perfect." To be sure not: for if we thought we had enough of Christ it would be more than half conviction that we had nothing at all. *Now, my soul, learn from Paul, in what the life of God in the soul consists: to be always pursuing the person of Jesus for the farther enjoyment of him; never sitting down satisfied with what is already attained; but "pressing (as the apostle did) towards the mark, for the prize of the high calling of God in Christ Jesus:"* in short, to make Christ the sum, the substance, the all of every desire; and ever to keep in remembrance that the more we receive the more Jesus hath to impart; the more he gives out the more he is glorified; and, like some rich spring, the oftener we receive from him the more rich and full he flows: Oh, the blessedness of such a state! Precious Lord! grant me this felicity, that, like Paul, I may say, 'Not as though I had already attained:" but all my longings are, so to apprehend and hold fast Christ Jesus, as Christ hath apprehended and doth hold me fast.

— *Robert Hawker*

January 16

It will be for Him, the truth-giving Spirit, when He comes, to guide you into all truth. He will not utter a message of His own; He will utter the message that has been given to Him; and He will make plain to you what is still to come. And He will bring honour to Me, because it is from Me that He will derive what He makes plain to you. I say that He will derive from Me what He makes plain to you, because all that belongs to the Father belongs to Me. — John 16: 13—15. — *Knox*

The Spirit is the custodian of all things belonging to Christ; to Him is committed the cause and credit of the Son of God. He is well entitled to take of what is Christ's especially considering that it is what the Father has that is Christ's, because He Himself is a divine Person, co-equal in power and glory with the Son. He is also qualified and able to receive what is Christ's because, as a member of the Trinity, He was in the great Council Chamber in the by-gone eternity when the glorious plan of redemption was conceived. Also He is a blessed Person whom Christ loves and can trust in this great undertaking. The Saviour sets His stamp of approval alone upon the blessed Spirit. As the Father could say, "This is my beloved Son, in whom I am well pleased", so the Redeemer was satisfied and pleased with the work of the Spirit in His own ministry. *Yes, and only the Spirit knows the "all things" of Christ!*

The resources at the disposal of the Holy Spirit are boundless and eternal. The perfect knowledge possessed by the Spirit of our Lord's mediatorial work placed Him in a position infinitely superior to all others as a witness and testifier to Jesus Christ. We dare to affirm that the Holy Spirit only could entirely glorify the Son of God. In reading carefully and prayerfully the precious prophecies of the Redeemer in the Upper Room, we see standing out before us the fact that the whole sum of the Spirit's ministry would culminate in the glory of the beloved Son. "He shall glorify Me." The Spirit glorifies Christ by taking of the things of Christ and revealing them unto us. *All the gifts and graces of the Spirit, all the preaching and the writings of the apostles under the influence of the Spirit, the tongues and the miracles, were to glorify Christ.* As J. C. Hare has clearly stated, *"The Comforter, in every part of His three-fold work, glorifies Christ.* In convincing us of sin, He convinces us of the sin of not believing in Christ. In convincing us of righteousness, He convinces us of the righteousness of Christ: of that righteousness which was made manifest in Christ going to the Father, and which He received to bestow on all who would believe in Him. And lastly, in convincing

25

of judgment, He convinces us that the prince of the world was judged in the life and by the death of Christ."

— *James A. Stewart*

Oh God! We bless Thee for the ministry of the Holy Spirit.

January 17

RABBONI! — John 20: 16

We notice that, this exclamation was called forth by the vision of the Risen Lord.

This word is not like the "Rabbi" of Nicodemus when he said, "Rabbi, we know that thou art a teacher come from God"; nor is it like the adoring exclamation of Nathaniel, "Rabbi, Thou art the Son of God; Thou art the King of Israel." *In this word there is a deeper adoration, and a more overwhelming wonder.* Remember, Mary had gone to the sepulchre to anoint the dead body of Jesus. She had found the stone rolled away from the sepulchre. She had seen Peter and John enter the sepulchre, and had heard their report of the clothes lying there; but that Jesus had risen, that her Lord was living, she did not believe. When the angels asked her, "Woman, why weepest thou?" she replied, "Because they have taken away my Lord, and I know not where they have laid Him." Even when she spoke to Jesus supposing Him to be the gardener, she said, "Sir, if thou have borne Him hence, tell me where thou hast laid Him, and I will take Him away." Up till that moment her eyes were blinded. But Jesus said to her, "Mary!" Then the scales fell from her eyes. The vision of the Risen Lord in His glory burst upon her, and that was what called from the depths of her soul, as she fell at His feet, the adoring cry, "Rabboni."

And as it was with Mary, so it must be with us. Until the Resurrection has become a reality to us, we can never rightly utter this word. The sight of Jesus on the Cross will not call it forth. That will call forth wonder, love, amazement. That will bring us peace from the burden of our sins, and fill our hearts with gratitude. *But it is the Risen Christ, the Christ who has been proved to be the Son of God with power, according to the Spirit of holiness by the resurrection from the dead, who becomes the accepted Lord of life.*

— *MacGregor*

May I catch a real glimpse of the risen Redeemer today!

January 18

STUDY TO SHEW THYSELF APPROVED UNTO GOD. — II Tim. 2: 15

There are Scriptures that I read at stated seasons. One of my earliest attempts at real Bible-study was to try to write out in order the doings and sayings of our Lord in the week of His Passion, and I go over those passages always in the Sacred Week. There are similar passages for Advent and other festivals of the Christian year. The first thing I do with a new Bible is to mark the passages in St. John in which our Lord makes His promise of the Paraclete, and those I read always between Easter and Pentecost, and then I find my inner chamber becomes my Lord's Upper Room.

There are three Sriptures that I have read on fixed days of the week for more than forty years. Every Sunday morning I read the fifth chapter of Revelation, and every Sunday night the seventh chapter from verse 9. Why do I do this? Sunday is the great day of my week. I preach other days, but there is one day in seven that is specially the Lord's Day. It is a day devoted to worship and the ministry of the Word. To me is given the responsibility of intercessor and prophet, teacher and evangelist. I have to represent Christ, preach Christ, plead for Christ. *For all this I need the vision of Christ,*

*and nowhere do I find the vision as He is there revealed
in the midst of the Throne, in the midst of the Redeemed,
in the midst of the Angels, and in the midst of Creation.*
I can face the day when I have beheld His glory, and
say Amen, Hallelujah! in His presence. At night I come
back to the vision of His ultimate triumph and commit
the day unto Him and rest my heart within the veil.

— *Samuel Chadwick*

January 19

THIS IS MY BELOVED SON. — II Pet. 1: 17
HIS SON. — Heb. 1: 1—2

*Joy comes through occupation with the person of
Christ, while peace comes from knowing His work.*
Peace is established and settled forever by knowing the
work of Christ for us, and the perfection of that work.
Faith brings peace (Romans 5: 1).

But joy comes in being occupied with the person of
the Lord Jesus Himself. Joy is a thing that grows. Peace
cannot grow, because it is established once and forever.
But as the Holy Spirit takes the things of Christ and
shows them unto us, they will produce increasing joy.

Simply going on rejoicing that I am saved is a very
poor affair, I don't rejoice so much that I am saved as
I rejoice *in the One that saves me! I am saved for the
purpose of being occupied with the person of Jesus Christ.*
Just get your eyes on Him and let the Holy Spirit point
out the glories of His person. And as you get Christ more
and more before you — your heart will rejoice.

*We should read the Word of God and be growing
every day.* We should have Christ fresh every time we
come to the Word. There is no joy in orthodoxy. For
a person can hold to any creed and still be unconverted.
But the person of Christ is the life of the soul — and
that's where the joy comes from.

When you have real joy you have forgotten yourself.

28

But the moment self comes in, joy is hindered. Old experiences can give little joy, as there is no freshness about that. It is solely by having Christ more and more before the eyes that joy can be produced.

"God . . . hath in these last days spoken unto us by His Son" (Hebrews 1: 1—2). In one epistle you see Christ in one way; in another, in another way. In each epistle Christ is the object. *Joy comes by being occupied with Christ and not with ourselves in any way whatsoever.*

— *Malachi Taylor*

Hallelujah!

January 20

BUT NOW THE RIGHTEOUSNESS OF GOD WITHOUT THE LAW IS MANIFESTED. — Rom. 3: 21

The key phrase which runs throughout this book is "The righteousness of God." An old theologian has defined the righteousness of God in this way, *"God's righteousness is that righteousness which His righteousness requires Him to require."* Since I cannot supply such a required righteousness, someone else must supply it, if I am to be justified. The answer to this need is found in chapter 3, verse 24, "Being justified freely by His grace, through the redemption that is in Christ Jesus." Christ Jesus then supplied this righteousness by His own death on the Cross. He and I exchange places; He takes my sin and I take His righteousness. The ground of our acceptance with God is the acceptability of the worth and work of Jesus Christ.

The term "justify" means *"to declare righteous."* Justification as used in this epistle, signifies the process of dealing with a guilty person legally and righteously in a way that makes him in the sight of God and angels as though he had never been guilty. In chapter 6, verse 7, we have a very interesting expression used. "For he that is dead is freed from sin." Being a legal term in a legal book, the word "freed" means "justified". If you pronounce the word "justified" as "Just-As-If-I'd-Died," the meaning becomes clear. An illustration from Scotland will help here. In the olden days, the legal term used by the Scottish court for "death by hanging" was the word "Justification." So it was common to see large posters on the streets announcing that a certain criminal was justified that morning by hanging. For example, one may have read the news on a large poster that "James Alexander Stewart was justified this morning at 6 A.M. when he paid the penalty of the law by hanging." What did this mean? It simply declared to the people of Edinburgh that James Stewart, having paid the supreme penalty for his crime by hanging, was now legally acquitted and justified. The law of Scotland could no longer punish him because he had met this righteous claim. The trouble was, the poor man was dead!

But in our case, Christ died in our stead. And it is "just as if I'd died." We live, and the law of God has no claim upon us. The righteous Judge cannot with justice inflict the second time a punishment that has already been borne.

Augustus Toplady, to my mind, has expressed this glorius truth above all other hymn writers:

> *If Thou hast my discharge procured,*
> *And freely in my room endured,*
> *The whole of wrath Divine;*
> *Payment God cannot twice demand,*
> *First at my bleeding Surety's hand,*
> *And then again at mine.*

— *James A. Stewart*

January 21

WHERE NO OXEN ARE, THE CRIB IS CLEAN; BUT MUCH INCREASE IS BY STRENGTH OF THE OX. — Proberbs 14: 4

I stood one day before the Lord, my soul dry and my heart cold.

"Give me the answer", I cried, "as to why I am so barren in my life and service".

As I read again the chapter in the Bible which lay open before me, my eye fell upon the fourth verse of the fourteenth chapter of Proverbs.

"Here is the reason" a still small voice whispered. "You would have increase in fruit without the trouble and expense of the ox. You like a clean crib and an orderly stall. You like to plan and organize and have things go smoothly. To have "the strength of the ox" whereby there is much increase — — to have the power of the Spirit in your life — — you must be willing for the bother, the irregular hours, extra burdens for prayer, interruptions of your nicely planned schedule, concern for the unlovely, and the suffering of the cross which accompanies the working of the Spirit in your life. Choose you then whether you will have ease and the satisfaction of the clean crib and no oxen or if you are willing to pay the price for the means by which there is much increase of fruitfulness."

I understood the rebuke and bowed myself low as I answered, "Come, Blessed Spirit, and disturb and upset and raise the battle cry against sin and wrong — — only come in power and glorify my Lord through me."

— *Ruth Stewart*

31

UNTO YOU THEREFORE WHICH BELIEVE HE IS PRECIOUS. — I Pet. 2: 7

Let Zion hear while I proclaim
My precious Saviour's matchless name;
He's wise and holy, just and true,
And altogether lovely too.

He's lovely from his head to feet,
His heart is love—his mouth is sweet;
Angels and saints delight to sing
Their altogether lovely King.

Essential deity He claims,
Reveals Himself in lovely names,
He lives, and dies, and reigns for us —
He's altogether lovely thus.

His loveliness has won my heart,
Dear Jesus, let us never part;
I'll sound Thy lovely name abroad,
My altogether lovely Lord.

Up to His throne I soon shall go,
More of His loveliness to know;
While ransomed millions shall declare
He's altogether lovely there.

— *Joseph Irons*

Oh God! I thank Thee for my glorious Redeemer today. Amen!

January 23

MY STRENGTH IS MADE PERFECT IN WEAKNESS. — II Cor. 12: 9

The Christian must be weak that he may be strong; weak in the deprivation of those things which the world connects with the idea of strength; deficient in the strength that men seek and extol; emptied of all thoughts of his own independent and personal power; stripped of his own righteousness and wisdom; sensible of the mighty power of the enemy; a mere ruin and a wreck apart from Christ. *Then there is indeed a preparation for strength.* A foundation is laid upon which Christ will build. Room is made for the wisdom and power and sufficiency of Christ. The Christian decreases, that he may in another and blessed sense increase. *He is made perfect in weakness, that he may be made perfect in true strength.* Look at Peter with his miserable sword in the garden of Gethsemane; look at him again on the day of Pentecost.

— *George Bowen*

Oh God! strip me today of my own strength.

January 24

IN ALL THY WAYS ACKNOWLEDGE HIM, AND HE SHALL DIRECT THY PATHS. — Proverbs 3: 6

Acknowledge him as thy guide, thine only, thy necessary guide. Refuse to stir a step without him, as the blind man that stops the moment he misses his guide. Without him thou art in utter darkness, and thy next step may be into a pit. He has made thee thus dependent. It is not enough that the sun shines for thee, the earth upholds thee, and all God's works wait upon thee; all these finite ministers cannot guarantee thee one safe step. God has ordained it. He created thee to be guided by himself, and unless thou canst call into existence another God like him for thyself, thou hast, without him, no guarantee in any of thy paths. Therefore acknowledge him as thy guide. In all thy ways. In thy worship. In thy study of his word. In thy intercourse with his people. In thy traffic with the world. In thy business and in thy recreation. At thy meals. In thy correspondence. In thy reading. In thy dress. What! in these petty matters? Yes! in all thy ways. Thinkest thou that God will have no word for thee on such topics? Be undeceived. *Thou shalt find a revelation of the will of God for every one of thy paths.* There is no need for thee ever to let go his hand. Not a single hair in thy head receives its aliment without him. Why then should a single step be taken without him? Think, and you shall see that the fate of millions may be involved in the least step that you may be ca'led to take.

— *George Bowen*

January 25

WHERE IS THE LORD GOD OF ELIJAH?
— II Kings 2: 14

Elisha's was a cry of Victory; the language of audacious faith. He knew Elijah's God was with him, and he marched with conquering strides to his first conquest. Where Elijah finished he began. Glory to God, the waters parted and the servant of the Lord passed through! *There is victory for the man who deliberately faces the problems of the work and takes his stand on the promises of God, and challenges Him to do the miraculous.* As my dear friend Lionel B. Fletcher has beautifully said, "It is useless for any man or woman to go into the work of God hoping to win victories with a mantle that has been riddled with holes by the moths of doubt and uncertainty. Such a mantle never yet opened a path for prophet or preacher, although it may have been wielded successfully by some other soul aflame with passion and power."

High are the cities that dare our assault,
Strong are the barriers that call us to halt!
March we on fearless, and down they must fall,
Vanquished by faith in Him, far above all.

*Elisha was bold enough to claim from God that which
ordinary people imagine God would only give to Elijah.*
Many dear saints go on in feebleness and despair, because
they cannot believe that God will give them also spiritual
power. This insignificant man of God, conscious of his
own weakness, cast himself in utter abandonment upon
God, and took the kingdom of heaven by force. Elisha
was really saying, "Did Elijah divide this river? No, it
was God Himself! Then where is the God of Elijah?" He
remembered that the mighty prophet was as human as
he, and that it was Jehovah Who wrought the miracles.
(James 5: 17).

— *James A. Stewart*

God is willing to do mighty things for you today!

January 26

AND THE PRIESTS... STOOD FIRM IN THE
MIDST OF JORDAN. — Joshua 3: 17

*So long as the feet of the priests "stood firm" in Jor-
dan's bed, they were absolutely safe, as safe as Jehovah
could make them.* And thus the whole host, men of war,
old men, and little children alike, passed "clean over"
Jordan, in the full light of day, and planted their feet on
the Canaan side.

*This inspiring sight has its typical lessons for the child-
ren of God.* The Paschal Lamb and the sprinkled blood
in Egypt pointed onward to the death of Christ, as that
which saves from the wages of sin and the wrath to come.
The Red Sea tells of deliverance from Satan's power, and
separation from the world, by the cross of Christ. Jordan

35

is a type of Christ's death and resurrection, as that by which death is abolished, judgment passed away, and a way opened into heaven for the people of God. Israel's passage through the dried-up river, tells of the believer experimentally and practically taking possession of this great truth in his soul, and reckoning himself dead, buried and risen with Christ. *To grasp these glorious truths by faith, to make them one's own, is the entrance to a wide and wealthy range of spiritual blessing.* That goodly land, in which "all spiritual blessings in heavenly places"—in which "the unsearchable riches of Christ," "the exceeding riches of His grace," "the exceeding greatness of His power," are things known and enjoyed by the believer, that land lies "beyond Jordan." The man who lives as a man in the flesh, a man of the world, may read about them, and even speak about them, but the enjoyment of them is only known to him who reckons himself dead and risen with Christ.

— *John Ritchie*

Oh God! help me to enter into this vital truth today.

January 27

I WILL DWELL IN THE HOUSE OF THE LORD FOR EVER. — Psalm 23: 6

THE CHRISTIAN PILGRIM WHEN NEARING THE CELESTIAL CITY.

My pilgrimage is almost o'er;
My Saviour now "stands at the door;"
And He is mine for evermore—
Hallelujah!

Oh, Jesus, Thou hast been my light!
Thy Word has been my heart's delight;
Thy presence made my journey bright—
Hallelujah!

36

Thy Holy Spirit led the way,
Restored me when I went astray,
And never left me, night nor day—
                        Hallelujah!

And now, when earth is nearly past,
And home appears in sight at last,
Into Thine arms myself I cast—
                        Hallelujah!

Thine arms! my shield when foes oppressed;
My sure resort when griefs distressed;
Where long ago I found my rest—
                        Hallelujah!

Those loving arms, now still more dear,
As heavenly scenes are drawing near,
And Thou in glory will appear—
                        Hallelujah!

                        — R. N. B.

January 28

ALL THE SAINTS SALUTE YOU, CHIEFLY THEY THAT ARE OF CAESAR'S HOUSEHOLD.

— Phil. 4: 22

SLAVES WHO WERE SAINTS

There, in the most unlikely place in all history, were Christians who were sufficiently saved from self to consider others; to send their Christian salutation to the Church of Jesus Christ at Philippi; and their greetings ringing down the corridors of time to you: "All the saints salute you, chiefly they that are of Cæsar's household." Well, *who were they?* They were slaves, bond slaves with fewer rights and privileges than our domestic animals enjoy today. When Paul walked the streets of the imperial city, three men out of every five he met were slaves, so much the property of their owners that if one of these owners, in a fit of pique, slew a dozen or a score of his slaves few men would care, and no man would dare to interfere. *The most unlikely material for the making of saints.* Yet in the court of Nero, the great antagonist of Christ and persecutor of His church, there were slaves who were saints, with "a heart at leisure from itself, to soothe and sympathize" so that they could send their saintly salutation to their fellow Christians in Philippi. The application is obvious. *The God who could create and control, make and maintain Christians out of slave material in Nero's court, can make and maintain Christians anywhere.*

— F. J. Miles

Oh Lord! Keep me from complaining about my circumstances.

January 29

Now unto Him that is able to do exceeding abundantly above all that we ask or think, according to the power that worketh in us, unto Him be glory in the Church by Christ Jesus throughout all ages, world without end. Amen. — Eph. 3: 20, 21.

In the great prayer which Paul had just indited, he had apparently reached the highest expression possible of the life to which God's mighty power could bring the believer. But Paul is not content. In this doxology he rises still higher and lifts us up to give glory to God as "able to do exceeding abundantly above all that we can ask or think." Pause a moment to think what that "exceeding abundantly" means.

Think of the words, "the exceeding great and precious promises." Think of "the exceeding greatness of His power toward us who believe, according to the working

38

of the strength of His might which He wrought in Christ when He raised Him from the dead." Think of the grace of our Lord as exceeding abundant with faith and love which is in Christ Jesus, so that where sin abounded grace did abound more exceedingly. He lifts our hearts to give glory to God as able to do "exceeding abundantly above all that we ask or think," according to the greatness of that power which worketh in us, nothing less than the exceeding greatness of the power that raised Christ from the dead. And as our hearts begin to feel that there is here a prospect of something that God will work in us beyond all our imagination, He lifts our hearts to join in the universal chorus: "Unto Him be the glory in the Church and in Christ Jesus, unto all generations, for ever and ever. Amen."

As we worship and adore, the call comes to believe in this Almighty God, who is working in our hearts, according to His mighty power, able and willing to fulfil every one of His exceeding great and precious promises, and, where sin abounded, to prove that grace abounds more exceedingly.

Paul began his great prayer, "I bow my knees to the Father." He ends it by bringing us to our knees, to give glory to Him as able to fulfil every promise, to reveal Christ dwelling in our hearts, and keep us in that life of love which leads to being filled with all the fullness of God.

Child of God, bow in deep adoration, giving glory to God, until your heart learns to believe: the prayer will be fulfilled, Jesus Christ will dwell in my heart by faith. Faith in this Almighty God, and the exceeding abundance of His grace and power, will teach us that the abiding indwelling of Christ in the heart is the secret of the abiding presence.

— *Andrew Murray*

January 30

A JUNIPER TREE. — I Kings 19: 4

The Christian is in most danger of a deep fall immediately after a great triumph. We should be especially watchful and prayerful immediately after great times of blessing. Elijah could boldly face the four hundred prophets of Baal, but he fled for life next day from one woman. "He went for his life." Accompanied by his servant and under cover of darkness, he hurried through the storm, across the hills of Samaria toward the extreme south of Judea. He was utterly demoralized and panic-stricken. The terrible reaction which so often comes to us after some tremendous tension and victorious battle over the enemy, seized hold upon God's servant. Elijah grew discouraged, possibly through a relapse of his physical powers. He was drained dry of his physical energy. How often we all have experienced this! Christ is saying to many a tired, weary worker, "Take My yoke upon you, and learn of Me; for I am meek and lowly in heart: and ye shall find rest unto your souls, for My yoke is easy and My burden is light" (Matt. 11: 28—30). To avoid such periods of discouragement we must "come apart and rest awhile" with our glorious Redeemer. *It is the rested workers that God wants.*

Angry and rebellious, the prophet crawled into a cave. Are you in a cave, tired, wearied and discouraged? Then the voice of God comes to you as to His servant, "What doest thou here, Elijah?"

Discouragement gets us out of touch with God. Discouragement gets us out of the line of God's will. Discouragement gives us wrong thoughts of our loving Father. Says Robert Murray McCheyne, "If I could hear Christ praying for me in the next room I would not fear a million enemies. Yet the distance makes no difference. He IS praying for me! Bless his name!"

— *James A. Stewart*

January 31

HE WAS WOUNDED FOR MY TRANSGRESSIONS.
— Isaiah 53: 5

SCARRED

The shame He suffered left its brand
In gaping wound in either hand;
Sin's penalty He deigned to meet
Has torn and scarred His blessed feet;
The condemnation by Him borne
Marred His brow with print of thorn.
Trespass and guilt for which He died
Have marked Him with a riven side.

Mine was the shame, the penalty:
The sin was mine; it was for me
He felt the nails, the thorns, the spear.
For love of me the scars appear
In hands and feet and side and brow.
Beholding them I can but bow
Myself a living sacrifice
To Him who paid so dear a price.
— *Bob Jones, Jr.*

They shall be unto me a special treasure — Malachi 3: 17, Spurrel.

Lord Thou Hast Bought Me To Possess Me!

February 1

And if it be a beast, whereof men bring an offering unto the Lord, all that any man giveth of such unto the Lord shall be holy. He shall not alter it nor change it, a good for a bad, or a bad for a good: and if he shall at all change beast for beast, then it and the exchange thereof shall be holy. And if it be any unclean beast, of which they do not offer a sacrifice unto the Lord, then he shall present the beast before the priest:

41

and the priest shall value it, whether it be good or bad: as thou valuest it, who art the priest, so shall it be. But if he will at all redeem it, then he shall add a fifth part hereof, unto thy estimation — Lev. 27: 9—13.

A clean beast, after it had been vowed, could neither be employed in common purpose nor exchanged for its equivalent; it must be sacrificed. If, through some discovered blemish, it was unfit for the altar, it might be sold and the money applied to the sacred service, but could not be exchanged. At the moment of consecration, God wrote across that offering, "Holiness unto the Lord." If, through some defect, it was unfit for sacrifice, and another beast was substituted, God said both were holy, and He followed the defective ram back to the flock, while "holiness unto the Lord" was ever upon it. The sin of misappropriation is so much the greater after we have devoted ourselves and our possessions to His service.

GOD WANTS THAT WHICH WE HAVE GIVEN HIM AND NOT SOMETHING ELSE. We know of young people who have offered themselves for full-time service unto the Lord, even for the foreign mission field, who later have exchanged that vow for one of working and giving part of their earnings to support missions. We know a young man who vowed to the Lord to sell his vehicle and give the money realised to a specific purpose. Later, he changed his mind, kept the vehicle, and paid his vow in another way. Little does that young man realise that that vehicle now belongs to the Lord.

GOD TAKES ALL THAT IS OFFERED TO HIM. How often, in a few hours it may be, our dedication is forgotten, and our money, for example, is spent without any reference to God. But has God forgotten? Oh no! He has written across every coin, "Holiness unto the Lord," though men and women indulge with impunity in the awful sin of misappropriation. Alas, for this playing at dedication! It is a travesty on our Christian life, and dishonoring to God. It is an insult to the

42

Son, and a grief to the blessed Spirit. It makes hypocrites of the men and women who indulge in it. *We forget that all our dealings with God are for eternity!*
— *James A. Stewart*

Oh God! Write this solemm truth on my heart.

February 2
THE SONG OF SONGS, WHICH IS SOLOMON'S.
— Song of Songs 1: 1

The Song of Songs begins with the cry of a soul who has had the heavenly vision of her high calling, and who surrenders wholly to the Well-Beloved, to be led on to "apprehend with all the saints what is the breadth and length and height and depth, and to know the love of Christ which passeth knowledge, that (she) may be filled unto all the fulness of God." (Eph. 3: 18, 19).

Solomon prefigured the crowned Conqueror of Calvary, the Risen and Ascended Jesus, when He had by Himself purged our sins and "sat down on the right hand of the Majesty on high." (Heb. 1: 3). It is important to remember that He is now the Glorified One, that He has completed His work of redemption, that He has sat down a triumphant Conqueror, that He is now a waiting expectant Lord; the One Who gave His life to redeem out of the earth, from among fallen sinners, a bride to share His Throne, lifting up a "beggar from the dunghill" to "inherit the throne of glory" (1 Sam. 2: 8, A.V.).

It is essentially the song "which is *Solomon's*," because it is the Song of the Heavenly Bridegroom over each soul who is a member of His purchased bride; and it is a song shared in by the purchased one, because it is *His* song in her, as she is brought into heart union with her Lord; for all in her is of Him, through the Holy Ghost.

— *J. Penn-Lewis*

The Banqueting House of your blessed Lord is open to you. — Song of Songs 2: 4.

43

February 3

MY BELOVED IS MINE, AND I AM HIS.
— Song of Songs 2: 16

While conducting an evangelistic campaign in the city of Neuchatel, Switzerland, with La Marechale, (Mrs. Booth-Clibborn, the eldest daughter of William Booth), she asked me to visit with her one of the most sacred spots to her soul. *This I discovered was a prison.* She had been sent by her father when a young lady to plant the flag of the Salvation Army in France, Holland and Switzerland. While evangelizing in Neuchatel, she was arrested and confined to a lonely cell in this prison. Now, many years later, she sang exultantly the very hymn that she wrote during this time of imprisonment:

> *Best-beloved of my soul,*
> *I am here alone with Thee;*
> *And my prison is a heaven*
> *Since Thou sharest it with me.*
> *All my life is at thy service,*
> *All my choice to share Thy cross;*
> *I am Thine to do or suffer,*
> *All things else I count but dross.*

— *James A. Stewart*

February 4

GOD LED THE PEOPLE. — Exodus 13: 18

As sinners we need a Saviour, as captives we need a Deliverer, and as pilgrims we need a Guide.

The God of love, Who from His holy habitation beheld us in our lost estate, and gave His Son to be our Saviour and Deliverer, has also given us *His Holy Spirit* and *His Word* to guide us. Father, Son, and Holy Spirit, have been all engaged in the work of our salvation; and they are all engaged in our home-bringing to the rest beyond!

Encamped in Etham, on the edge of the wilderness, and not knowing a step of the way that lay between them and their Canaan home, how it must have gladdened their hearts to see the pillar of cloud descend. Unasked, and we may say unexpected, God came down in the cloudy pillar to be their Guide; to walk with them, to defend them, and to be their Companion. What though the way be long and dreary, and the "great and terrible wilderness" beset with dangers, and filled with fiery serpents and scorpions, so long as God is with them! Every step and every danger are well known to Him, and if they only follow whither He doth lead, all will be well.

In the daytime the cloud was a covering, stretching over the entire camp, to screen them from the heat; and as the shades of evening fell, it became a pillar of fire, to give them light (Psa. 105: 39). *So they were never in darkness.* To travel by night, was as easy as by day, for the Lord God gave them light, and "there was no night there." How faithfully and lovingly He performed His guiding work as the Shepherd of Israel, the words of Deut. 32: 10—12 tell us: "He *found* him in a desert land, and in the waste howling wilderness; He *led* him about. He *instructed* him. He *kept* him as the apple of His eye. As an eagle stirreth up her nest, fluttereth over her young, spreadeth abroad her wings, taketh them, beareth them on her wings; so the Lord *alone* did *lead* him, and there was no strange god with him." And blessed to tell it, their failures, their murmurings, and their sins, did not drive Him away, nor make Him withdraw the cloudy pillar from them. *It accompanied them all the forty years of their pilgrimage, it hovered above them as they marched in triumph through the dried-up bed of Jordan, and at last it found its rest amid the glories of the temple, in the land. And "this God is our God for ever and ever."*

The threefold position of the cloud, tells us of God for us, God with us, and God in us. At the Red Sea

45

it stood between them and their foes (Exod. 14: 19); as they walked along the desert, it went before them, to seek out a resting-place (Num. 9: 17); and in the tabernacle it rested in their midst (Exodus 40: 34). When the cloud moved they followed; when it rested so did they. Jehovah was their Leader, and King. It was His to command; it was their's to obey. He was the Shepherd, they were the sheep. And He Who guided Israel across the dreary desert by the pillar of cloud and fire, has not left us unprovided for. He has given us *His Spirit* and *His Word*. These are to be our pillar of cloud and fire, till desert days are done. In their light we shall walk safely and securely—we shall walk with God.

Of the Word, it is written, "Thy Word is a *lamp* unto my feet, and a *light* unto my path" (Psa. 119: 105).

— *John Ritchie*

February 5

I BESEECH YOU . . . TO PRESENT YOUR BODIES A LIVING SACRIFICE . . . BE YE TRANSFORMED.
— Rom. 12: 1—2

The act of dedication places you of your own choice under the command of Christ, but it is only by the daily acceptance of His Lordship, the constant study of His will, as set forth in His Word, and the seeking of His face in prayer, that any act of dedication can be made really effective. *The reason why so many convention blessings evaporate is that people forget that a crisis which does not lead to a regular process is really no crisis at all, but merely a passing emotion.*

— *Selected*

Oh Father! deliver me from a mere passing emotion.

February 6

FOR AS OFTEN AS YE EAT THIS BREAD.
— I Cor. 11: 26

Therefore, no doubt, it is that when Paul was spe-cially inspired to recall to the saints the institution of the supper, the Holy Ghost put into his lips the now familiar words: "As often as ye eat this bread and drink this cup, ye do show the Lord's death TILL HE COME."

The guests at the table of the Lord are, by these words, pointed in a breath to His sufferings past, and to His glory to come. If there is in them a retrospect of deep solemnity and sadness, there is also a prospect of exceed-ing joy. The Lord's supper is graciously given to form the perpetual link between them. The Lord's death is here "remembered," that is, brought near—brought up from the distant past to be present to faith's eye and apprehension. It must not be, as to the heart, left be-hind, as a faded and hazy picture of an event that transpired time out of mind. This feast of commemora-tion acts to disentangle it from the ruins of ages, and present the cross a vivid reality, and rehearse its awful story to our very senses. So, in like manner, these words: "Ye do show the Lord's death *till He come*," bring near the promised return of Christ. They keep the heart of the worshippers expectant; so that, though an age of 2.000 years has passed since they were uttered, that hope lives still, the daily consolation of every believing suf-ferer, and the fulness of joy to every grateful saint.

The table is thus the living link between the past, which is the foundation of our blessing, and the future, which is its consummation—not so much a long con-necting chain, extending over weary centuries, but a single link, bringing the cross near as yesterday, the glory near as to-morrow. The table is thus, as it were, the closing scene of the sufferings of Christ, and the opening scene of His glory. It tells of the death, for the bread is *broken*, the wine *poured out;* it tells of the

47

glory, for the bread is *eaten*, and the wine is *drank*. Across that table lies the dark shadow of the cross, as of a substance only just out of view; and yet, athwart the shadow, stretch the bright beams and gleams of the coming glory, as of a day-dawn close at hand. And the morsel of bread we eat, the draught of wine we drink,. are the foretaste of the feast of fat things, of wine well refined, that we shall partake of at the coming of the Lord in His Father's kingdom.

— *George Trench*

February 7

WE PREACH CHRIST CRUCIFIED. — I. Cor. 1: 23

It is well for the evangelist to bear in mind, on every fresh occasion of rising to preach, that his unconverted hearers are totally ignorant of the gospel, and hence he should preach as though it were the first time they had ever heard the message, and the first time he had ever delivered it. For, be it remembered, the preaching of the gospel, in the divine acceptation of the phrase, is not a mere barren statement of evangelical doctrine— a certain form of words enunciated over and over again in wearisome routine. Far, very far from it. *The gospel is really the large loving heart of God welling up and flowing forth toward the poor lost sinner in streams of life and salvation. It is the presentation of the atoning death and glorious resurrection of the Son of God; and all this in the present energy, glow, and freshness of the Holy Ghost, from the exhaustless mine of Holy Scripture.* Moreover, *the* one absorbing object of the preacher is to win souls for Christ, to the glory of God. For this he labors and pleads; for this he prays, weeps, and agonizes; for this he thunders, appeals, and grapples with the heart and conscience of his hearer. His object is not to teach doctrines, though doctrines may be taught; his object is not to expound Scripture, though Scripture may be expounded. These things lie within the range of the teacher or lecturer; but let it never be forgotten, the preacher's object is to bring the Saviour and the sinner together—to win souls to Christ. *May God by His Spirit keep these things ever before our hearts, so that we may have a deeper interest in the glorious work of evangelization!*

— *C. H. Macintosh*

February 8

ALL THINGS WORK TO-GETHER FOR GOOD.
— Rom. 8: 28

When Colonel Brengle, the great soul-winner of the Salvation Army, was preaching on the street some years ago a big burly ruffian threw a brickbat at the Colonel, which struck him on the head, a blow which came very near taking his life. He was laid aside from active service for many long months, and while he was recovering he began to write those wonderful messages on Holiness which have blessed tens of thousands, and have been translated into several languages. When he was able to return home he found the missile that was hurled at him by the hand of hate, but oh, how transformed. Mrs. Brengle had gotten hold of it, painted and beautified it, and put these words on it: "Ye thought evil against me: but God meant it unto good." Had this not happened, the world and the Church might not have gotten those wonderful books. *Surely God can take the blunder of devils and the hatred of men and work it out for good.*

— *Hames*

February 9

I WILL BLESS THEE, AND MAKE THY NAME
GREAT, AND THOU SHALT BE A BLESSING.

— Gen. 12: 2

Gen. 12: 1—9

GOD'S call is imperative. There is no opportunity of
questioning His meaning. Nor is it an easy commandment for flesh and blood. *Get thee out from thy father's
house.* And still His injunctions ring as clearly in my
soul, and still they try my affections sorely. What shall
my attitude towards them be?

But GOD'S promise is gracious. It is astonishingly
munificent. It is the word of a King, liberal and irre-
vocable. *In thee shall all the families of the earth be
blessed.* Let me trust Him, and I shall discover that the
compensations outweigh the hardships a thousandfold.

Abraham's obedience is immediate. It cost him a
wrench. It was the tearing up of the roots of his being
from the old familiar soil. But his "not to make reply."
He *went, as the Lord had spoken unto him.* I would,
in the strength of the Spirit, practise a similar obedience,
instantaneous and unreserved. There is only impoverish-
ment in debate and delay.

And Abraham's religion is paramount. He *pitched
his tent, and there he builded an altar.* His own home
was a thing of fluttering canvas at the best. But GOD'S
oratory was permanent, a stable erection of durable
stone. Would that I understood as well the true pro-
portions of things! Would that I always gave my Lord
the best, and stayed content with little for myself! He
must increase; but I must decrease.

— *Alexander Smellie*

I WILL TRUST AND NOT BE AFRAID.

— Isaiah 12: 2

FAITH

Faith is not the blind outreach
Of groping hand
That seeks some solid thing to hold
Amid the sinking sand.

But faith is certain trust
In One well known
Who in the Saviour's cross
His love has shown.

And faith is sure repose
Of quiet love
That knows each step is ordered
From above.

It will not fuss or fret
When things go wrong
But in the valley dark
Sing a song.

It knows that God is near
When clouds arise
And looks to Him to clear
The storm-swept skies.

And should God's blessing fail
For some short while,
It knows that somewhere round the bend
God yet will smile.

— *David B. Stewart*

Then sing and bless the name of Jehovah!

February 11

STUDY TO SHEW THYSELF APPROVED UNTO GOD. — II. Tim. 2:15

There are mysteries of grace and love in every page of the Bible: it is a thriving soul that finds the Book of God growing more and more precious.

A careless reader of the Scriptures never made a close walker with God.

Spread the Bible before the Lord; ask Him to teach you what *your* ignorance and what *His* wisdom.

Meditation on the Word of God is the chief means of our growth in grace: without this even prayer itself will be little better than an empty form. Meditation nourishes faith, and faith and prayer are the keys which unlock the hidden treasures of the word.

The Book of God is a store of manna for God's pilgrim children; and we ought to see to it that the soul get not sick and loathe the manna. The great cause of our neglecting the Scriptures is not want of time, but want of heart, some idol taking the place of Christ. Satan has been marvellously wise to entice away God's people from the Scriptures. A child of God who neglects the Scriptures cannot make it his business to please the Lord of glory: cannot make Him Lord of the conscience; ruler of the heart; the joy, portion, and treasure of the soul.

— *Robert Chapman*

I covenant just now to no longer neglect my daily study of the Word under the illumination of the Blessed Spirit.

February 12

LIFT UP THY ROD. — Exodus 14:16

Here is an Old Testament picture of authoritative warfare against the powers of darkness. In a seemingly impossible situation Moses was victorious because he lifted up the rod in faith and defiance. God is calling us at this critical hour to "stand in the gap" and command situations in the face of all hellish onslaughts. The more hopeless the situation, the greater the triumph for God's eternal glory.

Let us go forward in partnership with the Almighty and command deliverances!

Lift up thy rod!

— *James A. Stewart*

February 13

I EXHORT... THAT... PRAYERS... BE MADE FOR ALL MEN. — 1 Timothy 2: 1

The vaster your prayers, and the more world-wide they are, so to speak, the more tremendous the forces set in motion in the unseen realm; and the longer God is working them out. If you ask a little thing, God can do that quickly, and many of the Lord's people are so happy if they get one thing "answered" in their daily life. Then they "ask" other small things, and think they understand "prayer", whilst they do not see how they might be brought to understand God's purposes, by the teaching of the Holy Spirit of the will of God, and *pray prayers that would go right down to the ages, in God's working out of His plans* (See Rev. 8: 3—5).

Do not undervalue "answers" in the little things of daily life, for they serve to confirm your faith, but God would have you matured in the spiritual life, so that you have the knowledge that your prayers are answered, without the need of having little "evidences" to keep your faith alive. Your knowledge of God's answer to prayer in His will, can grow so clear, that if you do not see a trace of visible answer for a prolonged time, still you know your prayers have been heard. Answer to prayer is as sure as cause and effect can be. If you pray for certain things, *in line with God's will and conditions,*

53

you are as certain of an answer as the working of cause and effect in other directions.

God wants men and women who can pray for the church of Christ, according to God's purposes for her, as revealed in His Word.   — *Selected*

February 14

BLESSED ARE THE PURE IN HEART; FOR THEY SHALL SEE GOD. — Matt. 5: 8

Exod. 3: 1—14

Four ingredients there are in the call of Moses. He is addressed by name, like the little lad Samuel in the holy house at Shiloh, like the persecutor Saul on the road to Damascus: twice over GOD'S voice says, *Moses! Moses!* He is warned that the place where he stands is holy. He is told Who it is Who addresses him, no angel, but the Very Lord Most High. And he is instructed what he must do; the mission is clear, plain, unmistakable; *I will send thee unto Pharaoh,* GOD announces from the burning heart of the thorn-tree in the wilderness.

There are the same ingredients in every call of the divine Spirit to the human spirit.

I must hearken to a personal and individual summons, as if my name were used by GOD, so that I cannot escape the conviction that now at length He claims me for His work. I must have impressed on me the sense of His lustrous and awful holiness, so that I recognise the responsibility and the sacredness of undertaking any labour with Him and for Him. I must meet with my Lord Himself, no one else, no one less, so that I accept my commission directly from His august and kingly hand. I must gain a clear indication of the field where I am to toil and the task which I am to finish, so that I shall not fight as one who beats the air.

Now, have I received this call, definite, solemn, imperative, illuminating?   — *Alexander Smellie*

54

February 15

AND CALL UPON ME IN THE DAY OF TROU-
BLE: I WILL DELIVER THEE. AND THOU SHALT
GLORIFY ME. — Psalm 50: 15

IN TIMES OF TROUBLE, GOD'S
TRUSTING CHILD MAY SAY:

FIRST: *He* brought me here; it is by His will I am in
this strait place: in that will I rest.

NEXT: *He* will keep me here in His love, and give
me grace in this trial to behave as His child.

THEN: *He* will make the trial a blessing, teaching
me the lessons He intends me to learn, and working in
me the grace He means to bestow.

LAST: In *His* good time He can bring me out again
— how and when He knows.

Say: I am here —
(1) By God's Appointment.
(2) In His keeping.
(3) Under His training.
(4) For His time.

— Andrew Murray

God tests our faith in order to strengthen it.

February 16

AS APPLES OF GOLD. — Prov. 25: 11
GOLDEN SAYINGS

God Himself, God alone, is sufficient for His work.
— Hudson Taylor

O, what I owe to the file, to the hammer, to the
furnace of my Lord Jesus!
— Samuel Rutherford

Attempt great things for God. Expect great things from
God.

— Grattan Guinness

In the spiritual life we learn to walk in naked faith, in closest communion with Him, never turning back to the life of feeling for one moment. Faith launches out on the bare Word of God, separated for ever from the emotional life.

— *Stockmayer*

February 17

THEY MINISTERED TO THE LORD. — Acts 13: 2

We are too busy in the work to be busy in the admiration of our Lord. Our ministry will be cold and lifeless unless we have a deep appreciation of the Person of the Lord Jesus. Ministering to the Lord is worshipping God. True worship is heart occupation with the Son of God. *It is the assembly's joy and glory in the Lamb of God that delights the Father's heart.* Worship is more important than service, because all true service springs from worship. How sad that we are too busy today to minister to the Lord! Even our Communion Services for "the breaking of bread" are hurried over, that the people might rush home for dinner. What a blessing would come to our churches if we could have a longer time to worship the Lord unhurriedly in the beauty of holiness.

— *James A. Stewart*

Gracious God, we worship Thee,
Rev'rently we bow the knee;
Jesus Christ, our only plea:
Father, we adore Thee.

Vast Thy love, how deep, how wide,
In the gift of Him Who died;
Righteous claims all satisfied;
Father, we adore Thee.

56

Lo, we bow before Thy face,
Sons of God, oh wondrous place;
Great the riches of Thy grace:
Father, we adore Thee.

By Thy Spirit grant that we
Worshippers in truth may be;
Praise, as incense sweet to Thee:
Father, we adore Thee.

Yet again our song we raise,
Note of deep adoring praise;
Now, and soon through endless days:
Father, we adore Thee.

— Trevor Francis

February 18

BUT THAT IT SPREAD NO FURTHER.

— Acts. 4: 17

If a handful of men and women on fire in Jerusalem
could set fire to the world, cannot the millions of profess-
ing Christians to-day win the whole world for Christ?
That depends on whether cold intellectuals continue to
dominate our thinking and acting, our work at home and
abroad—criticizing, dissecting everything connected with
the holy revelation of God, prayer, even our blessed
Saviour — and thus freeze the enthusiasm, the love, the
childlike trust that alone can prevail: or whether you
and I are going to love Him passionately, serve Him
self-sacrificingly, suffer for Him gloriously, and take
from Him the Holy Spirit to lead us out into the life
of prayer and power.

With this equipment the church shall live and conquer
as the early church did. This too shall be our experience:
"And the disciples were filled with joy, and with the
Holy Ghost" (Acts 13: 52).

Without it we shall become "neither cold nor hot" to be spewed out of the mouth of God. With it we shall be a flame of fire for His glory.

We must kneel to conquer — kneel in prayer — kneel in utter dedication and surrender; and then we shall rise up men and women filled with all the fulness of God, to go out as terrible as an army with banners against the powers of evil to acclaim Christ King of Kings and Lord of Lords, the one and only Saviour of the world.
— *Lionel B. Fletcher*

Oh God! give us the fire of Pentecost just now.

February 19

GOD WHO...HATH SPOKEN IN HIS SON.
— Heb. 1: 1—2

I would like to emphasize the value of that counsel and to recommend the practice of starting with silent worship. There must of course be full personal liberty in the use of the quiet hour. Some begin with prayer and then go on to read and ponder the Word of God, and others prefer to begin with reading. Such questions must be decided according to the requirements of each individual soul. As much time as possible must be given to worship, thanksgiving, and praise. *We should let our minds dwell on the glory of God the Father as it is manifested in creation, in His gracious dealings with man, and in the manifold gifts of His love; but it is His essential greatness and glory, His divine majesty, which should provide our chief subject of meditation, and call forth our worship.* The Father's gift in the Son, the sending forth of the Holy Spirit, the whole work of atonement and redemption give us *fathomless themes for adoring praise.* Then we come to the prayer of petition, when we can approach the Father in the Name of Jesus with childlike joy and confidence, and lay our requests before Him.
— *Sister Eva*

For whom he did foreknow, he also did predestinate to be conformed to the image of his Son, that he might be the firstborn among many brethren. — Rom. 8: 29

God's ultimate purpose in our creation was that we should finally be "conformed to the image of Christ." Christ was to be the firstborn among many brethren, and His brethren were to be like Him. All the discipline and training of our lives is with this end in view; and God has implanted in every human heart a longing, however unformed and unexpressed, after the best and highest it knows.

Christ is the pattern of what each one of us is to be when finished. We are "predestinated" to be conformed to His image, in order that He might be the firstborn among many brethren. We are to be "partakers of the divine nature" with Christ; we are to be filled with the spirit of Christ; we are to share His resurrection life, and to walk as He walked. We are to be one with Him, as He is one with the Father; and the glory God gave to Him, He is to give to us. And when all this is brought to pass, then, and not until then, will God's purpose in our creation be fully accomplished, and we stand forth "in his image and after his likeness."

Our likeness to His image is an accomplished fact in the mind of God, but we are, so to speak, in the manufactory as yet, and the great master Workman is at work upon us. "It doth not yet appear what we shall be: but we know that, when he shall appear, we shall be like him; for we shall see him as he is."

— *Hannah Whitall Smith*

Predestinated to be conformed. Oh! that I may live today in the goodness of this overwhelming truth.

February 21

THE DEPTHS HAVE COVERED THEM: THEY SANK INTO THE BOTTOM AS A STONE.

— Exod. 15: 5

Do not be filled with dismay at the might of your enemies. Keep praising! Keep trusting and standing on redemption ground and your "Man of war" will fight for you.

The foes that loom so big in your eyes will soon lie like a sunken stone at the bottom of the sea. Hallelujah!

— *James A. Stewart*

We should *always* be wearing the garment of praise, not just waving a palm now and then.

— *A. Bonar*

February 22

God ... did visit the Gentiles, TO TAKE OUT OF THEM a people for His name. And to this agree the words of the prophets ... After this I will return and WILL BUILD AGAIN the tabernacle of David.

— Acts 15: 14—17

Blindness in part is happened to Israel, until the fulness of the Gentiles be come in. — Rom. 6: 25

What does Paul mean by the term "fulness of the Gentiles"? The Apostle James tells us in Acts 15, that God has a definite purpose in all the events which He has been working out from the beginning in His dealings with Israel as a nation, and that at the present time, while they are set aside, He is visiting the Gentiles to take out of them a people for His Name. Since this is the great work of God in the present age, and His special aim has not so much to do with His ancient people (who are set to one side because of their rejection of their Messiah), but rather with the salvation of the nations, then we can readily understand what He means when He speaks of "the fulness of the Gentiles."

When, therefore, the Church, as the Body of Christ, is complete and is caught up to meet the Lord in the air, the fulness of the Gentiles will have come in, and Israel's blindness will begin to pass away. But Scripture shows us there is to be a brief but dreadful period called "the Great Tribulation," "the time of Jacob's trouble," intervening between *the fulness* of the Gentiles, and the end of *the times* of the Gentiles, during which period certain events will take place, in the land of Palestine and on the prophetic earth, which have been long predicted in the Book of God. Now I feel certain from a careful study of Scripture and from comparing it with the present world-events, that the fulness of the Gentiles has almost come in, and that in a very little while the Church of God will be taken out of this scene; then these events relating to the prophetic earth will have their fulfilment.

— *H. A. Ironside.*

February 23

HE SHALL GLORIFY ME, FOR HE SHALL RECEIVE OF MINE, AND SHALL SHEW IT UNTO YOU. — John 16: 14

Thus, we are reminded that the Spirit also glorifies Christ by making our Lord precious and real to us. In the measure that we allow the Holy Spirit, through meditation, prayer, and obedience, to take of the things of Christ and make them precious to us, do we glorify Him by our dynamic Christian witness. It is an utter impossibility to be an effective witness for Christ unless the Lord Jesus Christ is in us a "living bright reality."

61

Lord, Thou hast made Thyself to me
A living bright reality,
More present to faith's vision keen
Than any earthly object seen;
More dear, more intimately nigh
Than e'en the closest earthly tie.

As we have already stated, the Christian life is a supernatural, mystical life. We have never seen Christ with the naked eye, yet we would gladly die for Him. He is the altogether lovely One. This is the miraculous work of the Holy Spirit in our souls. It was He Who in the first place gave us a sight of the dying Lamb of Calvary. It was He Who drew out our heart's affections to that blessed One, so that we can exclaim like Paul in soul rapture, "The Son of God, who loved me and gave Himself for me" (Gal. 2: 20).

The twin marks of a Spirit-filled believer are a deep appreciation for the Person of our Lord Jesus, and a deep, spiritual, reverential hunger for an insight into the Word of God. Anything less is only a sham. How solemn, then, is our responsibility in the light of this glorious truth, and in the light of a dying world, to allow the Spirit daily to effect this blessed work in our souls.

— *James A. Stewart*

February 24

THEY CRUCIFIED HIM. — Math. 27: 35

They crucified Him — how pregnant the short sentence is!

Him they delivered up to the humiliation and the agonising death; and what a world of significance is in the pronoun! In character, He was holy and undefiled, flawless and radiant in His perfection, without a peer. Therefore He is well suited for me. Because He has neither secret fault nor presumptuous sin, He is free to atone

62

for my soul. Moreover, in person, He was both my Brother and my GOD; and so qualified to cope with my enemies and to save me to the uttermost. Him — how much it means!

Crucified — that is what they did to Him, and what He bore for me. But I may not read everything that is in the awful verb. He trod the winepress alone. He went out and down for my sake into a horror of great darkness. I have no standard by which I can estimate such an experience. It is deep as hell, for He Who is my Substitute endured my condemnation. It is broad as the world of sinning and dying men. It is high as heaven, for it raises me to the heart and the house of GOD. *Crucified* — such a word it is!

They; and now I have arrived at myself, because the Evangelist's *They* is spacious and comprehensive. Not only does it include Judas, and Pilate, and the priests, and the people of the Jews: it includes me. My unbelief, my pride, my sin, have pierced His hands and feet. Ah, but here are glad tidings also. As He had forgiveness and peace and eternal life even for those who slew Him on Calvary, if they would but take His gifts, so He has for me. "His blood so red for me was shed." *They* — it is love at its best!

— *Alexander Smellie*

February 25

FOR THEY ... DECLARE PLAINLY THAT THEY SEEK A COUNTRY. — Heb. 11: 14

Let no one apologize for the powerful emphasis Christianity lays upon the doctrine of the world to come. Right there lies its immense superiority to everything else within the whole sphere of human thought or experience. When Christ arose from death and ascended into heaven, He established forever three important facts, namely, that this world has been condemned to ultimate

63

dissolution, that the human spirit persists beyond the grave and that there is indeed a world to come.

There is about the Christian faith a quiet dogmatism, a cheerful intolerance. It feels no need to appease its enemies or compromise with its detractors. Christ came from God, out of eternity, to report on the things He had seen and heard and to establish true values for the confused human race. Then He drew a line between this world and the world to come and said in effect "Choose ye this day." The choice is between an earthly house which we can at best inhabit but a little while and the house of the Lord where we may dwell forevermore.

The Christian faith engages the profoundest problems the human mind can entertain and solves them completely and simply by pointing to the Lamb of God. The problems of origin and destiny have escaped the philosopher and the scientist, but the humblest follower of Christ knows the answer to both. "In the beginning" found Christ there at the creation of all things, and "the world to come" will find Him there at their regeneration.

The church is constantly being tempted to accept this world as her home, and sometimes she has listened to the blandishments of those who would woo her away and use her for their own ends. But if she is wise she will consider that she stands in the valley between the mountain peaks of eternity past and eternity to come.

— *A. W. Tozer*

February 26

Therefore, let all the house of Israel know assuredly that God hath made that same Jesus, whom ye have crucified, both LORD and CHRIST. — Acts 2: 35
The official title of our Redeemer is now "The Lord Jesus Christ," because of His resurrection and ascension. It is interesting to note that our Saviour is called by his earthly name, Jesus, 608 times *before* His ascension, and only 62 times *after* His ascension; that while He is never

mentioned as "The Lord Jesus Christ" before his ascension, He is called "The Lord Jesus Christ" 81 times after His ascension. It is also striking to notice that as the apostles preached the Lordship of the Redeemer, their listeners were cut to the heart and bowed in surrender to Him.

There is a tendency in our modern times to leave out the emphasis of the Lordship of Christ, but I fully believe that no one can truly receive Jesus as Saviour who does not recognize Him as his Lord. *Jesus Christ does not save rebels.* Why should a man seek a pardon if he intends to go on in rebellion and stand out in defiance of his King? When we preach the Lordship of Christ to the sinner, we are insisting that he lay down his arms of rebellion and submit himself to Christ as King over his life.

No evangelistic message is a true Gospel message which ignores the claims of the Lordship of Christ, as emphasized in the Book of Acts.

In the first Gospel sermon on the day of Pentecost, 3.000 souls were stabbed to the heart and were gloriously saved. The keynote of Peter's message on that historic day was the Lordship of Christ.

— *James A. Stewart*

Dear reader, is He thy Lord?

February 27

THE LAME TAKE THE PREY. — Isaiah 33: 23
HERE IS VICTORY!

"The lame shall take the prey,"
And I am lame —
Lame in my inmost soul,
But ever keep me lame enough to be
Of use to Thee.

If Thou shouldst make me strong —
Strong in myself —
To wrestle, fight and pray,
Toil for Thee night and day,
I might unwittingly soon cease to be
Wrecked upon Thee.

So leave me with the lameness Jacob had
Halting upon his thigh;
That when, amid the battle sorely pres't
The victory of the Cross is manifest
Through my prevailing prayer, the praise may be
Wholly to Thee.

For here is victory —
Give me the power
To fight until the sword cleave to my hand,
And "having overthrown them all, to stand,"
And be content for only God to know
Who wrought with Him that day.

— *Mary N. Garrard*

Jacob was crippled that he might be crowned. See Genesis 33: 27—29.

February 28

HE IS ALTOGETHER LOVELY.

— Song of Songs 5: 16

Jesus was absolutely and manifestly his heart's Lord. Mr. Spurgeon's favourite title for Jesus was "the Well-beloved." I never knew any other man who had tears so near the surface for his Lord. In a moment, although he might have been making you laugh your very heart out just before, if the conversation turned to Jesus Christ you would see his eyes filled with tears. Grief for the Saviour's sorrows was one of dear Spurgeon's grand characteristics. It was wonderful how he lingered at Calvary. He loved to go on talking about our Lord's unknown agonies. I have listened to him with awe and wonder, and marked the big tears running down his cheeks as he spoke, though, I believe, he was unconscious of their presence. *No man was ever more akin to Samuel Rutherford in the wonderful richness — the oriental splendour, if I may so put it — of his descriptions of his Well-beloved.* In my judgment it was one of the most wonderful things possible to hear his soliloquies at the Lord's table. I have no doubt that I am speaking to some who, with myself, have heard his remarkable prayers at the annual conference, when, on the last day, we gathered round the table. In my judgment he never appeared so solitary, so ahead of all, as when he talked to his Lord and about his Lord at the communion table. His language would have been considered extravagant if one had not known how perfectly real it was. *He would stand and soliloquize about his Lord until you felt that he was simply enraptured with Him. This characteristic comes out very beautifully in one of his own hymns:* —

> If now, with eyes defiled and dim,
> We see the signs but see not Him,
> Oh, may His love the scales displace,
> And bid us see Him face to face.
>
> O glorious Bridegroom of our hearts,
> Thy present smile a heaven imparts;
> Oh, lift the veil, if veil there be:
> Let every saint Thy beauty see.

In Spurgeon's heart the Lord Jesus stood unapproached, unrivalled. He worshipped Him; he adored Him. He was our Lord's delighted captive.

— *Archibald Brown*

Oh my soul! what sayest thou to this testimony? Oh! that I may be also completely enthralled. Amen!

February 29

Likewise also the Spirit helpeth our infirmities; for we know not what to pray for as we ought; but the Spirit itself maketh intercession for us with groanings which cannot be uttered. And He that searcheth the hearts knoweth what is the mind of the Spirit, because He maketh intercession for the saints according to the will of God. — Rom. 8: 26

This is the deep mystery of prayer. This is the delicate divine mechanism which words cannot interpret, and which theology cannot explain, but which the humblest believer knows even when he does not understand.

Oh, the burdens that we love to bear and cannot understand! Oh, the inarticulate outreachings of our hearts for things we cannot comprehend! And yet we know they are an echo from the throne and a whisper from the heart of God. It is often a groan rather than a song, a burden rather than a buoyant wing. But it is a blessed burden, and it is a groan whose undertone is praise and utterably joy. It is "a groaning which cannot be uttered." We could not ourselves express it always, and sometimes we do not understand any more than that God is praying in us for something that needs His touch and that He understands.

And so we can just pour out the fullness of our heart, the burden of our spirit, the sorrow that crushes us, and know that He hears, He loves, He understands, He receives; and He separates from our prayer all that is imperfect, ignorant and wrong, and presents the rest, with the incense of the great High Priest, before the throne on high; and our prayer is heard, accepted and answered in His name.

— *A. B. Simpson*

Oh! Thou blessed Paraclete, thou Divine Intercessor make the temple of my body Thy praying channel. Amen!

March 1

BETHEL. — Genesis 28:19

EL — BETHEL. — Genesis 36:7

Jacob, after his memorable experience in the wilderness, where he saw a ladder set up on the earth and saw God standing above it, called the place of his encounter Beth-el, which means "the house of God," *beth, being house and el, God.*

Many years later, after he had suffered and sinned and repented and discovered the worthlessness of all earthly things, had been conquered and blessed by God at Peniel *and had seen the face of God in an hour of spiritual agony, he renamed the place El-beth-el,* which means "the God of the house of God." *Historically the place was always known as Beth-el, but in Jacob's worshiping heart it would forever be El-beth-el.*

The change is significant. Jacob had shifted his emphasis from the house to the One whom he met there. God Himself now took the center of his interest. *He had at last been converted from a place to God Himself.* A blessed conversion.

Many Christians never get beyond Beth-el. God is in their thoughts, but He it not first. *His name is spoken only after a hyphen has separated the primary interest from the secondary, God being secondary, the "house" first.* The weakness of the denominational psychology is that is puts something else before God. Certainly there may be no intention to do so; the very thought may startle the innocent denominationalist; but where the emphasis is, there the heart is also. Loyalty to our group may be a fine thing, but when it puts God on the other side of a hyphen it is a bad thing. Always God must be first.

Every means of grace is but a "house," a "place," and God must be there to make it significant. Any means that can be disassociated from God can be a snare if we do not watch it. It has not done anything for us till it has led us to God and put *El* after it. But still it is incomplete, and will be until the *El* is placed *before* it. No soul has found its real place till all its places have God before them: God first—God on the near side of the hyphen.

We may judge our spiritual growth pretty accurately by observing the total emphasis of our heart. Where is the primary interest? Is it Beth-el or El-beth-el? Is it my church or my Lord? Is it my ministry or my God? My creed or my Christ? We are spiritual or carnal just as we are concerned with the house or with the God of the house. If we discover that religious things are first, separated from God by a hyphen, we should immediately go down in tender penitence before our Lord and pray that He will forgive us for this affront and correct our evil attitude. He will hear and, if we continue to seek Him in sincerity of heart, He will take His place in the center of our lives where He by every right belongs.

— *A. W. Tozer*

March 2

GOD...NOW COMMANDETH ALL MEN EVERY-WHERE TO REPENT. — Acts 17: 30

We must be careful in our invitations not to offer peace and rest to those who are not ready to meet the conditions laid down by the Prince of Peace. The finest illustration of this truth is brought out by John Bunyan, in his book The Holy War, concerning the seige of Mansoul. As you know, the town of Mansoul depicts the individual soul of man. And this soul is being beseiged by the evangelistic efforts of the Lord's people, under the leadership of Boanerges, or the apostle John. Boanerges and his captains are calling on the town to surrender in the name of their King El Shaddai. If they will lay down their arms and surrender to the king, no harm will come to them; in fact, all will be well with them. These attacks from the captains were making things so hot for the town of Mansoul that the leaders decided on a truce with Boanerges and his captains. Lord Wilbewill was the spokesman for the town, and he approached the captains with these words, "We will accept your invitation to surrender to your king upon the following conditions:

1. *That none of those who now serve the town under the great giant, Diabolus, will be put out of the town, or that their freedom will be taken from them.*

2. *That the citizens of Mansoul shall be allowed to carry on all the pleasures and enjoyments which they had known under their king Diabolus.*

3. *That no new law, officer, or executioner of law shall have any power over them without their choice or consent.*

We may be sure that such terms as those presented by Lord Wilbewill were catagorically rejected by Boanerges and his captains.

The lesson here taught by the old Puritan evangelist John Bunyan is that the soul-winner must be careful never to offer reconciliation and peace to those who wish to continue in defiance of God's way of holiness. But to all those who feel their need of a Saviour, the invitation is "Come now, and let us reason together, saith the Lord: though your sins be as scarlet, they shall be as white as snow; though they be red like crimson, they shall be as wool" (Isaiah 1: 18).

— *James A. Stewart*

March 3

Thou shalt love the Lord thy God with all thy heart, and with all thy soul, and with all thy mind.

— Matt. 22: 37

Speaking about the late beloved founder of the Salvation Army, Dr. Wilbur Chapman once said, "When I looked into his face, and saw him brush back his hair from his brow, heard him speak of the trials and conflicts and the victories, I said, "General Booth, tell me what has been the secret of your success!" He hesitated a second, and I saw the tears come into his eyes, and steal down his cheeks, and then he said, "I will tell you the secret. God has had all there was of me to have. There have been men with greater opportunities; but ... I made up my mind that God would have all of William Booth there was." ' *That's it! The difference between Christians lies fundamentally in the extent of their surrender, the extent of their possession, not of Him, but by Him.*

— *James A. Stewart.*

March 4

I HAVE BEEN CRUCIFIED WITH CHRIST.

— Gal. 2: 20

It is because the children of God do not apprehend the two aspects of crucifixion with Christ that they fail to realize abundant life in practical experience. The objective, or the finished work of Christ in His death and resurrection is the basis of the subjective work of the Holy Spirit in us.

Objectively the death of Christ was not only a propitiation for sin, but was, in the purpose of God, the death of all for whom He died. In our position before God, we who are believers are in Him, the Cleft Rock — planted into His death. The Holy One became a curse for the accursed ones, that the accursed Adam-life might be nailed to the Cross with the Substitute, the Lamb of God.

Subjectively it is the work of the Spirit of God to apply to us the power of Christ's death and resurrection; to bring us inwardly into correspondence with our "position" in Christ — crucified, buried, risen, and ascended in the Redeemer.

The "objective" and "subjective" aspects must both be made real to the soul by the power of the Holy Ghost, if "life out of death" is to be known in practical reality.

On our part, if we have been brought by the mercy of God to truly hate ourselves — our "own life" (Luke 14: 26) as well as our sins — and to recognize that all is accursed, being heartily willing to renounce all that we ourselves have, we may turn to Calvary, and see that in Christ we are delivered, being dead to that wherein we were held (Rom. 7: 6, A. V. m).

In dependence upon the Divine Spirit, we may appropriate the death of Christ as our death, and count upon the immediate inflow of the life of the Risen Lord, to possess us to the fullest capacity of the earthen vessel . . .

From this point — the faith position that we *have been* crucified with Christ — we may expect the Holy Spirit to bear witness, and "make to die the doings of the body" in ever-deepening power.

The Eternal Spirit — charged with the work of applying to us the death, and of communicating the resurrection life of Christ — will cause us always to bear about the dying of Jesus. Thus shall be manifested in our mortal flesh the life also of Jesus, and in the power of that endless life we shall be energised to labour according to His working, working in us mightily.

— *J. Penn-Lewis*

FOR TO ONE IS GIVEN BY THE SPIRIT THE
WORD OF WISDOM. — 1 Cor. 12: 8
HE THAT PROPHESIETH. — 1 Cor. 14: 3

*A prophet is one who knows his times and what God
is trying to say to the people of his times.*

What God says to His church at any given period
depends altogether upon her moral and spiritual condition and upon the spiritual need of the hour. Religious
leaders who continue mechanically to expound the Scriptures without regard to the current religious situation are
no better than the scribes and lawyers of Jesus' day who
faithfully parroted the Law without the remotest notion
of what was going on around them spiritually. They fed
the same diet to all and seemed wholly unaware that
there was such a thing as meat in due season. The prophets never made that mistake nor wasted their efforts
in that manner. They invariably spoke to the condition
of the people of their times.

Today we need prophetic preachers; not preachers of
prophecy merely, but preachers with a gift of prophecy.
The word of wisdom is missing. We need the gift of
discernment again in our pulpits. It is not ability to
predict that we need, but the anointed eye, the power of
spiritual penetration and interpretation, the ability to
appraise the religious scene as viewed from God's position, and to tell us what is actually going on.

There has probably never been another time in the
history of the world when so many people knew so
much about religious happenings as they do today. The
newspapers are eager to print religious news; the secular
news magazines devote several pages of each issue to the
doings of the church and the synagogue; a number of
press associations gather church news and make it available to the religious journals at a small cost. *Even the
hiring of professional publicity men to plug one or another preacher or religious movement is no longer un-*

74

common; the mails are stuffed with circulars and "releases", while radio and television join to tell the listening public what religious people are doing throughout the world.

Where is the man who can see through the ticker tape and confetti to discover which way the parade is headed, why it started in the first place and, particularly, who is riding up front in the seat of honor? What disturbs me is that amidst all the religious hubbub hardly a voice is raised to tell us what God thinks about the whole thing.

What is needed desperately today is a prophetic insight. Scholars can interpret the past; it takes prophets to interpret the present.

One hundred years from now historians will know what was taking place religiously in this year of our Lord; but that will be too late for us.

— *A. W. Tozer*

March 6

OCCUPY TILL I COME. — Luke 19: 13

A lady once asked John Wesley, "Suppose you knew that you were to die at twelve o'clock to-morrow night, how would you spend the intervening time?" "How, madam?" he replied, "Why, just as I intend to spend it now. I should preach this night at Gloucester and again at five to-morrow morning. After that I should ride to Tewkesbury, preach in the afternoon, and meet the societies in the evening. I should then repair to my friend Martin's house, who expects to entertain me, converse and pray with the family as usual, and wake up in glory."

This is the only right attitude for Christian men and women. The old cry must not fade from our lips, nor the old hope from our hearts, "Maranatha, the Lord cometh." But meanwhile He hath given to every man his work, and we may be sure that there is no better preparation for His coming than a steady faith and an eager obedience to His will, so that no emergency shall find us unprepared. "Blessed is that servant whom his Lord when He cometh shall find so doing."

— James A. Stewart.

Oh That I might be that blessed servant ready for Thy coming!

March 7

GOD HATH CALLED US. — I Cor. 1: 9

One of the wonders of the Christian life is that God should use us as instruments to the salvation of lost souls. The living God has limited Himself in man's redemption to the instrumentality of the Spirit of God, the Word of God, and the saints of God. He uses those, and only those, whom He has united to the Lord Jesus Christ, the Head of the body (Eph. 1: 22—23).

God has called us into partnership with the Lord Jesus. "God is faithful, by whom ye were called unto the fellowship (partnership) of his Son Jesus Christ our Lord" (I Cor. 1: 9). "And he gave some ... evangelists; and some, pastors and teachers; for the perfecting of the saints, for the work of the ministry, for the edifying of the body of Christ: Till we all come in the unity of the faith, and of the knowledge of the Son of God, unto a perfect man, unto the measure of the stature of the fulness of Christ" (Eph. 4: 11—13). "As Thou hast sent me into the world (Satan-ruled cosmos), even so have I also sent them into the world (Satan-ruled cosmos)" (John 17: 18). "But all things come from God, for He it is Who reconciled me to Himself, by Jesus Christ, and charged me with the ministry of reconciliation; for God was in Christ reconciling the world to Himself, reckoning their sins no more against them, and having ordained me to speak the word of reconciliation. Therefore I am an ambassador for Christ, as though God exhorted you by my voice; In Christ's stead I beseech you, be ye reconciled to God" (II Cor. 5: 18—20, Conybeare).

— *James A. Stewart*

> From the glory and the gladness,
> From His secret place;
> From the rapture of His Presence,
> From the radiance of His face
> Christ, the Son of God, hath sent me
> To the midnight lands;
> Mine the mighty ordination
> Of the pierced hands.

March 8

BEING ENRICHED IN EVERY THING TO ALL BOUNTIFULNESS. — II. Cor. 9: 11.

AND YOU ARE MADE FULL IN HIM.

— Col. 2: 10, margin.

> I am so weak, dear Lord, I cannot stand
> One moment without Thee;
> But, oh, the tenderness of Thine enfolding!
> And, oh, the strength of Thy right hand!
> That strength is enough for me.
>
> I am so needy, Lord, and yet I know
> All fullness dwells in Thee;
> And hour by hour, that never-failing treasure
> Supplies and fills in overflowing measure,
> My least and greatest need, and so
> Thy grace is enough for me.
>
> It is so sweet to trust Thy Word alone.
> I do not ask to see
> The unveiling of Thy purpose, or the shining
> Of future light on mysteries untwining.
> Thy promise-roll is all my own—
> Thy Word is enough for me.

— *Frances Ridley Havergal*

March 9

I will sing of the Lord, because He hath dealt so lovingly with me: yea, I will praise the Name of the Lord most Highest. Psalm 13: 6 P.B.V.

Such words of joy are like sluice-gates. Open them and floods pour through, floods of memories of a love which "hath dealt so lovingly" with us; floods of reasons for being sure that it will be to the end. It would be as impossible to think of these memories and reasons one by one, as it would be to separate the water-floods into separate drops; but two single drops from the great flood refreshed me this morning: "Thou maintainest [upholdest] my lot." (¹) So it is as though a hand gathered up the minutes of this new day, before ever it begins, as one might gather up a handful of pearls, and all that the day is going to mean is upheld from minute to minute. "Thou art maintaining my lot" is Rotherham's word, so that all is well for to-day. And for to-morrow: "As for me, I will behold Thy face in righteousness: I shall be satisfied, when I awake, with Thy likeness";(²) or, as Rotherham has it, "I . . . shall be satisfied when awakened by a vision of Thee."

— *Amy Carmichael*

My soul sing!
¹ Psa. 16: 5. ² Psa. 17: 15.

March 10

LET IT BE KNOWN THIS DAY THAT THOU ART GOD IN ISRAEL. — I Kings 18: 36

Never did a man of God stand forth in such solitary grandeur as did Elijah on Mount Carmel.

One man defies the hosts of hell. One man throws down the challenge to a back-slidden nation. One man dares to come forth from the presence of God to the heights of Carmel and give a living demonstration of the majesty and might of the God of Israel. With calm audacious faith God's lone prophet stands forth at a critical hour in the history of Israel and overthrows the powers of darkness. Here is hell-shaking faith at its very highest! Yes, one lone man with the power of God at his disposal turns the tide of battle.

— *James A. Stewart*

Oh, Thou mighty God! give me this moment the faith of Elijah.

March 11

YE KNOW HIM. — John 14: 17

No believer can have a dynamic Christian life in holiness and power, unless he knows the Holy Spirit in an intimate way. The Lord Jesus, in introducing the Spirit to His disciples, said "Ye know Him: for He dwelleth with you and shall be in you" (John 14: 17). Just as it is possible for an unbeliever to know all about the Lord Jesus and yet not know Him personally as Lord and Saviour, so it is possible for you as a believer to know all about the Holy Spirit and yet not know Him as Companion and Friend. Paul prayed fervently in his apostolic benediction, "The grace of the Lord Jesus Christ, and the love of God, and the communion of the Holy Ghost be with you all. Amen" (II Cor. 13: 14). *All such benedictions were originally supplications.* This verse is really a personal prayer: "Oh Father, let Thy love be manifested; Oh Lord Jesus, let Thy grace be with us; Oh Holy Spirit, let Thy saints enjoy much of Thy communion."

The Spirit of God loves us. He manifested His love to us in bearing our insults, as we rejected His strivings and pleadings to come to Christ (Hebrews 10: 29— "Despite"-insult). *Would it not be strange* indeed if one of the Persons of the Godhead, Who loves, comforts and helps us to live the Christian life, should hold

Himself aloof from sweet intercourse with the believer whom He indwells? He longs to commune with us; it is we who hinder the communion.

We can go to Him in every time of need. We can ask Him to help us to understand the Scriptures. We can ask Him to anoint us with fresh oil. We can ask Him to comfort us. We can ask Him to take of the treasures of Christ and reveal them unto us. We can ask Him to make Christ real to us. We can ask Him to glorify Christ in our lives.

— *James A. Stewart*

Oh! Let Thy saints enjoy glorious communion this hour.

March 12

HE . . . BECAME OBEDIENT UNTO DEATH, EVEN THE DEATH OF THE CROSS. — Phil. 2: 8

Crucifixion was not the ordinary Roman death for criminals. It was reserved for slaves and criminals of the deepest dye. So low did that blessed One stoop, dear reader, to show His wondrous love to us in the putting away of our sin! Oh, what marvellous grace to stoop so low for us guilty ones, even to the death of a Roman slave, a criminal of the deepest dye! O ye heavens shining forth in your unsullied and brightest glory, no wonder God should draw a veil of darkness over your splendour at the degradation of your Maker on that cross! But blessed be His Holy Name for ever for the lessons it teaches us of His Wondrous love! And as He hung there, what did that sight signify? What was the meaning of death by crucifixion? It meant that the one who hung there, betwen earth and heaven, was *fit neither for the one nor the other*—an outcast from both. Could insult go further? But could love stoop lower? *Yet all this He did, guilty, lost one, for thee!*

— *F. Whitfield*

March 13

MELODY IN OUR HEAVINESS.

— Isaiah 61: 3, P.B.V.

I do not think that such heaviness as was felt by the people who were led captive into Babylon is meant to be lightened by melody; but there is another kind of heaviness, the tired out feeling that may come, and that our Lord knew when He sat on the well. ([1]) I am quite sure that sometimes this kind of heaviness has to be. If it were not so, we should not know how to help other tired people. These words, "melody in our heaviness", show us one of the quickest ways out of the heaviness that depresses the spirit, even though all may be clear between us and our Lord. Try melody — try singing. If you cannot sing aloud, sing in your heart — "singing and making melody in your heart to the Lord".([2])

Sometimes we cannot sing much, but we can look up to our God and say a word or two. I did not know till one day last week that He calls that little word a song. In the Revised Version of Psalm 42.8 we have this: "In the night His song shall be with me, even a prayer unto the God of my life." (Other versions have the same thought — *prayer is song to God.)*

"If thou be tempted, rise thou on the wings of prayer to thy Beloved", and He will take that poor little prayer and turn it into a song.

From the midst of frustrations in Central Africa, Fred Arnot, who was the Livingstone of those regions, wrote, "I am learning never to be disappointed, but to praise."

I read that journal letter of his when it came home—it must be more than forty years ago—but that vital word in an ordinary letter remained with me ready for a moment of need. *I am learning never to be disappointed, but to praise.* God keep us so near to Himself that there will be little shining seeds like that scattered about our letters — seeds that will bear harvests of joy somewhere, sometime, and be melody to others in their heaviness.

[1] Jn. 4: 6.   [2] Eph. 5: 19.   — *Amy Carmichael*

March 14

THE VICTORY OF MY COUNTENANCE.

— Psalm 42: 5

Three times in the two psalms before us, there occurs a refrain in identical language. It varies somewhat in the Authorized Version, where the translators have employed different words. In the first instance of its use (42: 5), the last three words have been attached to the following verse, having probably been so arranged in some manuscript in order to remove what to some scribe seemed an abrupt transition of thought.

The following rendition applies in all three instances (42: 5, 11; 43: 5). It is quite literal:

> "Why art thou cast down, O my soul,
> And why art thou disquieted in me?
> Await God, for I shall yet praise him
> — *The victory of my countenance—and my God."*

God is here revealed not merely as the Deliverer of the soul of the psalmist. In the existing circumstances of spiritual oppression and physical depression that would have itself been a splendid achievement of faith. *Jehovah is represented in a larger way, as the Giver of victory to the countenance of the psalmist, so that his enemies fled before his face.* The Lord had endued His servant with His own authority from on high, so that, as he went forward in the name of God, opposing circumstances should give way and spiritual enemies would flee apace.

This is a New Testament truth in an Old Testament setting. It is one with which every saved and sanctified believer should be familiar. The purpose of the Father provides that each child of His may be a sharer of the throne and the authority of His risen and exalted Son. Over all the power of the enemy this authority extends. It is the believer's right to bind and loose in the name of

Him who has appointed him. As the psalm states it, God is Himself the Victory of the believer's countenance, so that he fears neither man, nor spirit, nor opposing circumstance.

THE WAY OF THE CROSS

It is the duty and privilege of every Christian to understand and enter into the divine desire for our perfecting, and to claim the place with Christ, both in His cross and resurrection and ascension, that the Father has appointed. God has reckoned each believer in His Son to have died with Him at Calvary. "Know ye not," demands Paul (Rom. 6: 3ff.), "that so many of us as were baptized into Jesus Christ were baptized into his death?" Alas, it is a truth of which very few who claim the saving grace of our Lord have any practical knowledge, but it is of vital importance. All of our growth into the stature of the risen Son of man depends upon our identification with Him. "Our old man," the apostle goes on to say (v. 6), "was crucified with him, that the body of sin might be annulled" (its power over us destroyed completely and for ever). We enter into the experience of this through faith: "Likewise reckon ye also yourselves to be dead indeed unto sin, but alive unto God through Jesus Christ our Lord" (v. 11). — *Macmillan*

March 15

BEHOLD, THE KEEPER OF ISRAEL WILL NEITHER SLUMBER NOR SLEEP.

— Psalm 121: 4, margin

God keeps His saints when storms arise
And watches with His love-worn eyes.
The perils of our coming night
Already lie before His sight.
He knows when clouds obscured the way
And blotted out the light of day.

He knows when we His help most need.
And to our aid His feet doth speed.
He comes on wings of healing love
And bids our hearts to look above.
The terrors of the endless night
Before His presence take to flight.
He smooths the path before our feet
And gives us strength our foes to meet.
We travel on to victory sure
For as He leads we are secure.
We know not what the future holds
But take each day as it unfolds.
The bitter with the sweet God blends
We wisely take what'ere He sends.
His dealings are in wisdom made
The warming sun or chilling shade.
On mountain top or in the dell
Our Father doeth all things well.

— David B. Stewart

I will trust and not be afraid!

March 16

CHRIST IN YOU, THE HOPE OF GLORY.
— Col. 1: 27

A cross Christian, or an anxious one, a discouraged gloomy Christian, a doubting Christian, a complaining Christian, an exacting Christian, a selfish, cruel, hard-hearted Christian, a self-indulgent Christian, a Christian with a sharp tongue or a bitter spirit; a Christian, in short, who is not Christlike may preach to the winds with as much hope of success, as to preach to his own family or friends, who see him as he is. There is no escape from this inevitable law of things, and we may as well recognize it at once. *If we want our loved ones to trust* the Lord, volumes of talk about it will not be one-thousandth part as convincing to them as the sight of a little real trust on our own part in the time of need. The longest prayer and the loudest preaching are of no avail in any family circle, however they may do in the pulpit, unless there is on the part of the preacher a living out of the things preached.

Some Christians seem to think that the fruits which the Bible calls for are some form of outward religious work, such as holding meetings, visiting the poor, conducting charitable institutions, and so forth. Whereas the fact is that the Bible scarcely mentions these at all as fruits of the Spirit, but declares that the fruit of the Spirit is love, joy, peace, longsuffering, gentleness, goodness, faith, meekness, temperance. A Christlike character must necessarily be the fruit of Christ's indwelling. Other things will no doubt be the outcome of this character; but first and foremost comes the character, or all the rest is but a hollow sham. A late writer has said: "A man can never be more than his character makes him. A man can never do more nor better than deliver or embody that which is his character. Nothing valuable can come out of a man that is not first in the man. Character must stand behind and back up everything—the sermon, the poem, the picture, the book. None of them is worth a straw without it."

— *Hannah Whitall Smith*

March 17

WHEN THE MORNING WAS COME. — Math. 27: 1

The day has just dawned — the most momentous, decisive, and eventful in the world. It greets our Lord with dreadful insignia. It approaches in a blood-stained robe, a crown of thorns to encircle His brow, in the one hand, and in the other, the scourge, the fatal cup, and the accursed tree; while it rises upon us with the olive-

85

branch of peace, the divine acquittal, and the crown of life. O sacred Friday, day of divine compassion, birthday of our eternal redemption, we bless thee, we greet thee on our knees!

— *Krummacher*

Pause, oh my soul, and contemplate on this wondrous display of God's grace to thee!

March 18

IT CAME TO PASS AFTER A WHILE, THAT THE BROOK DRIED UP, BECAUSE THERE HAD BEEN NO RAIN IN THE LAND.

— 1 Kings 17: 7

Week after week, with unfaltering and steadfast spirit, Elijah watched that dwindling brook; often tempted to stagger through unbelief, but refusing to allow his circumstances to come between himself and God. Unbelief sees God through circumstances, as we sometimes see the sun shorn of his rays through smoky air; but faith puts God between itself and circumstances, and looks at them through Him. And so the dwindling brook became a silver thread; and the silver thread stood presently in pools at the foot of the largest boulders; and the pools shrank. The birds fled; the wild creatures of field and forest came no more to drink; the brook was dry. Only then to his patient and unwavering spirit, "the word of the Lord came, saying, Arise, get thee to Zarephath."

Most of us would have gotten anxious and worn with planning long before that. We should have ceased our songs as soon as the streamlet caroled less musically over its rocky bed; and with harps swinging on the willows, we should have paced to and fro upon the withering grass, lost in pensive thought. And probably, long ere the brook was dry, we should have divised some plan, and asking God's blessing on it, would have started off elsewhere.

86

God often does extricate us, because His mercy endureth forever; but if we had only waited first to see the unfolding of His plans, we should never have found ourselves landed in such an inextricable labyrinth; and we should never have been compelled to retrace our steps with so many tears of shame. *Wait, patiently wait!*

— *F. B. Meyer*

March 19

LO, I AM WITH YOU . . . ALL THE APPOINTED DAYS. — Matthew 28: 20, *Variorum Version.*

HE MAKETH NO MISTAKE

My Father's way may twist and turn,
My heart may throb and ache,
But in my soul I'm glad I know,
He maketh no mistake.

My cherished plans may go astray,
My hopes may fade away,
But still I'll trust my Lord to lead
For He doth know the way.

Tho' night be dark and it may seem
That day will never break;
I'll pin my faith, my all on Him,
He maketh no mistake.

There's so much now I cannot see,
My eyesight's far too dim;
But come what may, I'll simply trust
And leave it all to Him.

For by and by the mist will lift
And plain it all He'll make,
Through all the way, tho' dark to me,
He made not one mistake.

— *A. M. Overton*

THIS CUP . . . THY WILL BE DONE.

— Math. 26: 42

A cup is a vessel which has its appointed measure, and is limited by its rim. The Saviour several times refers to the cup that was appointed for Him. In Matthew 20: 22, He asks His disciples, "Are ye able to drink of the cup that I shall drink of?" By the cup, He understood the bitter draught of His passion which had been assigned Him. We heard Him ask in Gethsemane, at the commencement, if it were not possible that the cup might pass from Him; and here we find Him mentioning, with the most unmoved self-possession, "the cup which his Father had given him." *We know what was in the cup. All its contents would have been otherwise measured out to us by divine justice on account of sin.* In the cup was the entire curse of the inviolable law, all the horrors of conscious guilt, all the terrors of Satan's fiercest temptations, and all the sufferings which can befall both body and soul. It contained likewise the dreadful ingredients of abandonment by God, infernal agony, and a bloody death, to which the curse was attached — all to be endured while surrounded by the powers of darkness.

Here we learn to understand what is implied in the words, "Who spared not his own Son, but freely gave him up for us all." "The Lord laid on him the iniquities of us all." "I will smite the Shepherd, and the sheep shall be scattered." "Christ hath redeemed us from the curse of the law, being made a curse for us." "God made him to be sin for us, who knew no sin." All that mankind have heaped up to themselves against the day of God's holy and righteous wrath—their forgetfulness of God—their selfish conduct—their disobedience, pride, worldly-mindedness—their filthy lusts, hypocrisy, falsehood, hard-heartedness, and deceit—all are united and mingled in this cup, and fermented together into a horrible potion. *"Shall I not drink this cup?"* asks the Saviour.

"Yes," we reply, "empty it, beloved Immanuel! we will kiss Thy feet, and offer up ourselves to Thee upon Thy holy altar!" He has emptied it, and not a drop remains for His people. The satisfaction He rendered was complete, the reconciliation effected. "There is now no condemnation to them that are in Christ Jesus." The curse no longer falls upon them. "The chastisement of our peace lay upon him; and by his stripes we are healed," and nothing now remains for us but to sing Hallelujah!

— *Krummacher*

March 21

NOT IN WORD ONLY. — I Thess. 1:5

Because it is the work of the Holy Spirit to convict and convince a man of his damning sin of Christ-rejection, it is necessary now for one to emphasize the difference between witnessing and the work of soul-winning. As we have said already, every Christian must witness to the saving power of the Lord Jesus. Witnessing is the divine method of preparing the way for soul-winning, but it does not necessarily result in the winning of all to whom we witness. We are to witness to all, without exception, but we can win for Christ only the people whom the Holy Spirit has convicted of their sin and their need for a Saviour. It is because many sincere workers fail to see this distinction and therefore fail to watch for the evidences of the Spirit's work in the life of the individual that we have so many false decisions. Some are urged, pushed, crowded, and sometimes almost forced to "make a decision", irrespective of the fact that the Holy Spirit has not yet done His preliminary work in their hearts. The Spirit's work is to plow up the ground through conviction and then insert the life-giving seed of the Word of God through the testimony of the soul-winner.

Then, by a creative act of the Holy Spirit, the new

*life of the Son of God is implanted in the heart of the
convicted and convinced sinner. This new life, implanted within the sinner, produces a new creation.* Thus, the
apostle cries out: "Therefore if any man be in Christ,
he is a new creature (creation): old things are passed
away; behold, all things are become new" (II Cor. 5: 17).
"I am crucified with Christ; it is no more I that live,
but Christ is living in me; and my outward life which
still remains, I live in the faith of the Son of God, Who
loved me and gave Himself for me" (Gal. 2: 20, Conybeare).

That old "I" — that old self — is nailed to the cross,
and in the new creation the Lord Jesus is the life. Consequently, nobody can become a child of God except by
being born again of the Holy Spirit through the Word
of God.

— James A. Stewart

Pause dear reader, and examine yourself and see if
you are truly born again.

March 22

IT IS NO LONGER I . . . but CHRIST.

Gal. 2: 20 Weymouth

> *"No longer I, but Christ.' O precious Lord,*
> *How can I speak the sweetness of this word,*
> *By which from bondage Thou hast set me free,*
> *Giving me perfect liberty in Thee.*
> *'No longer I, but Christ' —then am I 'dead';*
> *'Buried,' yet risen in my glorious Head;*
> *'Buried,' that self no longer come between*
> *His love and souls. Henceforth be only seen*
> *The beauty and the glory of my Lord*
> *Upon His child :—His power in every word,*
> *His life in every act, and look and tone;*
> *Mine the sweet peace, the glory His alone.*
> *'No longer I.' When comes temptation's hour,*

His is the kingdom, therefore His the power;
He knoweth how to keep in perfect peace
The soul in which His reign doth never cease.
'No longer I, but Christ,' —I may not choose,
But follow each command, nor e'er refuse
A call to service, whatsoe'er it be,
For Jesus calls and is enough for me.
O life of sweetest liberty so blest,
I yield Him all, and He does all the rest."

— *Freda Hanbury Allan*

March 23

HE . . . DEPARTED INTO A SOLITARY PLACE.
— Mark. 1: 35

THE SILENT SPACES OF THE SOUL

The soul needs its silent spaces. It is in them we learn to pray. There, alone, shut in with God, our Lord bids us pray to our Father which is in secret, and seeth in secret. There is no test like solitude. Fear takes possession of most minds in the stillness of the solitary place. The heart shrinks from being alone with God that seeth in secret! Who shall abide in His presence? Who can dwell with God Who is shadowless light? Hearts must be pure and hands clean that dare shut the door and be alone with God. *It would revolutionise the lives of most men if they were shut in with God in some secret place for half an hour a day.*

For such praying all the faculties of the soul need to be awake and alert. When our Lord took Peter and James and John with Him to the secret place of prayer, they were heavy with sleep. It was the same in the Mount of Glory and the Garden of Agony, and it was not until they were fully awake that they saw the glory or realised the anguish. There are some silent places of

91

rare wisdom where men may not talk but they find it possible to sleep. Mooning is not meditation, and drowsy repose is not praying. The secret place of prayer calls for every faculty of mind and heart.

Bless the Lord, O my soul;
And *all that is within me*
Bless His Holy Name.

— *Samuel Chadwick*

March 24

SANCTIFY YOURSELVES, FOR TOMORROW THE LORD WILL DO WONDERS AMONG YOU.
— Joshua 3: 5

This is a solemn verse, because our new relationship in Christ, although one of grace, has as its foundation the righteousness of God. "Grace reigns through righteousness." God is a Holy God. It is striking to notice in the Scriptures how that God put to death His people who had committed some trivial thing, while the uncircumcised were not put to death for committing even greater sins. The lesson is obvious; *God will not tolerate among His people what He tolerates among the unsaved.* As Christian workers, we must never forget the exortation of Paul; "Let us have grace, whereby we may serve God acceptably, with reverance and godly fear: for our God is a consuming fire." This clarion call of God was sounded throughout the camp of Israel on the eve of the memorial day, when after forty years of wilderness failure, they crossed over Jordan into the Promised Land; "SANCTIFY YOURSELVES, for tomorrow the Lord will do wonders among you."

The law, which underlies this command, is an eternal one. Every mighty movement of the Holy Spirit is preceded by a preparation of heart among God's people.

92

GOD'S TOMORROW OF WONDERS WAITS FOR OUR TODAY OF SANCTIFICATION. Upon us rests the responsibility of fixing the time of God's display of power, for there is no delay with Him. "The might of His power" is constant and unchanging, but His supernatural workings vary according to the receptiveness and obedience of the people of God.

— *James A. Stewart*

March 25

LET ALL THINGS BE DONE DECENTLY AND IN ORDER. — I Cor. 14: 40

If one were to particularise regarding this aspect of holiness, one could not be too circumstantial. It is important to fulfil every engagement punctually, to meet with exactness not only each specific promise but every reasonable expectation. We ought to answer our letters with scrupulous carefulness, to face the sometimes bewildering calls on time and patience with cheerfulness and alacrity, to receive interruptions, no matter how disturbing, with joyfulness. We should pass from one duty to another with unexhausted calmness, choosing with unerring precision those which have a prior claim, performing each in its own order without perturbation or undue haste, and always in the love of God. *Let no man think that he is fully sanctified, if he fails in things like these.*

If often happens that earnest servants of Christ accept responsibilities which they cannot suitably discharge. Perhaps we ought not to say quite without qualification that God *never* gives His children more to do than they are fully able to accomplish. But such an assertion would come extremely near the truth. As our Lord reminded His disciples, there are twelve hours in the day—the day is as long as the work. And if we could fill in the fleeting hours with carefulness and with diligence we should find, in almost every case, that the twelve hours which are entrusted to us are enough for all our need. Was any ministry ever so pressed by thronging and conflicting calls as was that of the Lord Jesus? Yet He did all things well, and at the last the work He came to accomplish was fully done. He failed in no duty; He missed no opportunity; He "finished" the task entrusted to Him.

— D. M. Mc Intyre

Lord I accept this kind rebuke!

March 26

And He called to the man clothed with linen, which had the writer's inkhorn by his side; and the Lord said unto him, Go through the midst of the city, through the midst of Jerusalem, and set a mark upon the foreheads of the men that sigh and that cry for all the abominations that be done in the midst thereof.

— Ezekiel 9: 3—4

Who is this mysterious seventh Person with the inkhorn, clothed with the linen garments of the High Priest? It is none other than the Lord of glory. He sighs over the abominations of the people whom He has redeemed by His precious blood. He sighs over their barren spiritual condition.

He sighs because He cannot deny His holiness and shut His eyes to their sins. "Son of man, these men have set their idols in their heart, and put the stumbling-block of their iniquity before their face: should I be enquired of at all by them?" (Ezekiel 14: 3). God cannot answer their prayers; they are an abomination unto Him. The mighty arm of Jehovah is paralysed in the midst of such awful conditions (Isaiah 59: 1—2).

We are living in a day when iniquity abounds and "the love of many shall wax cold." Compromise and callousness are among the crying evils of the present age. The Son of God is looking for Gethsemane companions.

Does He find one in you? As He has gone through your assembly, how many has He marked? Has He marked your forehead with His sacred sign of fellowship and identification? Does He find you among the godly remnant in these last days of a dying dispensation of grace, sighing for the abominations and sins of the Church? Are you among the believers to whom God has become a "little sanctuary"? (Ezekiel 11: 16).

The "Marked" ones are those who have claimed their "Magna Charta" of liberty from Romans 8, and have a heart free to enter into fellowship with Christ for others. Alas! Many Christians have to spend their time sighing and crying over their own sins and failures, so that they have no power to exercise the authority of their priestly function for others.

True intercession is the costliest of all Christian service. It is no mere lip service. It is the heart-agony of the Father expressed through us by the Holy Spirit, as He makes intercession through us (Romans 8: 26). We never really pray until our hearts and minds become the praying-ground of the Spirit.

What does this mark involve? In Ezekiel's case this mark meant intercession of the highest order — fullest indentification with the sufferings of God for His backslidden people; identifying himself with the people in their idolatry.

In the plans and purposes of God we are to be the instruments of the Spirit's intercession. When we seek the gifts and graces of this high and holy ministry, and allow our great High Priest and Saviour Jesus Christ to put His secret sign upon our forehead, we bear the burden in true identification for the condition of the Church and the world.

The moment we give ourselves to the Lord to be marked with the secret sign, that moment we must lay all on the altar of sacrifice and ourselves become "living" sacrifices (Romans 12: 1).   — *James A. Stewart*

Lord mark me with the secret sign!

March 27

THE LORD HAD SAID UNTO ABRAM, GET THEE OUT. — Gen. 12: 1

The call of God can never be stated explicitly, it is implicit. The call of God is like the call of the sea, or of the mountains; no one hears these calls but the one who has the nature of the sea or of the mountains; and no one hears the call of God who has not the nature of God in him. It cannot be definitely stated what the call of God is to, because it is a call into comradeship with God Himself for His own purposes, and the test of faith is to believe that God knows what He is after. The call of God only becomes clear as we obey, never as we weigh the *pros* and *cons* and try to reason it out. The call is God's idea, not our idea, and only on looking back over the path of obedience do we realize what is the idea of God; God sanctifies memory. When we hear the call of God it is not for us to dispute with God, and arrange to obey Him if He will expound the meaning of His call to us. As long as we insist on having the call expounded to us, we will never obey; but when we obey it is expounded, and in looking back there comes a chuckle of confidence — 'He doeth all things well.' Before us there is nothing, but overhead there is God, and we have to trust Him. If we insist on explanations before we obey, we lie like clogs on God's plan and put ourselves clean athwart His purpose.

Faith never knows where it is being led, it knows and loves the One Who is leading. It is a life of *faith*, not of intelligence and reason, but a life of knowing Who is making me 'go'.

— *Oswald Chambers*

March 28

THOU SHALT KNOW HEREAFTER. — John 13:7

UP THERE WE WILL UNDERSTAND

Not now, but in the coming years—
It may be in the better land—
We'll read the meaning of our tears,
And there, some time, we'll understand.

We'll catch the broken threads again,
And finish what we here began;
Heaven will the mysteries explain,
And then, ah then, we'll understand.

We'll know why clouds instead of sun
Were over many a cherished plan;
Why song has ceased when scarce begun;
'Tis there, some time, we'll understand.

Why what we long for most of all,
Eludes so oft our eager hand;
Why hopes are crushed and castles fall,
Up there, some time, we'll understand.

God knows the way, He holds the key,
He guides us with unerring hand;
Some time with tearless eyes we'll see;
Yes, there, up there, we'll understand.

— Selected

March 29

GOD IS FAITHFUL.

But God is faithful [to His Word and to His compassionate nature], and He [can be trusted] not to let you be tempted *and* tried *and* assayed beyond your ability *and* strength of resistance *and* power to endure, but with the temptation He will [always] also provide the way out — the means of escape to a landing place — that you may be capable *and* strong *and* powerful patiently to bear up under it.

— I Cor. 10: 13, The Amplified New Testament.

IN THE EARLIER PART OF THIS EPISTLE THE APOSTLE HAS WRITTEN:

"God is faithful — reliable, trustworthy, and (therefore) ever true to His promise, and He can be depended on; by Him were ye called into companionship and participation with His Son, Jesus Christ, our Lord."

— I Cor. 1: 9 Amplified N. T.

Now He would assure his readers that the faithful God Who called them can be depended on to keep them in all their ways, according to His promises.

If we would experience fully the reliability of our God, we must search out and claim for ourselves daily the promises He has given us in His Word; "great and precious promises", Peter calls them. There is no command from Him which is not met by a promise. *There is no need which can arise which is not matched with a promise.* There is no trial or temptation known to man which has no fitting promise in His Word.

No man has ever trusted in vain who has rested his head confidently on the promises of God.

"And the Lord gave them rest ... the Lord delivered all their enemies into their hand. There failed not ought of any good thing which the Lord had spoken unto the House of Israel: ALL came to pass (Joshua 21: 44—45).

— *Ruth Stewart*

BLESSED BE THE GOD AND FATHER OF OUR LORD JESUS CHRIST WHO HAS CROWNED US WITH EVERY SPIRITUAL BLESSING.

— Eph. 1: 3, Weymouth

Paul in verse 6 tells them they have been highly graced in the Beloved One. Again Weymouth's translation of this verse is faithful and accurate, and leads them to the gateway of the glorious deposits which are theirs: "to the praise of the splendour of His grace with which *He has enriched us* in the beloved One." As we scan our title deeds we discover that the word "riches" is the key word throughout this epistle. In chapter 2, verse 7, we read, "The exceeding riches of His grace". The word translated "exceeding" is that from which we get our English word "hyperbole", applied to exaggeration. The word literally means, "to shoot beyond the mark" and implies therefore the thought of excess. Paul means that although one uses the utmost wealth of language in speaking of these riches, he cannot shoot beyond the mark; the riches of God exceed all power of expression. The "transcendent riches", says Weymouth. Again in chapter 3, verse 8, the apostle speaks of the "unsearchable riches of Christ". The word "unsearchable" means "riches that can never be explored". We not only cannot measure them, and we not only form no estimate of them, but we can never get to the end of our exploration. *There is a boundless continent of riches that still lies before us, when we have carried our search to the limit.* Here our spiritual Geiger-counters are helpless in exploring all the riches which are potentially ours in Christ. Not only so, but these riches are *"untraceable"*. The thought is that of seeking to trace a path through the woods, and finding so many paths going out from each path, that the whole thing is untraceable. (Cf. "past finding out", Rom. 11: 33).

And all of these riches, the riches of His grace, the riches of His glory, the riches of His power, etc., are ours for the purpose of making and keeping us holy, "that we might be unto the praise of His glory".

— James A. Stewart

Hallelujah! Oh that I may appropiate my wealth in my blessed Redeemer today!

March 31

BEHOLD, THE VEIL OF THE TEMPLE WAS RENT IN TWAIN FROM THE TOP TO THE BOTTOM.

— Matt. 27:51

CHRIST DIES

Christ dies — the love of God commending
Christ dies — the temple veil is rending
Christ dies — His precious side is riven
Christ dies — behold an opened heaven.
Christ dies — the heart of God revealing
Christ dies — to give my soul its healing
Christ dies — the power of darkness shaken
Christ dies — "the Lonely One" forsaken.
Christ dies — the voice of mercy speaketh
Christ dies — there's life for him that seeketh.
Christ dies — His heart surcharged with sorrow
Christ dies — for me the cloudless morrow.
Christ dies — of victory the beginning
Christ dies — to end me of my sinning
Christ dies — but this is not disaster
Christ dies — of sin the proven master.
Christ dies — A Mercy Seat providing
Christ dies — within His wounds I'm hiding
Christ dies — His precious blood is flowing
Christ dies — eternal life I'm knowing.
Christ dies — it is a grievous sowing

100

Christ dies — and life from death is flowing
Christ dies — but soon He's raised in glory
Christ dies — proclaim the gospel story.

— David B. Stewart

Hallelujah! — In Him we have victory!

Through Him we have access!

Our Great high priest by His atonement has opened and inaugerated a new living way. — Heb. 10: 19—20

April 1

YE ARE . . . A ROYAL PRIESTHOOD. — I Pet. 2: 8.

A careful reader of the Scriptures need not be told how closely the ceremony of anointing was related to all the important offices and ministries of the servant of Jehovah under the old Covenant.

The priest was anointed that he might be holy unto the Lord (Lev. 8: 2).

The king was anointed that the Spirit of the Lord might rest upon him in power (1 Sam. 16: 15).

The prophet was anointed that he might be the oracle of God to the people (1 Sam. 19: 16).

No servant of Jehovah was deemed qualified for his ministry without this holy sanctified touch laid upon him. Imagine, if you can, a priest attemping to minister before the Lord and daring to touch the things of the sanctuary without having first of all been sprinkled with the holy anointing oil! God was so jealous for the sanctity of those who had been anointed for service that the penalty of failing to wash the hands and feet when they ministered before the Lord was death (Exod. 30: 19—21). What, then, but death in its most awful form must have

101

been the penalty of such presumption as that which we have suggested? The holy anointing was the outward, visible sign of the impartation to the priests of those gifts and graces which qualified them for being the ministers of the Lord; the teachers, the guides, and the intercessors of the Lord's people.

Under the new economy every born-again, blood-washed child of God is a royal priest to minister before and for the Lord, and hence needs the anointing of the Spirit. The Church is a kingdom of priests, and each individual believer is a royal priest (Rev. 1: 6; 1 Pet. 2: 9).

— *James A. Stewart*

April 2

THEY WENT BOTH OF THEM TOGETHER.

— Gen. 22: 8

There is a great mystery illustrated here: the mystery of the cross. Twice in this chapter we are told that Abraham, the father, and Isaac, the son, went both of them together to the place of sacrifice, the place where the only begotten son (Heb. 11: 17) was to be offered up, though at the last, as one has well said, God spared that father's heart a pang He would not spare His own. So throughout all the ages it might be said of the Eternal Father and the Eternal Son, that they went both of them together. The cross was ever before God. Christ was delivered to death by the foreknowledge of God. Redemption was planned and provided for, long ere sin lifted up its ugly head to mar God's fair creation. *All down the centuries the Father and the Son counseled together concerning the great redemption there to be wrought out.*

— *H. A. Ironside*

> *Son of God, Thy Father's bosom*
> *Ever was Thy dwelling-place,*
> *His delight, in Him rejoicing,*
> *One with Him in power and grace.*

Oh, what wondrous love and mercy!
Thou didst lay Thy glory by,
And for us didst come from heaven,
As the Lamb of God to die.

April 3

THAT THOU MIGHTEST . . . BE FILLED WITH THE HOLY SPIRIT. — Acts 9: 17

The normal experience of every New Testament believer is to be filled with the Holy Ghost at the threshold of his new life in Christ Jesus (Acts 9: 17). The New Testament teaches this. There is only one crisis demanded, and that is the one of regeneration — "Ye must be born again (John 3: 7). And through this new birth we ought to enter into all the fullness of God. There is growth in grace and in the knowledge of the Lord after this, however; and the new-born babe must walk in the Spirit until he reaches full stature in Christ (Eph. 4: 13). *It is when he fails to do this that he stunts his Christian growth, and then a new crisis is demanded if the life is to go on in blessing.* If you read the autobiographies or biographies of the holy men and women of God in the past, you will discover that *almost every one had a second crisis in his life* to which he attributed a real spiritual revolution in power and glory and knowledge. Many have called this a "second work of grace" since the change was almost as great as their conversion. We must try to keep to Scriptural terminology, or else we will confuse young believers. However, let us be careful not to criticize others who do not pronounce our "shibboleth."

If a believer is grieving and quenching the Spirit and not walking in Him, he needs to confess his sin and lay all upon the altar of dedication. This is a definite, new crisis in his life. Just as at regeneration one must have a definite dealing with the Lord Jesus for remission of sins, so there must be also a definite dealing with the Holy Spirit for the normal, New Testament life. *A young convert who does not possess his inheritance in Christ at conversion is left in the position of a potential backslider.*

— *James A. Stewart*

April 4

REJOICE IN THE LORD. — Phil. 4: 4

"*One Monday noon, at the close of the Brooklyn class, as I was about to start for New York, a lady who was at the class asked if she might accompany me, as she desired to talk with me.* I willingly consented, as I am glad to be of use to anyone who desires to know HIM better. As we rode along the Brooklyn elevated railway, my friend began to tell me her troubles, and I trusted the Lord for grace to listen as He would like me to. Having arrived at the Brooklyn end of the great bridge, and finding that the bridge cars were not running, and no one could tell when they would resume, my friend suggested that we walk over. It being only about a twenty minutes' walk, we did so; and as we walked, my friend continued her sad sory. When she stopped at a very sad part, and looked at me, as if for some word, all I felt led to say was, 'HE IS ALTOGETHER LOVELY'. She seemed a little surprised, but resumed her story. When she stopped again, I felt led to repeat the same words. She seemed more surprised, and said, 'Perhaps you do not want to hear my woeful tale.' I said: 'Yes, I am listening prayerfully. Go on.' She went on, till we reached the New York end of the bridge, where we were to part, and, as she took my hand to say 'good-bye,' 'Please say after me, HE IS ALTOGETHER LOVELY.' She did so, with some astonishment that I had nothing more to say to her, and so we parted."

— *D. M. Stearns*

CALL UNTO ME AND I WILL ANSWER THEE, AND SHEW THEE GREAT AND HIDDEN THINGS WHICH THOU HAST NOT YET SEEN.

— Jer. 33: 3, free translation

The greatest reason for my belief that God wants to send revival in these days, however, has to do with His plans and purposes for the lives of His redeemed ones. God is never content in any age for His people to live below the standard which He has set for His Son's Bride. Such passages from His Word as "Begin at My sanctuary" (Ezek. 9: 6). "Blow ye the trumpet in Zion" (Joel 2: 1), and "Remember therefore from whence thou art fallen, and repent, and do the first works; or else I will come unto thee quickly and will remove thy candlestick out of his place, except thou repent" (Rev. 2: 5) remind us that God is never content with the sub-normal life of the Church. *There is no parent who would be satisfied or happy about his children's being sick and perennially low in health.* It would indeed be startling, upon asking a father concerning the health of his children, to hear him say, "Most of the time my children are weak and sickly, but it doesn't matter, because for a few weeks each year they come back to normal and are rather healthy." No man is satisfied that his bride be sub-normal either physically or mentally. Far less can our Father be content for one moment to see His Church anything less than holy and powerful, living in vital communion with Himself, as He has purposed. *A sub-normal and back-slidden Church is an insult and a disgrace to a holy, powerful, almighty God.*

— *James A. Stewart*

Oh, Thou Holy God! Have mercy upon us and awaken us to Thy plans and purposes. Amen!

April 6

NOW UNTO HIM THAT IS ABLE TO DO.

— Eph. 3: 20

DIVINE POSSIBILITIES

I DARE to say that — IT IS POSSIBLE, for those who really are willing to reckon on the power of the Lord for keeping and victory, to lead a life in which His promises are taken as they stand and are found to be True.

IT IS POSSIBLE to cast all our care upon Him daily and enjoy deep peace in doing it.

IT IS POSSIBLE to have the thoughts and imaginations of our hearts purified, in the deepest meaning of the word, through faith.

IT IS POSSIBLE to see the will of God in everything, and to receive it, not with sighing, but with singing.

IT IS POSSIBLE, by taking complete refuge in Divine power, to become strong through and through; and, where previously our greatest weakness lay, to find that the things which formerly upset all our resolves to be patient or pure or humble, furnish to-day an opportunity — through Him Who loved us, and works in us an agreement with His will and a blessed sense of His presence and His power — to make sin powerless.

These things are DIVINE POSSIBILITIES, and because they are His work, the true experience of them will always cause us to bow lower at His feet and to learn to thirst and long for more. We cannot possibly be satisfied with anything less than — each day, each hour, each moment, in Christ, through the power of the Holy Spirit — TO WALK WITH GOD.

— *Handley Moule*

THE SON OF GOD WHO LOVED ME.

— Gal. 2: 20

And can it be that I should gain
  An int'rest in the Saviour's blood?
Died He for me, who caused His pain?
  For me, who Him to death pursued?
Amazing love! how can it be
That Thou, my God, shouldst die for me?

'Tis mystery all! The Immortal dies!
  Who can explore His strange design?
In vain the first-born seraph tries
  To sound the depths of love divine!
'Tis mercy all! let earth adore,
Let angel minds inquire no more.

He left His Father's throne above,
  So free, so infinite His grace;
Emptied Himself of all but love,
  And bled for Adam's helpless race:
'Tis mercy all, immense and free;
For, O my God, it found out me.

Long my imprisoned spirit lay
  Fast bound in sin and nature's night;
Thine eye diffused a quickening ray,
  I woke, the dungeon flamed with light;
My chains fell off, my heart was free;
I rose, went forth, and followed Thee.

No condemnation now I dread;
  Jesus, and all in Him, is mine!
Alive in Him, my living Head,
  And clothed in righeteousness divine,
Bold I approach the eternal throne,
And claim the crown, through Christ my own.

— C. Wesley

April 8

FOR I AM WITH YOU, SAITH THE LORD OF HOSTS. — Haggai 2: 4

What an encouragement for the weak and timid labourer in the Lord's vineyard! God's commands are assurances of power. He knows we cannot make ourselves strong. What He requires is, that we should be willing to be made strong. "Allow yourself to be empowered. You have no ability, but I have given you capacity. Your weakness and emptiness and need are your capacity to receive. Power belongeth unto Me. I have the ability to accomplish." It is thus that God equips us for service. He who bids us "work" is ready, by His own might, to make us "strong."

The encouragement is based on the fact that we have His Presence. "I am not only for you, but with you — close at hand, to succour and sustain." No duty or difficulty can be too great if the Lord of hosts is with us, and calls us to go forth.

Three things are intimately associated — the call to service; the work, or sphere of service; and the power, or equipment for service. They each come from God. Let us seek to let God have His right place in each of these parts of Christian service.

— *Evan H. Hopkins*

April 9

A VESSEL UNTO HONOUR . . . PREPARED UNTO EVERY GOOD WORK. — II Tim. 2: 21
A PLAN FOR EVERY LIFE

The Divine purpose of the ages implies a personal plan for each individual life, for the wider purposes of God are carried forward upon the united obedience of individual lives; sometimes even seemingly upon the tiny pivot of one life. *For every life there must therefore be a distinctive will of Good that fits in with the whole scheme.* And the richness of the life will depend upon how perfectly it achieves its own ordained purpose. The sovereignty of God guarantees that if the individual fails the ultimate divine purpose will still move forward; but the personality loses the rich joy, to say nothing of the everlasting reward, of co-working with the Almighty to an eternal design.

— *Donald Gee*

Oh, Thou great Architect I pray Thee fervently this moment that I will not miss Thy plan for my life.

April 10

TO HIM THAT OVERCOMETH. — Rev. 2: 7

The condition of enthonement with Christ is expressed in His own words sent to the Church by His Apostle: "Unto him that OVERCOMETH will I grant to sit with Me in My Throne." *So we labour toward making believers "overcomers".* We seek to teach them to war in order that they may reign. We strive to cause them to overcome in order to share Christ's Throne; for he that has been girt by the panoply of God, and has wielded the sword, shall be honoured to stretch out the sceptre of the Most High.

— *Evan Roberts*

Overcomers are desperately needed today!

April 11

THEY HAVE MOSES AND THE PROPHETS.
— Luke 16: 29

A Family Which Had Every Needed Chance to be Saved.
Here was a big family, a rich family, one of them dead, one of them in Hell, five others on the way. And

109

now one last word. It was a family that had every chance it needed to be saved. That man did not have to go to Hell. His five brothers did not have to go. They had Moses and the prophets. They had a testimony. They could have been saved. But listen! You are this side of Calvary. You are this side of the open tomb. You have a chance greater than they had. You have the gospel. You are in the Holy Ghost dispensation. You are in the church age. You are in the gathering-out period, when God is getting a bride for His Son. You have a chance. If you never had one before tonight, you have this one tonight. If you never hear the gospel again, you are hearing it now. If you never have another call, you have a call tonight. Why don't you settle it tonight? Do not go out of this house without settling it; please do not. Let me beg you to settle it. I want to do you a favor. I want you to be saved. It is wonderful to be saved! You feel so safe when you are saved. You can go to bed at night and rest in peace. Won't you come to God tonight? Won't you trust Jesus? Don't lose this chance. Now is your chance. *Your last chance will come some day; this may be it. Don't let it pass! Trust Him tonight!*

— *Bob Jones, Sr*

April 12

SPEAK, LORD, FOR THY SERVANT HEARETH.

— 1 Sam. 3: 9

Only a word, O Lord,
I crave from Thee!
One little word will give
Full victory
O'er every doubt and fear and anxious care:
One little word will answer all my prayer.

Only a word, O Lord,
    Will cheer my heart
Like that of lovers who
    Are long apart.
A word from Thee assures forgiveness sweet,
And blessedly confirms Thy friendship meet.

Only a word, O Lord,
    Will start the song
That gives me faith that Thou
    Wilt right all wrong.
A word from Thee in dark temptations' maze,
Will light my lonely path with heaven's rays.

Only a word, O Lord,
    I crave of Thine!
Each morning, as I read
    Thy Book divine,
Cause me to hear Thy well-beloved voice;
Plan Thou my day submissive to Thy choice.

— *C. H. Pridgeon*

April 13

BY THEIR FRUITS YE SHALL KNOW THEM.
— Math. 7: 20

It is a holy-making gospel. Without holy fruit, all evidences are vain. Dear friends, you have awakenings, enlightenings, experiences, and many due signs; but if you lack holiness, you will never see the Lord. A real desire after complete holiness is the truest mark of being born again. Jesus is a holy Saviour. He first covers the soul with His white raiment, then makes the soul glorious within — restores the lost image of God, and fills the soul with pure, heavenly holiness. Unregenerate men among you cannot bear this testimony.
— *Murray McCheyne*

111

April 14

THEY THAT DWELL UNDER HIS SHADOW SHALL RETURN; THEY SHALL REVIVE AS THE CORN AND GROW AS THE VINE.

— Hos. 14: 7

The predominant meaning of the word "revival" in the Old Testament is "to recover", "to restore", "to return" to God's original standard for His people.

Coldness, callousness, deadness, and back-slidings are abnormal, and the Chruch will never become normal until she sees revival. *The glorious splendour of the church which shines out as the result of revival is the true standard our Lord has set up in the New Testament, and this is what He expects to see among His redeemed ones at all times. There is nothing abnormal about the revived Church of God. The only thing abnormal about the Church today is that she needs to be revived.* There is nothing abnormal about being filled with the Spirit, according to Ephesians 5: 18. There is nothing abnormal about sanctifying Christ in the heart, as we are commanded in 1 Peter 3: 15. There is nothing abnormal in a Christian's "reigning in life by Christ Jesus", as mentioned in Romans 5: 17. There is nothing abnormal in a redeemed child of God presenting his body a living sacrifice, as Paul adjures us to do in Romans 12: 1. There is nothing abnormal in receiving a mighty baptism of power for winning lost souls to Christ. These things represent the normal Christian life, as set forth for us in the New Testament. *Adolf Monod, when dying, gasped out four telling utterances:* "All in Christ — By the Holy Spirit — For the glory of God — All else is nothing!"

— *James A. Stewart*

April 15

OUR SUFFICIENCY IS OF GOD. — II Cor. 3: 5

GRACE SUFFICIENT

The other evening I was riding home after a heavy day's work. I felt very wearied and sore depressed, when swiftly and suddenly as a lightning flash, that text came to me, "My grace is sufficient for thee.' I reached home and looked it up in the original, and at last it came to me in this way. 'My grace is sufficient for THEE' and I said, 'I should think it is, Lord,' and burst out laughing. I never fully understood what the holy laughter of Abraham was until then. It seemed to make unbelief so absurd. It was as though some little fish being very thirsty, was troubled about drinking the river dry, and Father Thames said, 'Drink away, little fish, my stream is sufficient for thee.' Or it is like a man on a lofty mountain saying to himself, 'I fear I shall exhaust all the oxygen in the atmosphere'; but the earth might say, 'Breathe away, O man, and fill thy lungs ever, my atmosphere is sufficient for thee.' O, brethren, be great believers. Little faith will bring your souls to heaven, but great faith will bring heaven to your souls.

— *C. H. Spurgeon*

Sing then my soul!

April 16

WOE IS ME IF. — I Cor. 9: 16

Remember this, too, that God's claims, as well as man's become outlawed if not settled on time. We hear talk about a second probation for sinners who, while living, neglected their opportunity of grace. I do not believe in that doctrine. Neither do I believe in any second probation of Christians who failed to do their duty to the world in their day and generation. There will be no chance for us to preach the Gospel to the heathen after we have passed through the narrow portals of the grave. *There will be no chance to give to the cause of missions when our hands are stiffened in death. Skeleton fingers cannot turn a safe key, or sign a check or open a pocket-book.* The present is our opportunity; and opportunity is but another word for importunity; as though God did beseech you by us to use the present moment for doing all possible for making known the grace of God to all those who have not heard it.

This incident occurred in a bank recently. A plain man, evidently not accustomed to the ways of business, called for the cashier of the bank. "Bank closed at two o'clock," was the gruff reply. "But I called to pay that note of mine." "Too late," was the reply, "it has gone to protest." "But here is the money," insisted the farmer. "Sorry, but we cannot receive it." "What," exclaimed the astonished debtor, "don't you receive money that is due you when I have it in hand?" "No, sir," was the inexorable verdict, "it is too late." And the iron gate was shut in the man's face.

It is a sort of parable and prophecy of what may occur on a larger scale by-and-by. Belated servants will crowd around the judgment seat to pay the dues of which an awakened conscience has now at length reminded them. I see them reaching out eager palms toward the judge. "Lord, I am ready to pay my debt to the unevangelized world, though I have neglected to pay it for so long." "Lord, I desire to give myself for the salvation of the lost, though I am very slow in reaching the decision." And the Saviour stretches out His nailed-pierced hand, and answers. "Too late! Too late! This is judgment-day and not pay-day. Oh that thou hadst known in thy day the things that belonged to thy peace."

— *A. J. Gordon*

Oh! That I may have no blood spots on my hands.

114

April 17

WHO THROUGH FAITH... OBTAINED THE PROMISES. — Heb. 11:33

Turning promises into facts.

It is recorded of Hudson Taylor that on a day of deep depression, in his daily reading he came across God's significant statement of the believer, "My cup runneth over." "Yes, Lord, if *Thou* dost say so, it must be true, but yet it really is very far from running over, for there is not enough money for the missionaries." And he read again, "My cup runneth over." "Yes, Lord, Thou sayest it, but there are dissentions among some of the missionaries." But again, "My cup runneth over," and still other very real burdens and difficulties came to mind. "But, Lord, Thou art eternal, and Thy Word is eternally true. So, in spite of appearances, it must be true just now for me.

'My Cup Runneth Over!'

I do now believe it and count it true, and thank Thee for it." So by God's grace that burdened heroic missionary was enabled in a time of great difficulty to rest upon that gracious statement and promise of God, and to appropriate it as true for him just then. *So he "obtained"* (Heb. 11:33) *that promise, and turned it into a present happy fact by a definite act of faith.* And the effect was very much more than the mere subjective effect of cheering his own heart. For God very soon showed him that it *was* literally true at that moment by dissolving all the difficulties in His own wonderful way, so well known to us in the mission field. That, to me, is a perfect instance of turning a promise into a present fact by an act of faith, by a man who had learned to walk on both feet, by praying and believing, by asking and then taking.

And it is a habit one can most humbly and thankfully recommend after some years of experience, as most practical and profitable, indeed as being often the only pathway open to the burdened believer. How very often in years past in the conflict of the mission field spiritual defeat has only been changed into victory by a deliberate taking hold in faith, and by

Holding on in Spite of Feelings

to some such promise of God till He has intervened and given deliverance.

— *Northcote Deck*

April 18

OH! THAT THOU WOULDEST REND THE HEAVENS. — Is. 64: 1

A sense of the Lord's presence was everywhere. It pervaded, nay, it created the spiritual atmosphere. It mattered not where one went the consciousness of the reality and nearness of God followed. Felt, of course, in the Revival gatherings, it was by no means confined to them; it was also felt in the homes, on the streets, in the mines and factories, in the schools, yea, and even in the theaters and drinking saloons. The strange result was that wherever people gathered became a place of awe, and places of amusement and carousal were practically emptied. Many were the instances of men entering publichouses, ordering drinks, and then turning on their heels leaving them on the counters untouched. The sense of the Lord's presence was such as practically to paralyse the arm that would raise the cup to the lips. Football teams and the like were disbanded; their members finding greater joy in testimony to the Lord's grace than in games. The pit-bottoms and galleries became places of praise and prayer, where the miners gathered to worship ere they dispensed to their several stalls. Even the children of the Day-schools came under the spell of God. Stories could be told of how they would gather in any place they could,

116

where they would sing and pray in most impressive
fashion.

If one were asked to describe in a word the outstanding feature of those days, one would unhesitatingly reply
that *it was the universal, inescapable sense of the presence of God.* Revival is the exact answer to such a sigh
as that of Isaiah 64: 1, "Oh that Thou wouldest rend the
heavens, that Thou wouldest come down, that the mountains might flow down at Thy presence." *In 1904 the
Lord had literally rent the heavens, and had scattered the
satanic foes entrenched therein.* The Lord had come
down! The mountains were gloriously melted down in
His presence.

— *R. B. Jones*

April 19

IN A MOMENT, IN THE TWINKLING OF AN EYE,
AT THE LAST TRUMP. — 1 Cor. 15: 52

> *"In a moment." O how wond'rous!*
> *In the twinkling of an eye*
> *We shall hear the shout and trumpet,*
> *And shall meet Him in the sky,*
> *Jesus Christ our Lord and Saviour,*
> *Who for sinners came to die.*
>
> *"In a moment." O what rapture!*
> *All earth's fetters shall be gone,*
> *And our frail and feeble bodies*
> *Immortality put on.*
> *"In a moment" we shall see Him,*
> *And be like that blessed One.*
>
> *"In a moment." O what wonder!*
> *Those who sleep in Christ shall rise.*
> *Living ones caught up together*
> *Re-united in the skies.*
> *We shall dwell in His fair Mansions,*
> *Where Eternal Glory lies.*

For a moment, here affliction,
Yonder, it will all be o'er.
Trials now may sorely press us,
There we'll know them nevermore.
In a moment we shall see Him,
What a prospect lies before!

— F. B.

April 20

BUT HE, BEING FULL OF THE HOLY GHOST.
— Acts 7: 55

A visitor from England visited Christmas Evans in Wales, of whom he had heard much, and with whom he was sore displeased because of his disorderly meetings and unbecoming zeal. The Englishman preached coldly, fully determined not to countenance any of the wild notions of the Welsh. When he had finished, Christmas Evans commenced, and out of respect to the brother from England he tried to speak a little broken English as well as he could. While he was describing the glory of Christ, the greatness of His sufferings and the infinite merits of His sacrifice, in a most powerful manner, the Englishman quite forgot himself and cried out with all his might: "Oh my God, is this my Saviour?" and fell down on the floor. *This was only a natural sequence of an experience previously known by the Welsh revivalist.* Riding on horseback to a preaching engagement over the hills, being weary of a cold heart in the pulpit, in secret prayer, and in the study, he dismounted from his horse and spent three hours in the woods, crying to God to break his cold heart and fill him with a burning love for lost souls. "Having begun," he said, "in the name of Jesus, I soon felt, as it were, the fetters loosening and the old hardness of heart softening and, as I thought, mountains of frost and snow dissolving and melting within

118

me. There stole over me a sweet sense of His forgiving love. As the sun was westerning, I went back to my appointment. On the following day I preached with such power to a vast concourse of people, gathered on the hillside, that a revival broke out that day and spread through the whole Principality."

— *James A. Stewart*

Seek the Lord to-day and give Him no rest until you are broken and anointed.

April 21

Thy name shall be called no more Jacob, but Israel: for as a prince hast thou power with God and with men, and hast prevailed. — Gen. 32: 28

This story of the angel wrestling with Jacob is an instance of God's earnest desire to take from us all that hinders our best and highest life, whilst we resist with might and main. There was much evil in Jacob that needed to be laid aside, and so the love of God drew near to him in the form of an angel to wrestle with him. At first he held his own, but whatever it is that enables a soul whom God designs to bless to stand out against Him, God will touch. It may be as *natural* as a sinew, but if it robs us of spiritual blessing, God will touch it; it may be as *small* as a sinew, but its evil influence will compel the Almighty Lover of our souls to take notice of it, to cause our scheming to miscarry, and the sinew of our strength to dry up.

Then Jacob abandoned the posture of defence and resistance, and clung to his Adversary. It is good when we come to this attitude, for there is nothing which God will not do for the soul that clings to Him in absolute weakness (2 Cor. 12: 7—9).

Three things happened: *The changed name,* which indicated a changed character. Israel means "prince with

119

God." The supplanter, cheat, and weak vacillator became royal! There is only one road to royalty, it is the path of self-surrender and faith. *Power:* as a prince hast thou power with God, and with men thou shalt prevail. (R. V. marg.) He who would have power and authority with his fellows must first secure it by yielding to God. *The Beatific Vision:* "I have seen God face to face." Our moments of vision come after the night of wrestling. The price is high, but the vision more than compensates. Our sufferings are not worthy to be compared to the glory which shall be revealed. Such is life! As the dawn of heaven breaks we see the Angel of Love, and as Christ meets us we awake to the royalty of the sons of God.

— *F. B. Meyer*

Art thou a prince?

April 22

BUT HE, BEING FULL OF THE HOLY SPIRIT.
— Acts 7: 55

We cannot dictate to the Holy Spirit. We cannot lay down what we think should be the avenues of our service. Personally, I cannot tell you what will be the consequences of your fulness, but one thing I do know from experience, it will be a life of constant sacrifice for the Person and work of our blessed Lord. Are you prepared, like John the Baptist, to have only six months of ministry, and then imprisonment, only to have your head chopped off at the end of it? Are you prepared, like Stephen, to thunder forth the message of God in such a manner that your congregation will hate you to the gnashing of their teeth and the stoning you out of the ministry? Are you prepared like Barnabas, to obey the voice of the Spirit and sell your possessions as well as giving yourself to the Lord? We had the joy once of leading a dear business man in Europe into the experience of the Fulness. Within a week the Spirit had told him to give several thousands of dollars for the work of the Lord. Are you prepared, dear father and mother, that the Holy Spirit should take your children for foreign mission work? Are you prepared, dear young couple, to be lonely sentinels of the Cross of Christ on the mission field?

In a word, the terms on which God is prepared to give this most peerless gift to a believer are that the life shall be absolutely at God's own disposal, as He has purposed after the counsel of His own will (Eph. 1: 11).

— *James A. Stewart*

Anything Lord!

April 23

WOE IS ME! FOR I AM UNDONE. — Isa. 6: 5

Christ always comes in lowly guise, and always brings His cross with Him. No one who has been used by God in revival ministry can ever forget the melting, the brokenness, and the humiliation before Him. Spontaneous New Testament revivals begin in the secret of holy obscurity, with insignificant and broken instruments; instruments which have passed through a Gethsemane experience and have become worms before a Great God. Great respect is certainly due to these blessed men and women of God, but we must be careful never to magnify them in an idolatrous way, as the world worships its film stars and sportsmen, and its heroes. *When such idolatry takes place, the Holy Spirit is grieved and quenched and soon withdraws Himself from the revival movement.*

— *James A. Stewart*

April 24

HE SHALL BE LIKE A TREE PLANTED BY THE
RIVERS OF WATER. — Psalm 1: 3

OUT OF HIM SHALL FLOW RIVERS OF LIVING
WATERS. — John 7: 38, free translation

Meditation of the Word, and watchfulness unto prayer,
keep the soul in that freshness of communion with the
Lord which fits for His service. *"He that abideth in me,
and I in Him, the same bringeth forth much fruit." "If
any man thirst, let him come unto me and drink."* And
when his own soul has been refreshed, from him shall
flow forth *"rivers of living water,"* for the refreshment
of others.

*Every service we undertake ought to be the result of
fresh, personal communion with the living Head, the
Fountain of all supply.* Nothing short of this will meet
the need. There must be enjoyed association with the
source of life and blessing, in order to become the channel
of life and blessing to others. Ability, however great —
gift, however distinct — are not enough without personal
communion. Unless we drink ourselves from the Foun-
tain-head, our ministries will be dry and profitless.

— Selected

April 25

HOW SHALL WE ESCAPE. — Heb. 2: 3

GOD'S HELL

In these civilized lands of ours we have large prisons.
What a shame it is to put men and women in such places
of torment, robbing them of their liberties, and privileges;
separating men from their homes and families, and bringing pain and shame on their friends. Many a time men
are in jail because they have committed one crime, and
some of them we hang.

122

We have large asylums all over the land. Thousands of people are kept there against their will. Isn't it a shame to have such places, and treat people like that. You would look with pity on me if I talked like this, and wonder where I came from. You would say, "Don't you know that these people are lawbreakers and insane? It is for their own good and the safety of the country and the people that we put them there."

Do you think we have more sense than God? Who are the people who go to hell? They are men and women who rebelled against God, and refused to be saved by the blood of His Son. What else can God do with them but put them in prison? Surely a man is mad who damns his own soul by willfully rejecting Jesus Christ as his Saviour. Men and women, hell is God's penitentiary; hell is God's madhouse. If you continue to rebel against God, God has a jail for you; and if you are so foolish as to refuse His salvation, God has an asylum for you.

Let me give you some of the terms used by God to describe the nature of this place: "A lake of fire — A bottomless pit — A devouring fire — A place of sorrows — Where they wail — A place of weeping — A furnace — A place of torments — Everlasting burnings — A place of filthiness — Where they curse God — Everlasting destruction — A place of outer darkness — Where they have no rest — Everlasting punishment — Where they gnaw their tongues — A place prepared for the devil and his angels — Where they cry for a drop of water — Tormented with fire and brimstone — Hell fire — Hell — Wrath to come."

If God had not been love He might have made the way to hell easy and fast, but He has hedged the way there with thorns and barriers, and a man must work hard to get there. He has to stifle conscience again and again. He has to trample over the tears and prayers of God's people. He has to silence God's Word, quench the

Holy Spirit, and trample under foot the precious Blood of Christ; all this before he succeeds in damning his soul for ever.

— W. P. Nicholson

Oh God! have mercy on me now and save my soul! Amen!

April 26

BLESSED ... WITH EVERY SPIRITUAL BLESSING IN THE HEAVENLIES IN CHRIST.

— Eph. 1: 3, Rotherham

If salvation of the soul from hell were the sum-total of all our evangelistic efforts, then the major portion of the New Testament would be unnecessary. A few Gospel texts would suffice, such as John 1: 12, John 3: 16, John 5: 24, Acts 4: 12, Romans 10: 9, and the like.

In the Old Testament we find that almost the whole of this volume is occupied in describing the life and journeys of a redeemed people in their relationship to a holy God. When Jehovah redeemed His people by the blood and power from Pharaoh's tyranny and Egypt's bondage, He was not satisfied to leave them in the wilderness. *Oh no! He had a plan and purpose for the people He had redeemed.* His plan and purpose was that these saved souls should be brought into the Land of Canaan to live there the life of victory. The Word of God says, "And he brought us *out* from thence, that he might bring us into the land which He sware unto our fathers" (Deut. 6: 23). *If it is true that the new-born babe has been sealed with the Holy Spirit: (Eph. 1: 3); if it is true that the new-born soul is blessed with all spiritual blessings in Christ: (Eph. 1: 3); if it is true that the new-born soul is united to Christ the Vine: (John 15: 5.); if it is true that the new-born soul is now an heir*

*of God and joint-heir with Jesus Christ: (Romans 8: 17.);
if it is true that the new-born soul has a life which is
hid with Christ in God: (Col. 3: 1), then surely it is a
spiritual disaster for us not to tell him so.*

— *James A. Stewart*

April 27

CAST THY BURDEN UPON THE LORD, AND HE SHALL SUSTAIN THEE. — Psalm 55: 23

BEING CARRIED

Henry Moorhouse, when engaged in a work that seemed to call upon him for a more than usual exercise of faith, received what seems like a most tender answer from God. His little daugther, who was a paralytic, was sitting in her chair as he entered the house with a package in his hand for his wife. Going up to her and kissing her, he asked, "Where is mother?" "Mother is upstairs." "Well, I have a package for her." "Let me carry the package to mother." "Why, Minnie dear, how can you carry the package? You cannot carry yourself." With a smile on her face, Minnie said, "Oh, no father, but you give me the package, and I will carry the package, and you will carry me." Taking her up in his arms, he carried her upstairs — little Minnie and the package too. And then it came to him that this was just his position in the work in which he was engaged. He was carrying his burden, but was not God carrying him? "Cast" (Psa. 55: 22). "Carry" (Isa. 46: 4).

— *Selected*

Lord I know that Thou wilt sustain me!

Awake, awake; put on thy strength, O Zion; put on thy beautiful garments, O Jerusalem, the holy city: ... shake thyself from the dust; arise, sit down, O Jerusalem; loose thyself from the bands of thy neck, O captive daughter of Zion. — Isa. 52: 1—2

THE CLARION CALL comes to us from Isaiah's prophecy:

Notice the pathos in the challenge and rebuke, "O Jerusalem, the holy city! O captive daughter of Zion! Rouse thyself, clothe thyself, cleanse thyself, shake thyself, loose thyself." What a terrible condition to be in — how God-dishonoring! "Captive daughter of Zion"! What a contradiction! The Church has compromised and dragged the dear Name of the Saviour in the dust. Therefore she is in captivity. *The sin of the Church is that it is earth-bound.* "Shake thyself from the dust." Many are longing for a tidal movement of the Spirit to sweep through our churches, but we do not need to wait for that. The remnant of old cried to Jehovah, "Awake, awake, put on strength, O arm of the Lord; awake, as in the ancient days, in the generations of old." (Isa. 51: 9). God answered them with this pathetic rebuke, "Awake, awake, put on thy strength, O Zion." (Isa. 52: 1). It is not the Lord who is asleep, but His people. We must repent and get right with God, and humble ourselves to the dust in sack-cloth and ashes. "Put on thy strength, O Zion." Strength is at our disposal. The garment of power is hanging on the door of Pentecost. (Acts 1: 8). Power is at our disposal. *We read the menu, but fail to order.* "He that believeth on Me, out of him shall flow rivers of living water." *We must appropriate our resources. They are not dried up. The Church's potential is the same as in apostolic days.*

— *James A. Stewart*

AN HIGH PRIEST... TOUCHED WITH THE FELLOW-FEELING OF OUR TRIALS.

-- Heb. 4: 15, free translation

PRIESTHOOD

In reference to the priesthood of our Lord, the Holy Spirit tells us, "Seeing then that we have an High Priest that is passed into the Heavens, Jesus the Son of God" (Heb. 4: 14). *As His Sacrifice takes its value from the worth of His Person, so the Holy Spirit is careful to point out that His Priesthood is that of "Jesus the Son of God."* Do we need a tender, sympathising priest, one who has a fellow-feeling for us in our infirmities? We have Jesus. Do we need a priest with Almighty power? We have "Jesus the Son of God." If he were only human He might enter into our sympathies, but He could do no more. He is both human and divine, and therefore He can help as well as sympathise.

A dear sister, whose husband had been killed in a colliery accident, had a great many callers to sympathise with her in her sad bereavement. They did their best, but none of them had passed through the same sorrow, and therefore could not enter fully into her feelings. At last one woman came in and waited for a few moments, but the widowed sister, after her departure, said she got more comfort from her visit than from all the others put together. When asked what the visitor had said and done, she replied, "She said nothing; she merely sat down on that stool, took my hand in hers, and we both wept together, and her tears went to my heart." The visitor had lost her husband, and could therefore enter into the widow's grief. *Blessed be God, the Christian can say he has "a great High Priest" who has been in every condition on earth He may find himself, save one* — He "knew no sin." Do our friends despise us? He was "despised and rejected," indeed His own brethren did not believe in Him. Even amongst His own disciples there was a traitor. But sympathy was only one side of His priesthood. He sympathised with the sisters of Bethany. "Jesus wept" (John 11:35). He did more, He raised Lazarus from the dead. Our Priest is not only "Jesus" — the One who sympathises — He is the "Son of God." If He does not work a miracle on our behalf, it is not that He has not the power. If it were for our good He would do so. People say the age of miracles is past. Well, such a statement is only true so far, for every saved sinner is a miracle of grace. *When we get to Heaven we shall see that it has been miracles all along the line.*

— J. G.

April 30

IF WE WALK IN THE LIGHT. — 1 John 1:7
IF WE CONFESS OUR SINS. — 1 John 1:9

Brokenness is obedience; indeed, revival is the simple outcome of obedience to the light. But for many of us the brokenness to which we are now referring, including openness before men, starts by being really costly. The reason is obvious. The walls of reserve and self-esteem have gone so high, probably without our ever realizing it, and so the first step into this brokenness is probably a big one. It is the walls of Jericho which have to fall down flat! I certainly found that, and so have many others. In my own case I suddenly found myself face to face in Central Africa with a brother whom I had met and disliked in England! I had disliked him only because he was too open for my taste, although I had not at that time traced the real cause of my dislike; I was not ready enough for the light in those days. But here I was in a revival company where dislike was only another word for hate which was faced and brought to the light as sin; and I was carefully pretending that I had brotherly love for a man whom in the white and black terms of I

128

John, I "hated!" It was then I found how high those walls of pride are. I just could not bring myself to admit in public that I had the sin of dislike against him, and equally the sin of hypocrisy against all my brethren in pretending that I did like him. As a senior visiting missionary, I could not let on that I had such a "foolish" thing in my heart. But it was not foolish, it was sin which crucified my Lord. To say I could not bring it out was to deceive myself; I could, but I wouldn't, that was all. I had to learn obedience to the light. At last, after two days, under the constant inner compulsion of the Spirit, I just took the step of cold-blooded obedience, brought it into the light before the brother and all, and of course the blood reached me at once; there was the cleansing, the love of God in my heart, and the joy of the whole company. I love and honour that brother to-day. *That is why the first step into brokenness is probably a big break.*

N. G.

To obey is better than sacrifice.

May 1

LET US GO UP AT ONCE, AND POSSESS IT; FOR WE ARE WELL ABLE TO OVERCOME IT.
— Numbers 13: 30

The best illustration of overcoming is the life of an Overcomer. The incontrovertible proof of its possibility is that it has been done. The most powerful incentive to live such a life is to see it lived. Herein lies the value of a study of Caleb's life. *He was an overcomer.*

"Hebron therefore became the inheritance of Caleb ... because that he wholly followed the Lord God of Israel" (Joshua 14: 14).

Standing alone, Caleb would be one of the most winsome characters in Biblical history. But when we see his life *silhouetted* against that of the ten spies, who represent also the congregation of Israel, it is nothing short of majestic. *Caleb saw himself only in his relationship to his God.* He was God's chosen, redeemed, sanctified one. Therefore, he looked upon himself as the one who had the right to the inheritance in Canaan and the power to possess it.

— *Ruth Paxson*

To him that overcometh will I grant to sit with me in my throne. — Rev. 3: 21.

May 2

WHAT? DO YOU NOT KNOW THAT YOUR BODY IS THE INNERMOST SHRINE OF THE SPIRIT. — I. Cor. 6: 19, free translation.

The Bible teaches us that the Body of Christ is the company of the faithful. These words are taken generally in their spiritual sense, while the Bible asks us positively whether we know not that our bodies are the members of Christ. In the same way, when the Bible speaks of the indwelling of the Holy Spirit or of Christ, we limit their presence to the spiritual part of our being; our soul, or our heart. Nevertheless the Bible says expressly, *"Know ye not that your body is the temple of the Holy Spirit?" When the Church understands that the body also has part in the redemption which is by Christ, by which it ought to be brought back to its original destiny, to be the dwelling place of the Holy Spirit, to serve as His instrument, to be sanctified by His presence, she will also recognize all the place which divine healing has in the Bible and in the counsels of God.*

Faith puts us in possession of all that the death of Christ and His resurrection have procured for us, and it is not only in our spirit and our soul that the life of the risen Jesus manifests its presence here below, it is in the body also that it would act according to the measure of our faith.

130

"Know ye not that your body is the temple of the Holy Spirit?" Many believers represent to themselves that the Holy Spirit comes to dwell in our body as we dwell in a house. Nothing of the kind. I can dwell in a house without its becoming part of my being. I may leave it without suffering; no vital union exists between my house and me. It is not thus with the presence of our soul and spirit in our body. The life of a plant lives and animates every part of it; and our soul is not limited to dwell in such or such part of the body, the heart or the head, for instance, but penetrates throughout, even to the end of the lowest members. The life of the soul pervades the whole body; the life throughout proves the presence of the soul. It is in like manner that the Holy Ghost comes to dwell in our body. He penetrates its entirety. He animates and possesses us infinitely more than we can imagine.

In the same way in which the Holy Spirit brings to our soul and spirit the life of Jesus, His holiness, His joy, His strength, He comes also to impart to the sick body all the vigorous vitality of Christ as soon as the hand of faith is stretched out to receive it. When the body is fully subject to Christ, crucified with Him, renouncing all self-will and independence, desiring nothing but to be the Lord's temple, it is then that the Holy Spirit manifests the power of the risen Saviour in the body *Then only can we glorify God in our body, leaving Him full freedom to manifest therein His power, to show that He knows how to set His temple free from the domination of sickness, sin and Satan.*

— *Andrew Murray*

FROM HENCEFORTH LET NO MAN TROUBLE ME: FOR I BEAR IN MY BODY THE BRAND-MARKS OF THE LORD JESUS.

— Galatians 6: 17, Free Translation

The words of my text are the battle-cry of a harassed, yet proud fighting soldier of the Cross. "Leave me alone! for I bear in my body the brand-marks of Jesus."

Paul had been used of God to found the Galatian church, and upon visiting them after three years of absence, he found them in danger of departing from the simple faith of the Gospel. False teachers had come and unsettled them in their faith and in their confidence in their spiritual father.

The letter is rough and rugged. In this fighting epistle the apostle gets down to the root of the trouble right away. "I am ashamed," he writes, "that you so quickly deserted the Gospel of God's grace. I know these false prophets have also asserted that I preached a message of my own compilation. This is not true. I never received it from man nor was I taught it of man. These false teachers, moreover, fail to preach the gospel of the Crucified Redeemer. *Let it be clearly known that I, myself, glory in the stigma, shame and reproach of Calvary.* God forbid that I should glory, save in the cross of our Lord Jesus Christ, by whom the world is crucified unto me, and I unto the world. I am a crucified man."

Brands Of The Cross

The apostle brings his message of correction and castigation to a final conclusion: "Oh Galatians, here is my final word: to all those who would trouble and harass me, — leave me alone; I bear branded on my body the 'stigmata' of the Cross.' "

The believers at Galatia immediately knew the illuminous meaning of the word "slave". All around them were slaves, including some of the believers. A slave was a person who had no power over his own body, no rights of his own. He could not resign; he could not give up his master's work just when he felt like it. Paul was sold out completely to his glorious Lord. "Go where I may", he says, "I cannot turn traitor, or I shall be a traitor with my Master's 'stigmata' upon me."

The word "Stigmata" speaks of ownership

As a slave bore upon his body the branded marks of slavery, proving him to be a slave, so Paul gloried in his marks as evidence that he was the bond-slave of Christ. Read his letters, and you will see that he thrilled at the thought of being a "doulos", the bond-slave of Christ. "God has honored me", he says, "by putting His stamp of ownership upon me. I bear in my body the brand-marks of the Lord Jesus."

Paul had surrendered all to the domination of the Redeemer; he wholly belonged to Christ. "If you have anything against me," he says in effect, "go to my Master. I am responsible to Him. Do you not see in my body the marks of His ownership?"

The Son of God desperately needs warriors today! May God help us to stand with Paul, come what may, and cry out, "Henceforth let no man trouble me, for I bear in my body the ownership-marks of the Lord Jesus."

— *James A. Stewart*

May 4

COMMIT THY WAY UNTO THE LORD.

— Psalm 37:5

Begin at once; before you venture away from this quiet moment, ask your King to take you wholly into His service, and place all the hours of this day quite simply at His disposal, and ask Him to make and keep you ready to do just exactly what He appoints. Never

133

mind about to-morrow; one day at a time is enough. Try it to-day, and see if it is not a day of strange, almost curious peace, so sweet that you will be only too thankful, when to-morrow comes, to ask Him to take it also, — till it will become a blessed habit to hold yourself simply and "wholly at Thy commandment for *any manner of service." The "whatsover" is not necessarily active work. It may be waiting (whether half an hour or half a lifetime), learning, suffering, sitting still.* But shall we be less ready for these, if any of them are His appointments for to-day? Let us ask Him to prepare us for all that He is preparing for us.   — *F. R. Havergal*

May 5

For God, who commanded the light to shine out of darkness, hath shined in our hearts, to give the light of the knowledge of the glory of God in the face of Jesus Christ. But we have this treasure in earthen vessels, that the excellency of the power may be of God, and not of us. — 2 Cor. 4: 6, 7

Our minds are carried back in these verses to the time when God said, "Let there be light," and dispelled the darkness of the primeval chaotic world, and then to that incident related in the book of Judges *where Gideon's army* went to battle against the Midianites with a sword in one hand and a lamp hidden in a pitcher in the other. At Gideon's command they broke the earthen vessels and the lights shone out striking terror to the hearts of the enemy who could not account for the clash and the blaze of light in the midnight hour. So we who are saved, having been turned from darkness to light, now have the responsibility of shining for God in this world. *But in order that this may be, these earthen vessels of our humanity must be broken. Then others can behold the light.*   — *H. A. Ironside*

Lord break me that Thy glorious light will shine forth!

134

May 6

But we all, with open face beholding as in a glass the glory of the Lord, are changed into the same image from glory to glory, even as by the Spirit of the Lord.

— 2 Cor. 3: 18

The secret of Christian holiness is heart-occupation with Christ Himself. As we gaze upon Him we become like Him. Do you want to be holy? Spend much time in His presence. Let the loveliness of the Risen Lord so fill the vision of your soul that all else is shut out. Then the things of the flesh will shrivel up and disappear and the things of the Spirit will become supreme in your life. We do not become holy by looking into our own hearts. There we only find corruption. But as we look away from self altogether, "looking unto Jesus," as He is the object in which we delight, as we contemplate His holiness, purity, love, and compassion, His devotion to the Father's will, we shall be transformed, imperceptibly to ourselves, perhaps, but none the less surely, into His blessed image. There is no other way whereby we may become practically holy, and be delivered from the power of the flesh and of the principles of the world.

— *H. A. Ironside*

Turn your eyes upon Jesus,
  Look full in His wonderful face,
And the things of earth will grow strangely dim
  In the light of His glory and grace.

May 7

FOR BY GRACE ARE YE SAVED THROUGH FAITH. — Eph. 2: 8

Our English word "FAITH" coming as it does from a root which indicates "trust," is connected with the Anglo-Saxon word "Faegan" (to covenant). Saving faith

135

is the faith of a transaction. The simplest form of covenanting is that in which one of the covenanting parties gives and the other receives. God conveys Christ to us by deed of gift, and faith "nakedly and alone" receives Him. It is a full Christ that is given and embraced, Christ in all His offices, Christ with all His benefits.

The well-known story of the Scottish theologian, Thomas Chalmers, will help a seeking soul here. While visiting an anxious elderly lady in a mountain glen in Scotland, he sought for hours to lead her to a saving faith in the Lord Jesus. Somehow, Granny could not see the way. On leaving the humble cottage, the minister pretended that he was afraid to cross the plank of wood which forded the small stream. Hesitating to place his foot on the board, he was met with a cry from the doorway, "Why are ye afraid? It's all right. Just lippen! just lippen!" Triumphantly, the mighty preacher turned again to the anxious soul and pointing to her, cried, *"Granny, just lippen til Jesus!"* Instantly the light of God's glorious salvation shined into her darkened soul, and Granny "lippened til Jesus." "For God so loved the world, as to gie His Son, the only begotten Ane, that ilke ane wha lippens til Him sunda dee, but hae life for aye" (John 3:16, broad Scottish dialect).

The Gospel does not make light of sin. It reveals to us the terrible sword of God's justice when He smote His beloved Son in order to deliver us from the penalty and slavery of sin. Calvary supplies the most solemn and awe-inspiring spectacle of God's hatred of sin that time or eternity will ever furnish.

— *James A. Stewart*

Oh, dear reader! cast away your works of self-righteousness now and trust in the merit of Christ alone.

Oh, Lamb of God, I come!

BUT WE SEE JESUS . . . CROWNED WITH GLORY AND HONOUR. — Heb. 2: 9

We need, as instantly as possible, to apprehend Him where He is now, to come into living communion with Him in His present exaltation at the right hand of the Father. That is the divinely arranged order. First, Christ died on the cross; then Christ raised from the dead, the great Shepherd of the Sheep brought again from the dead through the blood of the everlasting covenant; Christ as indwelling the believer; then the King coming in His manifested glory.

Now, I want to turn your gaze for a little time to Christ at the right hand of the Father; and I remind you that we have the testimony of Stephen to that effect. The heavens were opened for him, and he said: "I see the Son of Man." And observe, there is no inaccurate or careless use of the Divine names in the perfect Word of God. It was the Son of Man whom dying Stephen saw standing for that moment; not His characteristic attitude, which is sitting; but it is as if He rose to receive His dying martyr, the first martyr of the church. "I see the Son of Man standing at the right hand of the glory." *Well, now that is a very significant fact, and I venture to say that it is not apprehended with anything like the distinctness it ought to be by us for our comfort, but there is a Man in the glory now.* I fear that there is a very general looseness of apprehension of this fact — a Man in the glory; a Man who had lived on this earth for thirty-three years, who died the sacrificial death for us, and then in His resurrection body, visible before the eyes of His assembled disciples on earth, was received into the clouds and taken up, until He was seated on His Father's throne in the glory, and He is there for us now. Not a disembodied spirit, but a Man, and this Man, of course, is the Eternal Son of God, and in time the Son of Glory, the Son of David. He has for us entered as a forerunner into that Glory into which we shall come by His grace. *It is a great deal when you apprehend this simple truth, that there is representing us and appearing for us in the Glory of the Father, at this very moment, a Man, our representative there.* Oh, how it makes everything solid and sure, does it not? How it antagonizes all this vaporizing and indefinite and unsatisfactory romancing about heaven.

— C. I. Scofield

May 9

BECAUSE I HAVE YOU IN MY HEART.
— Phil. 1: 7

EVER REMEMBERED

I want you to know you are ever remembered —
The kindliest feelings encircle your name;
Though life's pressing claims may have silence
engendered,
Your place in remembrance remaineth the same.

I want you to know that, as busy thoughts travel
On busiest days — as most surely they do —
Perhaps when some problem seems hard to unravel,
My thoughts may instinctively travel to you.

And when at His footstool, untired, I would linger,
And think of the many God-given as friends —
There comes gainst your name an invisible finger,
And forthwith some word for you surely ascends.

— J. Danson Smith

May 10

WE PREACH CHRIST CRUCIFIED. — 1 Cor. 1: 23

It must not be overlooked that when Jesus is received as Lord, He must be received as a crucified Lord. The One Who is now exalted "in the midst of the throne" is represented as a "Lamb as it had been slain" (Rev. 5: 6). It is not as though He was Christ only in His sufferings for us, and is now Lord since His exaltation. No, He was "the Lord of glory" when He was crucified; and it is as the "Lamb that was slain" that He now receives the worship of the redeemed in Heaven (I Cor. 2: 9, and Rev. 5: 11, 12). So then it is as the crucified Lord that He must reign in our hearts now. To receive the crucified One as our Lord means to be despised and rejected with Him. We must bear the stigma and the reproach of the Cross of Christ. *The acceptance of Christ as Lord means also the crucifixion of the old life of selfishness and sin.* "They that are Christ's have crucified the flesh with the affections and lusts" (Gal. 5: 24). *If the crucified One is Lord of our lives, the hand that rules will be a nail-pierced hand. He, as the Captain of our Salvation, will lead us in a path of crucifixion and shame.* That is what it means to accept Christ as Lord.

— *James A. Stewart*

May 11

AND THERE WAS A FAMINE IN THE LAND.
— Gen. 12: 10

There is a difference between our circumstances and our environment. We cannot control our circumstances, but we are the deciders of our own environment. Environment is the element in our circumstances which fits the disposition. A man convicted of sin and a man in love may be in the same external circumstances, but the

139

environment of the one is totally different from that of the other. Our environment depends upon our personal reaction to circumstances. 'Circumstances over which I have no control' is a perfectly true phrase, but it must never be made to mean that we cannot control ourselves in those circumstances. No matter into what perplexing circumstances God's providence may lead us or allow us to go, we have to see to it that in our reaction to those circumstances, which dance around us so perplexingly, we exhibit a personal relation to the highest we know. *It is only by living in the presence of God that we cease to act in an ungodlike manner in perplexing circumstances.*

— *Oswald Chambers*

May 12

THE YOUNG LIONS DO LACK AND SUFFER HUNGER: BUT THEY THAT SEEK THE LORD SHALL NOT WANT ANY GOOD THING.
— Psalm 34: 10

There is one remarkable instance that I cherish because of the way the story came to me. There are two buildings in the city of Bristol which are monuments of answered prayer. One is Müller's Orphanage, and of the other I am not at present at liberty to speak. Dr. A. T. Pierson was my friend, and he was the friend and biographer of Müller. It was from him I got the first half of the story. He told me of an occasion when he was the guest of Müller at the orphanage. One night when all the household had retired he asked Pierson to join him in prayer. He told him that there was absolutely nothing in the house for next morning's breakfast. My friend tried to remonstrate with him and to remind him that all the stores were closed. Müller knew all that. He had prayed as he always prayed, and he never told anyone of his needs but God. They prayed. At least

Müller did, and Pierson tried to. They went to bed and slept, and breakfast for two thousand children was there in abundance at the usual breakfast hour. *Neither Müller nor Pierson ever knew how the answer came.* The story was told next morning to Simon Short of Bristol, under pledge of secrecy till the benefactor died. The details of it are thrilling, but all that need be told here is that the Lord called him out of bed in the middle of the night to send breakfast to Müller's Orphanage, and knowing nothing of the need, or of the two men at prayer, he sent provisions that would feed them for a month. That is like the Lord God of Elijah, and still more like the God and Father of our Lord Jesus Christ.

— *Samuel Chadwick*

May I grow in child-like trust in Thee that I may become a giant in faith! Amen.

May 13

THEY . . . OFFERED BURNT OFFERINGS, AND PEACE OFFERINGS; AND THE PEOPLE SAT DOWN TO EAT AND TO DRINK, AND ROSE UP TO PLAY. — Exodus 32: 6

The scene before Mount Sinai has been repeated again and again in the history of Christendom. The Lord Jesus has gone up on high to the immediate presence of God. His people, His church, which bears His name and calls Him Lord is left on earth in the place of dependence and obedience to keep His word, to bear testimony to His name and to own His Lordship until the time of his return. "To serve" and "to wait" (I Thess. 1: 9—10) was the employment, and the attitude of saints of early times, but this continued only for a little time. "The hope" became obscured; the minding of "earthly things" (Phil. 3: 19) usurped its place: "My Lord delayeth His coming" became the language of the many, and then the traditions of men, the fashion of

141

the world, clerisy, priestcraft, and doctrines of demons, rolled in like a flood, and apostasy from God supervened. The molten calf — the worship of Egypt; or what men now call "Natural Religion" — something to appeal to men's senses and fill their eyes, took the place of "Jesus in the midst." The voice of leaders, the creeds and liturgy of men supplanted the Word of God and the place of Christ as Son and Lord over God's house (Heb. 3: 6). *What is that which calls itself "The Church" to-day, but a defiled camp, where man's will, and man's word rule supreme.* The voice of the people ever "set on mischief" (Exod. 32: 22) can always find some in high places, such as Aaron, who ought to know better, but fear the people more than God, to carry out their desires, and thus the apostasy of Christendom has been accomplished. *What a sight before high heaven, that zealous host, at early morning, offering their burnt-offerings and their peace-offerings — notably no sin-offering — before their calf, and immediately after, filling up their busy day in ungodly revelry!* "They sat down to eat and to drink, and rose up to play." Such is the world and its religion: a combination of hypocrisy and lewdness: from the sacrament to the ballroom; from the church to the theatre; from the altar rail to the gambler's board and the drunkard's cup. And the darkest blot, the deepest insult to a Holy God is this, that men like Aaron, are abettors of this unholy sham. Verily they shall have their reward!

— *John Ritchie*

May 14

Behold, I come as a thief. Blessed is he that watcheth, and keepeth his garments, lest he walk naked, and they see his shame. — Rev. 16: 15

That blessed Hebrew Christian, Joseph Rabinowitz, in talking with Dr. A. J. Gordon on one occasion, opened his New Testament and read to him this solemn verse.

"The admonition of the Lord," he said, "affected me

very deeply when I first read it, for I knew at a glance its meaning. All night long the watchmen in the Temple kept vigilance. The overseer of the Temple was always likely to appear at unexpected hours to see if these were faithfully attending to their charges. If he came upon any watchman who had fallen asleep, he quietly drew his loose garments from him and bore them away as a witness against him when he should awake.

"My Lord is likely to come any moment. He may come in the second watch or in the third watch. Therefore I must be ready, lest coming suddenly He find me sleeping and I be stripped of my garment."

The solemnity of these words of Christ, "Behold I come as a thief" is of startling moment. The preposition EPI rendered "on" and "upon" signifies being over an object with a distinct direction and purpose toward it. As the thief comes to take something away from another, so Christ will take away the defiled garments which will be evidence against us of our unfaithfulness. At our Lord's return we shall be judged regarding our new life in Christ: our use, misuse, or abuse of it.

In this dispensation Christ is calling out and commissioning those who are to be His cabinet ministers and colleagues. "To him that overcometh will I grant to sit with me in my throne, even as I also overcame, and am set down with my Father in His throne" (Rev. 3: 21).

— *James A. Stewart*

May 15

BEAR YE ANOTHER'S BURDEN, AND SO FULFIL THE LAW OF CHRIST. — Gal. 6: 2

Our own burden is lightened as we bear the burdens of others in our intercession. It is all wrong when people say, "I have enough myself to bear; I cannot add to it by taking up the burdens of others." Open wide the windows of thy heart, turn away from that which oppresses thee, bear the burden of another, and thou wilt see how it lightens thine own. Fresh air will rush into thine exhausted heart, and with it new elasticity, new breadth and endurance in bearing thine own burden. In ceasing to be self-seeking with thine own burden and task, thou wilt not give way under what presses upon thee. *The closer thou comest into relation with Christians, so much the more indispensable to thee will be Christ, the Foundation-stone, on whom all depends, and so much wider will become thy horizon.* Out from Him thou canst extend, north and south, east and west; for Christ has become for thee thy Starting-point, thy Centre, and thy Goal.

— *Stockmayer*

Oh, Heavenly Father forgive me for my selfishness! Amen.

May 16

HE SHALL NOT SPEAK OF HIMSELF.

— John 16: 13

I have found, in times past, a very great blessedness in this short but sweet account which Jesus gives of the gracious office of the Holy Ghost; and therefore I would make it the subject of my present evening meditation. I find what the Lord Jesus said concerning the blessed Spirit, in this most delightful part of his divine ministry, to be true. For, look wherever I may, through the Bible, it is of Jesus only the Holy Ghost is continually speaking, and not of Himself. And hence, by the way, I learn how to form a most decided testimony of the faithful preachers of the Word. For if God the Holy Ghost, in his glorifying the Lord Jesus, is never found to be speaking but of Jesus, surely all his faithful servants, who act by His authority, and are commisioned and ordained by Him to the work, will never preach themselves, but Christ

144

Jesus the Lord. And how blessed is it to be taught of Jesus, by the Holy Ghost! It is astonishing, when we take into one mass of particulars the agency of the Holy Ghost in His glorifying the Lord Jesus, to observe the patience, the compassion, the tenderness and love, which that blessed Spirit manifests in the Church of Jesus, in holding up to their view, and in bringing home to their heart, the person, work, character, and relations of Jesus! *How sweetly and effectually doth He speak of him, plead for Him, and win over the affections to Him, by His saving light, His illuminating grace, and persuasive arguments in the heart!* It is the Holy Ghost that takes of Christ, and the things of Christ, and makes both appear lovely and desirable in our eyes. It is His blessed work to bring about the gracious union, when, as the Bridegroom of His Church, God the Spirit represents Him in His beauty, and persuades the soul of the sinner to receive Him and accept Him as her maker and her husband to whom she is betrothed for ever! And from whom, but the Holy Ghost, do those sweet influences arise from day to day, and from one degree of grace to another, by which the life of the believer in Christ is kept up, maintained, and carried on in the soul, from the first beginning of the spiritual life until grace is consummated in eternal glory. Oh! Lord the Spirit! I beseech thee, glorify my adorable Redeemer in my poor, cold, and lifeless heart, and sweetly lead over the whole of my affections to all-precious Jesus, that I may live upon His glorious person, and feel my interest in His great salvation increasingly precious. *And oh, Thou holy Lord! keep alive, I beseech Thee, Thine own saving and powerful influences in my heart, that I may never — never by sin — quench Thy divine flame, nor grieve the Holy Spirit, whereby I am sealed unto the day of redemption.*

— *Robert Hawker*

For whether we be beside ourselves, it is to God: or whether we be sober, it is for your cause. For the love of Christ constraineth us; because we thus judge, that if one died for all, then were all dead: And that he died for all, that they which live should not henceforth live unto themselves, but unto Him which died for them, and rose again. — II Cor. 5: 13—15

"The love of Christ constraineth us!" The apostle's magnificent outburst is the key to his rugged life of utter abandonment.

Constraineth! What is the weight and content of the word? The Greek word *sunecho,* which is translated *constrain* is one of the most expressive words in the New Testament. This fine muscular, masculine word graphically portrays the deep, overwhelming mastery which the love of Christ held over His servant. Its usage in other connections in the New Testament reveals its force and grip. By using this picturesque word, Paul would say:

THE LOVE OF CHRIST CAPTIVATES ME

The word *sunecho* is found in Acts 18: 5 used to describe the effect of the Word of God upon Paul. The Authorized Version says, "Paul was *pressed* in the spirit." Berkeley translates, "Paul was *completely possessed* by the message." Moffatt says, "Paul was *engrossed* in the preaching of the Word." Knox would have it, "Paul was *much occupied* with preaching."

In the same way Paul is possessed, engrossed, occupied and utterly absorbed with the wondrous love of Christ. As he gazes at the Crucified Lord, he cries out in holy rapture, "The Son of God, Who loved me and gave Himself for me!"

— *James A. Stewart*

Oh my soul! may I this day be captivated by my dear Redeemer's Love.

CONSTRAINETH. — 2 Cor. 5: 13—15

THE LOVE OF CHRIST CROWDS
EVERYTHING OUT OF MY LIFE

Another New Testament usage of the word is found in Luke 8: 45 where we read, "The multitude *throng* Thee." The very word which is here translated *throng* lends its color and intensity to the text.

Have you ever been caught by the grip and the current of a thronging multitude? I can vividly recall an experience I had with my wife on a train in Poland. It was in 1939 just before the Germans invaded Warsaw. We were conducting a Bible conference in the suburb of the city and had made our way into the city by trains. As we neared the station my wife slowly made her way toward the sliding doors, prepared to step off as soon as the train stopped. Suddenly, however, before she could move, the door had opened and a pressing, pushing, rushing, multitude heaved its way into the train, each striving to be first. There was no means of resistance so that she was lifted up and pressed back by the force of the multitude into the one direction away from the open door.

"The multitude throng thee." And it is that word *throng,* descriptive of such a mass movement, which the apostle uses to describe the effect upon him of the love of Christ. *The love of Christ swept the apostle off his feet and thus shut him up to his Lord alone.* Yes, the love of Christ crowded everything else out of his life.

Alas, the vast majority of belivers today know so little of the constraining love of Christ! Constrained and compelled by their own selfish ambitions, they are swept away by the resistless current of human affairs. The crying need of the hour is for more saints to be constrained by His matchless love.

— *James A. Stewart*

What will it constrain us to do, to be, or bear, to serve?

> *Were the whole realm of nature mine,*
> *That were a present far too small;*
> *Love so amazing, so divine,*
> *Demands my soul, my life, my all.*

May 19

HE BROUGHT ME TO THE BANQUETING HOUSE, AND HIS BANNER OVER ME WAS LOVE.
— Song of Songs 2: 4

Oh, my dear reader, have you been captivated by this love? It is an utter impossibility to be captured by the love of Christ and not be captivated by it. Your profession of faith is an utter sham if Calvary's love has not captivated you.

Samuel Rutherford in his quaint way, writing from his lonely, damp prison cell in Scotland some three hundred years ago, gives expression to words of adoration which stagger us in their boldness and spiritual depth:

"I must tell you what lovely Jesus, fair Jesus, King Jesus, hath done to my soul. Sometimes he sends me out a standing drink and whispereth a word through the wall and I am well content of kindness *at the second hand.* His bode is ever welcome to me, be what it will, but at other times He will be messenger, Himself, and I get the cup of salvation out of His own hand. He is drinking with me, and we cannot rest till we be in other's arms. And, oh, how sweet is a fresh kiss from His holy mouth! His breathing that goeth before a kiss, upon my poor soul is sweet, and hath no fault but that it is too short."

"I have been before a court, set up within me, of terrors and of challenges, but my sweet Lord Jesus hath taken the mask off His face and said, "Kiss thy fill," and

I will not smother nor conceal the kindness of my King Jesus. He hath broken in upon the poor prisoner's soul like the swelling of Jordan. I am banked and brim full; a great, high spring tide of the consolations of Christ have overflowed me. *They have sent me here to feast with my King.* His spikenard casteth a sweet smell. The Bridegroom's love hath run away with my heart. Oh, love, love, love! Oh, sweet are my royal King's chains! How sweet were it to me to swim the salt sea for my new Lover, my first Lord. ... I would not exchange Christ Jesus for ten worlds of glory. I am swelled up and satisfied with the love of Christ that is better than wine."

His last words from his damp cell have blessed the Church down the years from 1637:

> *Oh, Christ, He is the fountain,*
> *The deep, sweet well of love!*
> *The streams on earth I've tasted,*
> *More deep I'll drink above.*
> *There to an ocean fullness*
> *His mercy doth expand,*
> *And glory, glory dwelleth*
> *In Immanuel's land.*

— James A. Stewart

May 20

FOR I HAVE LEARNED, WHATEVER BE MY OUT-WARD EXPERIENCES, TO BE CONTENT.
— Phil. 4: 11, Weymouth

I have learned to see a need of everything God gives me, and want nothing that He denies me. Whether it be taken from or not given me, sooner or later God quiets me in Himself without it. I cast all my concerns on the Lord, and live securely on the care and wisdom of my heavenly Father.

— Joseph Eliot, 1664

149

Sing, then, my soul! and keep away the sighing;
Sing, now, yes, sing, and stay thy fount of tears;
Sing of His goodness, and His love undying,
And, singing, lose thy griefs, thy cares, thy fears.

— *J. Danson Smith*

May 21

But when the fulness of the time was come, God sent forth His Son, made of a woman, made under the law, that we might receive the adoption of sons. And because ye are sons, God hath sent forth the Spirit of His Son into your hearts, crying, Abba, Father. — Gal. 4: 4—6

Sonship is more than new birth. Through that we become children of God. This was true of believers in all dispensations. But now by the reception of the Holy Spirit, who is the Spirit of adoption, we become sons. *This is the distinctive blessing of the present dispensation of grace.* Old Testament saints were as children in their nonage. New Testament Christians are sons who have attained their majority and are joint heirs with Christ. We are all children of God by the second birth and sons of God by adoption. This is what is unfolded here in Galatians, as also in Romans 8: 14—17. In Roman law all born in the family were children, but only those legally adopted were reckoned as sons.

— *H. A. Ironside*

"Abba," Father — thus we call Thee,
(Hallowed name!) from day to day; —
'Tis Thy children's right to know Thee,
None but children "Abba" say.
This high honor we inherit,
Thy free gift, through Jesus' blood;
God the Spirit, with our spirit,
Witnesseth we're sons of God.

May 22

For we have not followed cunningly devised fables, when we made known unto you the power and coming of our Lord Jesus Christ, but were eyewitnesses of His majesty. For He received from God the Father honour and glory, when there came such a voice to Him from the excellent glory, This is My beloved Son, in whom I am well pleased. — 2 Peter 1: 16, 17

It is in 2nd Peter 7, Verses 16 to 18, that we learn the true significance of the transfiguration. It was the coming Kingdom in miniature. Christ Himself appearing in glory was the center of that wondrous scene. In Moses we see pictured the state of those who pass through death, but will be raised in glorified bodies. Elijah pictures the living saints who will be changed and caught up to be with Christ at His coming. Then the three disciples in their natural bodies set forth the earthly saints who will enjoy the blessings of the kingdom in this world during the millennial reign of the Lord Jesus, when blessing will flow forth to all mankind from the exalted Saviour reigning in righteousness as King of kings and Lord of lords. *All this confirmed the word of prophecy and made clearer to the disciples, in after days, what God has in store for His saints and the world at large when the hour of Christ's glory shall come.*

— *H. A. Ironside*

We have the word of prophecy confirmed or made more sure.

Oh God! we thank Thee for the light of Thy prophetic lamp in this dark confused space age.

May 23

Thus saith the Lord of hosts, Hearken not unto the words of the prophets that prophesy unto you; they make you vain; they speak a vision of their own heart, and not out of the mouth of the Lord ... The prophet

151

that hath a dream, let him tell a dream; and he that hath my word, let him speak my word faithfully . . . And the burden of the Lord shall ye mention no more for every man's word shall be his burden; *for ye have perverted the words of the living God*, of the Lord of hosts our God. — Jer. 23: 16, 28, 36

In these strange days the servants of the Lord must be careful to preach the true Gospel. Before the Gospel can be preached clearly, it must be apprehended clearly. The Christian worker must prayerfully and carefully study the great words of the Gospel, and the presentation of that blessed message as found in the Book.

Paul, the greatest of all preachers, exhorts young Timothy, "Study to shew thyself approved unto God, a workman that needeth not to be ashamed, rightly dividing the word of truth." The word, "rightly dividing" could be translated "handling aright," or as the modern Greek version says, "teaching accurately" the word of truth. The Greek word *Orthotomeō*, which is used here, is a metaphorical word. In present-day Greece it is used also in describing a carpenter drawing a straight line to divide a piece of wood. He does not draw a zig-zag line, but cuts straight, and is accurate in his work. He handles the tools aright in following the blueprint, and is thus a workman that needs not to be ashamed.

What is needed, therefore, is not only a mental knowledge of the Scriptures, but a strict adherence to its doctrine, and to the way in which its truths are presented. It was Chrysostom who gave the faithful warning, "He who swerves ever so little from the pure faith, soon proceeds from this to graver errors and becomes entirely corrupted." Only by an assiduous care in the accurate use of the words of Scripture, can we be Gospel workmen that need not be afraid of the coming Bema.

We must firmly hold the blessed evangel, and let neither earth nor hell, men or demons, turn us one hair's breadth from its truth.

— *James A. Stewart*

May 24

BE KINDLY AFFECTIONED ONE TO ANOTHER WITH BROTHERLY LOVE. — Rom 12: 10

A vexation arises, and our expressions of impatience hinder others from taking it patiently. Disappointment, ailment, or even weather depresses us; and our look or tone of depression hinders others from maintaining a cheerful and thankful spirit. We say an unkind thing, and another is hindered in learning the holy lesson of charity that thinketh no evil. We say a provoking thing, and our sister or brother is hindered in that day's effort to be meek. How sadly, too, we may hinder without word or act! For wrong feeling is more infectious than wrong doing; especially the various phases of ill temper, — gloominess, touchiness, discontent, irritability, — do we not know how catching these are?

— *F. R. Havergal*

May 25

HE THAT IS SPIRITUAL. — 1 Cor. 2: 15

There are four planes — broadly speaking — in the spiritual life of the believer, and of the Christian worker: The first plane we may call the *"EVANGELISTIC" plane;* that is, the plane where the soul knows the new birth; knows that he has eternal life in Christ; where he becomes a soul winner, preaches salvation from the penalty of sin, and is used to lead others to Christ; where the entire objective is winning souls for Christ; where he is faithful in proclaiming the gospel of salvation in Christ.

Then there is the second plane, which may be called the "REVIVAL" plane; or the stage in personal experience where the believer receives the Fulness of the Holy Spirit, learns to know Him and to obey Him; to rely upon Him and to look to Him to work as he co-operates with Him, and is used to lead others into the experience of the Fulness of the Spirit.

Then there is the third plane, which we may call the plane of the "PATH OF THE CROSS", where the believer experimentally apprehends his position in Romans 6 in fellowship with Christ's death; is brought into "conformity" to His death (Phil. 3: 10); learns the fellowship of His sufferings, and is led to walk in the path of the Cross in every detail of practical life. Here the believer is able to interpret to others the way of the Cross, and to lead others to know Romans 6 and 2 Cor. 4: 10—12 in experience.

The fourth plane is the plane of spiritual warfare. It is really the "ascension" plane, where the believer knows his union with Christ, seated with Him "far above all principality and power"; and where, in service, he is in aggressive warfare against the powers of darkness; learns to have spiritual discernment to detect the workings of the devil; and learns the authority of Christ over all the power of the enemy (Luke 10: 19).

To put it concisely —
The first is the plane of Salvation,
The second is the plane of the Spirit,
The third is the plane of Victory over sin,
The fourth is the plane of Victory over the power of darkness.

— *J. Penn-Lewis*

May 26

Then took Mary a pound of ointment of spikenard, very costly, and anointed the feet of Jesus, and wiped His feet with her hair: and the house was filled with the odour of the ointment. — John 12: 3

THE FRAGRANCE OF WORSHIP
Worship is heart occupation with Christ in what He is in all the matchless beauty of His Person.

154

Worship is the most spiritual of all Christian activities and thus the hardest and highest to obtain. All true service for God springs from worship.

Mary did what no one had ever done before. Others had fallen down at the Redeemer's feet before this, but no one had broken his alabaster box over Him. They had come as petitioners or beggars, but Mary came as a worshipper. How sad must the heart of God be to see so few worshippers today. Oh! dear child of God, prostrate thyself before thy majestic Lord and learn the joy of worship.

The worshipful attitude is that which simply gazes, contemplates and adores; the adoring contemplation of God as He is revealed in Christ.

— *James A. Stewart*

Let the ointment flow!

May 27

WITH CHRIST...WHICH IS FAR BETTER.

Phil. 1: 23

SAFELY HOME

I am home in heaven, dear ones;
Oh so happy and so bright
There is perfect joy and beauty!
In this everlasting light.

All the pain and grief is over,
Every restless tossing passed;
I am now at peace for ever,
Safely home in heaven at last.

Did you wonder I so calmly
Trod the valley of the shade?
Oh, but Jesus' love illumined
Every dark and fearful glade.

155

And he came Himself to meet me
In that way so hard to tread;
And with Jesus' arm to lean on,
Could I have one doubt or dread?

Then you must not grieve so sorely,
For I love you dearly still;
Try to look beyond death's shadows
Pray to trust our Father's Will.

There is work still waiting for you
So you must not idly stand;
Do it now, while life remaineth
You shall rest in Jesus land.

When that work is all completed,
He will gently call you Home;
Oh, the rapture of that meeting,
Oh, the joy to see you come.

— *Selected*

May 28

Now may the God of peace ... strengthen (complete, perfect) *and* make you what you ought to be ... that you may carry out His will. Heb. 13: 20—21

Blessed Redeemer, what wonderful grace that Thou callest us to share in Thy intercession! We pray Thee, arouse in Thy redeemed people a consciousness of the glory of this their calling, and of all the rich blessing which Thy Church in its impotence can, through its intercession in Thy Name, bring down upon this earth. May Thy Holy Spirit work in Thy people a deep conviction of the sin of restraining prayer, of the sloth and unbelief and selfishness that is the cause of it, and of Thy loving desire to pour out the Spirit of prayer in answer to their petitions — for Thy name's sake. Amen.

— *Andrew Murray*

O for a passionate passion for souls,
O for a pity that yearns!
O for the love that loves unto death,
O for the fire that burns!
O for the pure prayer-power that prevails,
That pours itself out for the lost!
Victorious prayer in the Conqueror's Name,
O for a Pentecost!

May 29

As they ministered to the Lord and fasted, the Holy Ghost said, Separate me Barnabas and Saul for the work whereunto I have called them. — Acts 13: 2

The Spirit needed new full-time workers for His vineyards. Into the busy prosperous church at Antioch, He steps and lays His hand on two choice servants, Barnabas and Saul. How strange it seems to us today, who are living so far from the New Testament pattern to read of the distinctive call of these two men by the Spirit! The church did not call them. A committee did not call them. They were chosen, called, separated and empowered to go forth by the Spirit. Surely one of the chief reasons there is so little fruit in our ministry today is that so few full-time Christian workers are *divinely* separated for the ministry. In the last analysis, only the Holy Spirit can call.

It is necessary, however, to see the other side of the picture. The church at Antioch laid their hands upon the men the Spirit had elected. The Holy Spirit not only told the two men of His choice of them, but He also told the church. When the Spirit speaks, there is no confusion. He is never the author of confusion. I am sure, dear brother and sister, that if you are called and separated by the Spirit for a distinctive ministry, it will be clearly evident to some others around you. I know there are extreme cases in these days, when the Church is not enjoying times of revival, for the Spirit's voice to go unheeded. *I know that some of the Lord's dear servants have to strike forth into the vineyards, while a sleeping church does not approve.* However, in most cases a spiritual assembly will know that you have been set apart for full-time Christian ministry.

Well I remember when the Spirit spoke to me in the Orkney Islands and told me to give up my evangelistic ministry as a boy-preacher and proceed to Eastern Europe. The call of the Spirit was so urgent and so definite to me and yet few around me seemed to believe that I was in the will of God. What the Spirit of God had told me to do was so fantastic that none seemed to believe that it was the Lord of the harvest thrusting me forth.

On reaching my destination, I was deeply disturbed about this. "Surely," I told the Spirit, "according to Acts 13 you must have told someone else that you have called me to this missionary ministry. O Lord, I am only human. Please give me the joy of confirmation from another source."

To my great delight, I received a letter from a pastor in Scotland whom I had never met. Writing from a thousand miles distance he said, "Dear Brother, the Spirit revealed to me some months ago that you were a chosen vessel to carry the gospel to the Slavic races in Eastern Europe. I praise God that you have been obedient to the heavenly vision."

— *James A. Stewart*

May 30

THE FELLOWSHIP, COMMUNION, PARTNER-SHIP OF THE HOLY SPIRIT BE WITH YOU ALL.
— 2 Cor. 13: 14, Margin

This is a day of the denial of the personality of the Spirit. There is a grave danger in our high-powered evangelistic machinery that we may organize the blessed Spirit out of the church. *It is easier to organize than to agonize!* Unless the Holy Spirit is given the prominent

158

place in the seat of authority, there will be only false fire, no matter how big the organization and no matter how big the financial budget may be. How many evangelistic campaigns I have known in which the executive member of the Godhead was completely ignored!

Revival comes from the Holy Spirit and it is only as He is honored and obeyed that there can be a true spiritual awakening. Since the day of Pentecost when He was installed as the administrator of the church, it has been His prerogative to undertake the leadership of all gospel conquests. *Throughout the Acts we see Him as a divine Person residing in and over the church.*

In the general assembly gathering in the fifteenth chapter, the chairman James recognizes the Spirit's leadership by announcing to the delegates: "It seemed good to the Holy Ghost, and to us . . ."

How extraordinary these words would sound in a Christian convention today! *So far have we removed ourselves from the authority of the Spirit of God that such language would bring only a knowing smile from the delegates.* Yes, the sin of the church today is the denial of the personality and presidency of the Spirit of Pentecost.

Campaign after campaign is conducted without Him. An occasional reference may be made to His Name; but alas, He is outside the camp and wounded in the house of His friends. The Holy Spirit is the source of all true revival. All our efforts apart from Him no matter how big they may be are like som much beating of the air. *A church without her Pentecostal experience is utterly powerless to move herself or others.*

Can it be that the church of Christ has so denied the Spirit of God His rightful place of authority and administration that it is too late in the day for Him to return? This is a very solemn and heart-searching question that ought to drive us to our knees in deep humiliation. Something is vastly wrong when we see so little results for our efforts.

— *James A. Stewart*

May 31

HE WILL GUIDE YOU INTO ALL TRUTH.
— John 16: 13

May we be able to spread our Bibles on the mercy seat and read them by the light of the cloud of Glory!

When we pray in the morning to be filled with the Spirit, we may expect to be filled all day with thoughts of Christ.

In prayer in the wood for some time, having set apart three hours for devotion; felt drawn out much to pray for that peculiar fragrance which believers have about them, who are very much in fellowship with God. It is like an aroma, unseen but felt. Other Christians have the beauty of the Rose of Sharon. These have the fragrance too.

— *Andrew Bonar*

June 1

BEFORE THE COCK CROW, THOU SHALT DENY ME THRICE.
— Math. 26: 34

The Cock crowed thrice,
And in the night — a startled face . . .
Of ashen white, sank low, in deep despair,
For Peter heard it —
Ling'ring there,
And Peter knew! — that he had done . . .
The very act, against the One,
To whom, he had His service sworn,
The cock crowed thrice, and nite was torn —
With more than sound!
For all the air, did thus resound . . .
With Peter's broken cry!
That all his loyalty should die!

In weakness!
Nurtured by a Maid . . .
In loud denials, he had made!
'Tis then the bitter price! — he paid,
All sorrow to endorse,
For Peter knew, in that dark night —
The valley of remorse.
And Lord:
The cock, is crowing still . . .
And we have often found — our will,
To pay in dividends of pain,
As we refuse — deny — again,
We find our weakness oft gives o'er,
And we forsake, Thy love once more,
'Tis in such nights of lonely sin,
We hear that crowing cock, begin —
And Lord: we stand, as Peter stood:
And cry in anguish — that we could!
Have e'er denied our matchless Lord,
Who in our lives, such blessing poured,
But give us strength,
We humbly pray,
That we might live — from day to day,
Secure, within Thy perfect will,
Each purpose of Thy plan — fulfill,
We ask Thee Lord — remove! each stain . . .
And may the Cock . . .

N'er crow! — again!

— Connie Calenberg

June 2

. . . [in His love] He chose us — actually picked us
out for Himself as His own — in Christ before the
foundation of the world; that we should be holy (consecrated and set apart for Him) and blameless in His
sight. — Eph. 1: 4, The Amplified New Testament.

Study universal holiness of life. Your whole usefulness depends on this, for your sermons last but an hour or two; your life preaches all the week. If Satan can only make a covetous minister a lover of praise, of pleasure, of good eating, he has ruined your ministry. Give yourself to prayer, and get your texts, your thoughts, your words from God. Luther spent his best three hours in prayer.

— *Robert Murray McCheyne*

John Wesley gives us a glimpse into a church which had been so restored to apostolic devotion, purity and power. Writing of his visit among the Moravians, he says, "God has given me at length the desire of my heart. I am with a church whose conversation is in Heaven, in whom is the mind that was in Christ, and who so walk as He walked. Here I continually meet what I sought for — living proofs of the power of faith, persons saved from inward, as well as outward sin, by the love of God shed abroad in their hearts. I am extremely comforted and strengthened by the conversation of this lovely people."

He has picked me out to be holy.

— *James A. Stewart*

June 3

AND THE YIELD OF RIGHTEOUSNESS SHALL BE PEACE. — Isa. 32: 17, Rotherham.

Humility is perfect quietness of heart. It is for me to have no trouble, never to be vexed or irritated or sore or disappointed. It is to expect nothing, to wonder at nothing that is done to me, to feel nothing done against me. It is to be at rest when nobody praises me, and when I am blamed or despised. It is to have a blessed home in the Lord, where I can go in and shut the door, and kneel to my Father in secret, and be at peace as

162

in a deep sea of calmness when all around is in trouble. *It is the fruit of the Lord Jesus Christ's redemptive work on Calvary's Cross, manifest in those of His own who are definitely subjected to the Holy Spirit.*

— *Andrew Murray*

June 4

TAKE YOU HENCE . . . TWELVE STONES.

Josh. 4: 3

MEMORIALS OF JORDAN

The passage of Israel across Jordan was not to be forgotten. Twelve chosen men — one from each tribe — returned to the emptied bed of the river, to the place where the priests' feet still stood, and from thence, each lifted a stone, which he carried on his shoulders to the Canaan side, and set it up on the promised land. These stones were to be memorials of the Lord's power in cutting off the waters of Jordan, and in bringing His people into the land. They were to be witnesses to generations yet to come of the power of the Lord's right hand. *These memorial stones, raised up from the place of death, and borne by a power outside themselves to a new position, in which they were to bear witness for God, remind us of the present place of those who are risen and seated with Christ.* Once like these stones they lay in death, under judgment, but now by the grace and power of God, they have been raised up, and seated together in heavenly places in Christ. Believers living in the power of this position, and manifesting by a daily life for God that their affection is set on things above, will soon attract the world's attention. The question will still be asked, "What mean ye by these stones?" Gilgal — where Israel's "reproach" was rolled away, was a continual witness to "all the people of the earth"

163

of what the hand of the Lord had wrought for His people Israel (Josh. iv. 24).

Another memorial, in a different place, must also be erected. In the deep bed of Jordan, in the place where the priests' feet stood, Joshua set up twelve more stones, to be overflowed and buried by the waters of Jordan when they returned in their strength. Here we have the other side of the picture, the countertruth we may say. The twelve stones lifted out of Jordan, and set up in Canaan, tell of the new standing of the believer, as risen with Christ. The twelve stones buried in Jordan, never more to be seen by human eyes, tell of the believer's death and burial with Christ.

— *John Ritchie*

Dear young believer, ask God now to lead you into this vital truth.

June 5

LET THE WORD CONCERNING CHRIST REMAIN AS A RICH TREASURE IN YOUR HEARTS.
Col. 3: 16, Weymouth.

The Bible should be read repeatedly.

We have a warrant for repetition in Phil 4: 1, "To write the same things to you, to me indeed is not grievous but for you it is safe"; and you must have noticed that Christ repeated Himself a great deal. If, then, repetition is one of the arts of teaching it must be also one of the arts of learning. Just because we never can know any part of Scripture well enough, we should read every part over and over again. The serious student of literature will read the ancient and modern Classics hundreds of times, and the serious student of the Bible will read it as often as is possible. Each time any of these Writings is read some special object should be in view. *For instance, Romans should be read to discover its broad out-*

164

line; then, again, for the sweep of its argument; then, each of its three parts should be read carefully on three separate occasions; then, the whole should be read again for the purpose of marking its dominating words, such as faith, sin, righteousness; then, again, to consider its quotations from the Old Testament. That would make an interesting week for any eager soul.

— *W. Graham Scroggie*

June 6

IN THE LAST DAYS PERILOUS TIMES WILL COME. — II Tim. 3: 1

Potpourri Evangelism

Mix together an unending parade of star performers whose notoriety has been achieved upon what they can do or have done, add a liberal quantity of syncopated rhythm, spice the mixture with clever quips, highschool slang and a generous sprinkling of jokes, prepare the potion under such high-pressure and extravagent advertising as befits Hollywood, and the resultant brew is sufficient to effectively thwart all attempts at scriptural revival and true evangelism. Yet in almost every direction today we observe this tendency in various states of development.

— *Kenneth H. Good*

O blessed Spirit strike a death blow to this Hollywood Evangelism.

June 7

THERE IS A LAD HERE WITH FIVE BARLEY LOAVES. — John. 6: 9

May I here give a word of testimony? I think the Lord wants me to give it. It is this: I never go to a Convention, least of all this Convention, without being severely tested by the great enemy of souls along this line. He says, "What are you taking? *Only a few barley loaves? Of what use are they?* Why don't you take some rich cake with plenty of almond icing on it?" He can tell the truth when it suits him. It is true that to me they are, indeed, little barley cakes; nobody who listens to me ever realises that as much as I do. God only knows all about it, but I go to my Lord and I say, "But, Lord, it is my all." There is yearning behind, there are prayers behind, tears behind, effort behind, sacrifice, blood of soul behind even the little barley cake. *There was a time when I did try to bring the rich cake and the almond icing into the pulpit, but I never saw a miracle then.* But the Lord has taught me just to bring the barley loaf, and I place it in His pierced hand and I say to Him, "Take it and give thanks for it, and bless it and break it; so break it that I can hardly recognise it again as my own," and then, with a smile that banishes all my poor misgivings, He hands it back to me, and oh, I have seen Him feed the hungry multitudes in desert places all over the world, thousands and tens of thousands of them.

The Lord had to break the bread; that was the condition of distribution — the breaking of the sacrifice. There is a great truth there that has been gripping my soul the last twenty-four hours: I do not know whether I can put it before you — that the sacrifice, however complete, cannot reach its ultimate measure of blessing until it is first broken. The sacrifice of a broken heart is the moment of the miracle of sanctification, and the supreme moment in the life of Jesus came when His dear body became a broken body: that was the moment when He completed and perfected the redemption of a lost and ruined world. Of the moment when the disciples, after His death and His resurrection, got that vision of Him, we read: "He was known in the breaking of bread." How did they know Him, do you think? Did not they, in that moment, know Him as the One of the broken body? I think they did. *I am very glad there are missionaries here this morning, because you understand it as people at home hardly do: it is one thing to place the sacrifice in His hands: it is another thing to have it broken.* David Livingstone, when a mere boy in Blantyre, having given his own heart to Jesus, placed all upon God's altar when he worked at that little spinning-jenny in the cotton factory. The sacrifice was complete then. But oh, read his diary! Talk about a broken sacifice, broken and broken, and always a condition of a larger distribution of blessing; and because he was so broken, and so continually broken, Africa to-day is in some sense a new continent.

— *Charles Inwood*

June 8

And even now I rejoice in the affliction which I bear for your sakes, and I fill up what yet is lacking of the sufferings of Christ in my flesh, on behalf of His body which is the Church. — Col. 1: 24, Conybeare.

The mighty warrior cries to the saints at Colossae:

"I am filling in what is lacking of the sufferings of my dear Saviour. I am complementing in my own sufferings the unfinished sufferings of Christ."

It is not that Paul could add anything to the merit of the redemptive sufferings of the Redeemer. Oh no! These sufferings were complete and final (Heb. 10: 12). There is nothing lacking in that divine blood-shedding. There is nothing left for us to "fill in" by our co-sufferings. His was a perfect salvation wrought out by His precious death on that accursed Tree (Gal. 3: 13). Blessed be God, there is nothing left for the sinner to do but to rest on that finished work (John 19: 30).

The sufferings of which Paul writes to the Colossians are those of the Saviour as THE HEAD OF THE

167

CHURCH. Our Kinsman-Redeemer is now our Head, of Whose Body we are the members. So great is the oneness of the body with its glorious Head that the Church in I Corinthians 12:12 is referred to as "The Christ." "For as the body is one, and hath many members, and all the members of that one body, being many, are one body: so also is Christ."

Our redemption cost the life blood of God's beloved Son. It cost Him so much anguish and suffering to become a curse for us on Calvary as our Surety that He cannot be indifferent to the spiritual condition of the members of His body.

Oh my brother, my sister, let us never forget that the sufferings of our Saviour are not yet over. Oh Church of Christ, let this startling truth arrest us. Our dear Redeemer is suffering untold anguish just now. He is suffering on behalf of His Body. He is suffering for the sanctification of His people. Christ died, not only to redeem His Body, but to sanctify it wholly. He died not only to save our souls from hell, but that He might raise up a conquering people assaulting the gates of hell. The Church must be beautiful with the garments of her blessed Lord and mighty in battle.

"Thou art beautiful, O my love . . . terrible as an army with banners." (Songs of Solomon 6:4)

Just as the Head suffers for the body, so the members of the body should suffer with the Head. The burning question is, am I suffering with my blessed Head, or am I causing the Head to suffer? *Have I entered into the fellowship of His sufferings, or do I drift along, careless and indifferent to His groans, tears and bloody sweat? The Saviour is travailing on behalf of His Church.*

— *James A. Stewart*

June 9

Let us be glad and rejoice, and give honour to Him:
for the marriage of the Lamb is come". Rev. 17: 7
*This is the actual union, the consummation of the
glory.* Caught up into the royal pavilion to meet her
Lord in the air, she is not only for ever with the Lord,
but for ever His own chosen Bride, to sit upon His
throne, to wear His crown, to share His love, to be
invested with His glory. All this when He comes the
second time to be glorified in His saints. Round this
great event the fortunes of God's universe revolve. That
marriage hall is to be the centre of all blessing to Heaven
and earth.

— *Horatius Bonar*

Blessed Lord, prepare me!

June 10

GET THEE UP. — Josh. 7: 10

UP, SANCTIFY THE PEOPLE. — Josh. 7: 13

*Have you noticed how much praying for revival has
been going on of late — and how little revival has
resulted?*
I believe our problem is that we have been trying to
substitute praying for obeying; and it simply will not
work.
To pray for revival while ignoring or actually flout-
ing the plain precept laid down in the Scriptures is to
waste a lot of words and get nothing for our trouble.
It has been quite overlooked in recent times that the
faith of Christ is an absolute arbiter. It preempts the
whole redeemed personality and seizes upon the individual to the exclusion of all other claims. Or more
accurately, it makes every legitimate claim on the Christian's life conditional, and without hesitation decides the

place each claim shall have in the total scheme. The act of committal to Christ in salvation releases the believing man from the penalty of sin, but it does not release him from the obligation to obey the words of Christ. *Rather it brings him under the joyous necessity to obey.*

Look at the epistles of the New Testament and notice how largely they are given over to what is erroneously called "hortatory" matter. By dividing the epistles into "doctrinal" and "hortatory" passages we have relieved ourselves of any necessity to obey. The doctrinal passages require from us nothing except that we believe them. The so-called hortatory passages are harmless enough, for the very word by which they are described declares them to be words of advice and encouragement rather than commandments to be obeyed. *This is a palpable error.*

The exhortations in the epistles are to be understood as apostolic injunctions carrying the weight of mandatory charges from the Head of the Church. They are intended to be obeyed, not weighed as bits of good advice which we are at liberty to accept or reject as we will.

— *A. W. Tozer*

June 11

FOR THIS GOD IS OUR GOD FOR EVER AND EVER. — Ps. 48: 14

He was better to me than all my hopes,
He was better than all my fears;
He made a road of my broken works
And a rainbow of my tears.
The billows that guarded my sea girt path
But carried my Lord on their crest;
When I dwell on the days of my wilderness march
I can lean on His love for the rest.

170

He guided by paths that I could not see,
By ways that I have not known,
The crooked was straight and the rough made plain,
As I followed the Lord alone.
I praise Him still for the pleasant palms
And the water-springs by the way;
For the glowing pillars of flame by night
And the sheltering clouds by day.

There is light for me on the trackless wild
As the wonders of old I trace,
When the God of the whole earth went before
To search me a resting place.
Has He changed for me? Nay! He changes not
He will bring me by some new way,
Through fire and flood and each crafty foe,
As safely as yesterday.

Never a watch on the dreariest halt
But some promise of love endears;
I read from the past that my future will be
Far better than all my fears.
Like the golden pot of the wilderness bread,
Laid up with the blossoming rod,
All safe in the ark, with the law of the Lord,
Is the covenant care of my God.

— *Anna Shipton*

Hallelujah!

June 12

TO ONE IS GIVEN. — I Cor. 12: 8

TO ANOTHER. — I Cor. 12: 9

Being baptized with the Holy Spirit, as Dwight L.
Moody was, (and here we need to distinguish between
the *fact* of such an experience and the *form* which it
may assume) *will not make you or me a second Moody.*

171

Yet in one sense it will do for us precisely what it did for him: it will release the maximum of what we are capable of doing in the service of our Lord even as it released his maximum. The clamant need today, as it has always been, is for servants of Christ, heralds of the evangel, whether clergymen or laymen, *who, refusing to live on spiritual minimums, insist upon maximums. God loves their holy audacity. He will never let them down!*

— *Selected*

June 13

APPLES OF GOLD IN PICTURES OF SILVER.
— Prov. 25:11

GOLDEN SAYINGS

Beloved brother, I have no time to be in a hurry.
— *R. C. Chapman*

There are many who preach Christ, but not many who live Christ: my great aim will be to live Christ.
— *R. C. Chapman*

The Lord Jesus is invisible to the world except through His Church, and as the people among whom we dwell see us, they see Christ so far as we represent Him.
— *A. J. Gordon*

Some fine morning you will see in the newspaper, "D. L. Moody is dead", Don't you believe it: I shall be more alive that morning than ever before.
— *D. L. Moody*

Mrs. Spurgeon's favorite verse:
*His love in times past forbids me to think
He'll leave me at last in trouble to sink;
Each sweet Ebenezer I have in review
Confirms His good pleasure to help me
quite through.*

172

And the saying pleased the whole multitude: and they chose Stephen, a man full of faith and of the Holy Ghost, and Philip, and Prochorus, and Nicanor, and Timon, and Parmenas, and Nicholas a proselyte of Antioch. — Acts 6: 5

In Acts 6: 5 we are told of two men, Stephen and Philip who were full of the Spirit. Now, notice it does not say they were filled with the Spirit but that they were "full" of the Spirit. There are many believers who receive fresh infillings of the Holy Spirit, but there are very few who *remain* full of the Spirit. A brother once prayed in a prayer meeting, "O God, fill me with Thy Spirit." Immediately a sister nearby prayed, "O Lord, don't. He leaks!"

The tragedy is that many of the Lord's people do leak. *The normal habitual experience of the child of God ought to be the constant fullness of the Spirit.* We do not deny the special need for fresh infillings and enduements in times of spiritual crises, but we do assert that God's norm for us is the continual fullness. We remain full by abiding in Christ. The qualification of these elders was that they must be "full of the Spirit".

Let us pause a moment to reiterate this glorious truth, that to be filled with the Spirit is to be dominated, possessed and controlled by a divine Person. The similes such as "rivers of living water" and "spiritual channels" are only human terms of accommodation. The Holy Spirit is a Person, co-equal in power and glory with the Father and the Son. So "power" is a Person. The Holy Spirit is the Spirit of power. The power of the Spirit is inseparable from His person. "Ye shall receive power, after that ye have received the Person!" His power cannot be detached from His Person. The Holy Spirit does not rent out His attributes. *We must be perfectly clear in our minds as to our desires. Do we want the gift of power or the Giver of power?*

— *James A. Stewart*

173

June 15

And when they had prayed, the place was shaken where they assembled together; and they were all filled with the Holy Ghost, and they spake the word of God with boldness. Acts 4: 31

They had just been beaten, and the enemy had told them not to dare utter another word in the name of the Lord Jesus. The gospel epidemic was spreading and the enemy was anxious that "it spread no further." As the liberated apostles came away from their place of confinement, did they start saying, "O Lord, it was awful. We were beaten. We had a hard time. O Lord, we are not going to preach again!"? Did they say, "O Lord, have mercy on us; take away this persecution?" Did they plead, "O Lord, give us wisdom that we may not offend again?"

No! They prayed fervently *"As to the present things then, O Lord, look upon their threats and grant unto Thy servants with all freedom of utterance to be speaking Thy word, by stretching forth thy hand for healing, and by the coming to pass of both signs and wonders through the Name of Thy holy Servant Jesus."* Acts 4: 20—30, Rotherham.

God answered their prayer for boldness of utterance so that we read, *"They were all filled with the Holy Ghost and they spake the word of God with boldness."* Holy boldness comes through a holy empowering. The Spirit is given to equip us for divine warfare, to make us victorious over all persecution, to make us overcomers so that we may not be ashamed or afraid to witness to the glory of God.

— *James A. Stewart*

June 16

This book of the law ... thou shalt meditate therein day and night, that thou mayest ... do ... for then shalt thou make thy way prosperous, and then thou shalt have good success. Have I not commanded thee? be strong and of a good courage, be not afraid, neither be thou dismayed, for the Lord thy God is with thee. — Josh. 1: 8—9

To be freed from all fear and dismay of the forces of the enemy, our great remedy is to have God's Word strengthening us day and night, so that we lose sight of man, and all fear of man. The Word is strength to you. You would be strong souls, if you were so filled with the Word of God, that everything you heard around you, would cause to spring into your mind instantly the Word, which would meet or explain the need; so that whatever question was asked you, or whatever doubt came to you, in one moment there would come the right answer to your mind from the Scriptures.

Are you being kept by God at this point? Are you *strong and very courageous?* Are you dismayed, are you afraid, are you fearful? Will you allow all fear to be swept from you, and go forward meditating on this Book day and night? It means when you awake in the morning the Word that is new will be in your mind. When you go to sleep, it means that you will not have troublesome thoughts in your mind to prevent your sleeping. One great, strong, mighty equipment for unbroken victory is to be filled with Divine strength by this Word dwelling in you richly. This was the equipment for Joshua as he was starting out, and if you are to be a "leader", you can only have the true vision to lead, as the Word dwells in you, and you meditate upon it, as Joshua was bidden to do.

Remember, too, they were not all Joshuas! Joshua had his place, and commission, and the people had theirs. *If you try to be a Joshua when the Lord wants you to be one of the people, it will only mean confusion and disorder.* True, God can make you a Joshua in your own centre and sphere to lead those around you into the

175

heavenly places; but it is necessary to ask you, if you are ready to recognize others with a commission from God not granted to you.

— *Selected*

Oh God! give me this holy grace to meditate on Thy Word day and night.

June 17

We love him because he first loved us. If a man say, I love God, and hateth his brother, he is a liar: for he that loveth not his brother whom he hath seen, how can he love God whom he hath not seen? — 1 John 4: 19—20

May we be in earnest, — may we live while we live! *May we know more of that love which will take a brother's failings to a throne of grace while throwing over them a cloak of charity; which will fix on His grace in a brother, and render thanks for it; which will be faithful in reproof, as well as jealous in defence.* May the beam be more and more extracted from our own eyes, that we may see fewer motes in our brother's!

— Lady Powerscourt.

Simply trusting Thee, Lord Jesus,
I behold Thee as Thou art,
And Thy love, so pure, so changeless,
Satisfies my heart;
Satisfies my deepest longings,
Meets, supplies my every need,
Compasseth me round with blessings,
Thine is love indeed!

June 18

He that believeth on me, as the Scripture hath said, out of his innermost being shall flow rivers of living water. —

But this spake he of the Spirit, which they that believe on him should receive. — John 7: 38—39.

If, some summer day, you were tramping down a certain mountain pass, you would, by-and-by, come to one of the most famous of Swiss glaciers. In the perpendicular wall of that great glacier, summer sun and warm winds have hollowed out a great ice cavern. You enter the arch, and, as you stand in the fantastic cave, you are chilled through with its cold. Ice above you; ice before you; ice all about you; — masses of ice; miles of ice. And now, as you gaze, there springs up at your feet a crystal stream of water from the very heart of the glacier, and begins its journey down the valley. You could almost step across it where it finds its birth. But, like the true Christian life, as it goes it grows, and a few miles down the valley, it is a strong, deep, leaping stream. The birds dip their bills into it, and, drinking, lift their heads to God as if in thanksgiving. The trees slip their roots down the bank and draw up its moisture. The lowing herds sink their nostrils in its pools and drink of its refreshing. By and by it enters a great lake, and seems lost. But it finds issue, and crossing central France, it takes a sudden turn and runs southward, and then, at its mouth, broad enough for great ships to sail upon its bosom, it is at last in Europe's greatest inland sea. And this beautiful, sparkling river, with all its refreshing and blessing, springs from the frozen heart of a great Swiss glacier!

Have you ever looked up into the Lord's face and cried, "O, Christ, how cold my heart is! How cold when I study Thy blessed Book with all its wondrous words of life; how callous it seems in the sacred chamber of secret prayer; how icy as I look with such seeming unconcern upon the sin and suffering of the lost world; how frozen in its lack of love for the Christless millions of heathendom! O Christ, is there anything that will melt this ice-berg heart of mine and cause a river of love and peace and power to flow forth from it to the world about me?" And Jesus Christ says, "There is. I have it." The God who can cause a river of refreshing to break forth from the frigid heart of an Alpine glacier can make a river of life burst forth from your cold heart.

— *J. H. McConkey*

June 19

I WENT INTO ARABIA. — Gal. 1: 17

Calvary and Pentecost are inseparable and they are indispensable for the preaching of the Gospel. Calvary creates the preacher and the teacher, and Pentecost equips the preacher and the teacher. Big learning will never make us preachers or teachers, although big learning has its place and a very great place; but there is one theological seminary into which we must go, and from which we must graduate if we are to be preachers and teachers of the Gospel. It is sometimes called Arabia, and Arabia means for you some place where you come face to face with the need in your life and fight it out in the presence of God. If you will do that you will learn what Paul learned in his Arabia, you will learn the meaning of the cross, and you will learn much about the purpose and power of the Holy Ghost, for Calvary and Pentecost are inseparable.

We may stand in pulpits and we may teach classes, and we may organize Christian work, and people may praise us, and we may have outward success, but if we do not know Calvary and we do not know Pentecost except in a superficial manner, those people we speak to and teach will never have cause to glorify God in us, and see God mighty in and through us as they saw in the apostle Paul.

— *Gordon Watt*

178

June 20

SUPER CONQUERORS. — Rom. 8: 37, Lit.

The cross is the source of all victory, and there is a fivefold victory for the Christian to win. First, "But thanks be to God which giveth us the victory through our Lord Jesus Christ," victory over death (1 Cor. 15: 57). *Second,* "I am crucified with Christ: nevertheless I live; yet not I, but Christ liveth in me: and the life which I now live in the flesh I live by the faith of the Son of God, who loved me, and gave himself for me," victory over self (Gal. 2: 20). *Third,* "And they that are Christ's have crucified the flesh with the affections and lusts," victory over the flesh (Gal. 5: 24). *Fourth,* "But God forbid that I should glory, save in the cross of our Lord Jesus Christ, by whom the world is crucified unto me, and I unto the world," victory over the world (Gal. 6: 14). *Fifth,* "And having spoiled principalities and powers, he made a shew of them openly, triumphing over them in it, " victory over Satan (Col. 2: 15). *And Satan can be defeated on no ground except that of Calvary.* There on the cross the Lord Jesus Christ bruised the serpent's head and broke the serpent's power, and to-day we stand facing a conquered foe. Do not let us forget it. The cross embraces all these things, and gives to you and to me a full and complete victory.

— *Gordon Watt*

June 21

AND THE NUMBER OF THEM WAS TEN THOUSAND TIMES TEN THOUSAND AND THOUSANDS OF THOUSANDS. — Rev. 5: 11

> *Hark! ten thousand voices crying,*
> *"Lamb of God!" with one accord:*
> *Thousand thousand saints replying,*
> *Wake at once the echo'ng chord.*

179

"Praise the Lamb!" the chorus waking,
  All in heaven together throng;
Loud and far each tongue partaking
  Rolls around the endless song.

Grateful incense this, ascending
  Ever to the Father's throne;
Ev'ry knee to Jesus bending,
  All the mind in heaven is one.

All the Father's counsels claiming
  Equal honors to the Son,
All the Son's effulgence beaming,
  Makes the Father's glory known.

By the Spirit all pervading,
  Hosts unnumbered round the Lamb,
Crowned with light and joy unfading,
  Hail Him as the great "I AM."

Joyful now the new creation
  Rests in undisturbed repose,
Blest in Jesu's full salvation,
  Sorrow now nor thraldom knows.

Hark! the heavenly notes again!
  Loudly swells the song of praise;
Through creation's vault, Amen!
  Amen! responsive joy doth raise.

— *J. N. Darby*

Hark! and worship.

June 22

I BARE YOU ON EAGLES' WINGS. — Exodus 19: 4

"They that wait upon the Lord shall renew their strength; they shall mount up with wings as eagles; they shall run, and not be weary; and they shall walk, and not faint." Or as Rotherham's Version renders it, *"They who wait for Jahweh shall renew their strength, they shall mount on strong pinion like eagles, they shall run and not grow weary, they shall walk and not faint."* The difference in the Versions being that Rotherham's speaks of those who wait *for the Lord* (not wait upon Him) and again of those who mount *on* strong pinion like eagles, not of those who mount up *with* wings as eagles. The eagles' wings being given not to them but belonging to another.

For they belong to God. The God of whom Moses spoke when he said. "As an eagle stirreth up her nest, fluttereth over her young, spreadeth abroad her wings, taketh them, beareth them upon her wings, so the Lord alone did lead him."

The simile commences with the eaglets' extreme dilemma. Brought up from the first to enjoy the security and safety of their nest, suddenly they find their home being stirred so violently and so ruthlessly that safety and security vanish. While beneath them is the unknown dread abyss, and overhead the expanse where their helpless wings can never take them.

Until they become aware of the strong wings of the parent eagle fluttering over them, and being spread out so that she may take them, and bear them on her wings to a place of safety.

"They who wait for Jahweh shall mount on strong pinion like eagles." Here again the picture begins with extreme dilemma, that of fainting youths confronted with some situation for which they find they have no might, and where a great deliverance is needed; needed just as desperately as it was with the frightened eaglets.

181

But a deliverance which will only come if they "wait for the Lord," or hope expect, or look for Him is the alternate meaning, expect and look for the deliverance which He has promised in His Word. For God says that they who do so shall mount on strong pinion like eagles, on the wings of the One who fainteth not neither is weary, and who will face, through those who are themselves so hopelessly unable, all that they are called upon to do.

And consequently they shall renew their strength, or the Hebrew is they shall change it. *For just as it is not the helpless wings of the eaglet, but the strong pinions of the mother eagle which bear it to a place of safety, so also "not I, but Christ that liveth in me" will face the otherwise impossible situation.* Not I, but Christ will run and not grow weary; not I but Christ will walk or, as the literal Hebrew rendering is, will *go on* (running) and not faint.

— *Aphra White*

June 23

DELIGHT THYSELF ALSO IN THE LORD; AND HE SHALL GIVE THEE THE DESIRES OF THINE HEART. — Psalm 34: 4

Come, therefore, my dear Lord and Saviour, whilst thy servant is breathing after thee, and possess my heart with the spiritual blessings of grace and faith, peace and charity; and let none of these empty and transient delights of this world stand in competition with them! Thou art the source and centre of all my wishes and desires; even as the hart panteth after the water brooks, so panteth my soul after thee, O God!

— *Bishop Beveridge*

> *Thou art enough for me —*
> *Thou art enough for me —*
> *My precious, living, loving Lord,*
> *Yes, Thou art enough for me!*

June 24

IN JEHOVAH MY LORD HAVE I TAKEN UP MY SHELTER. — Psalm 73: 28, Spurrell

Meditation must lead to prayer. It provides matter for prayer. It must lead on to prayer, to ask and receive definitely what it has seen in the Word or accepted in the Word. Its value is that it is the preparation for prayer, deliberate and wholehearted supplication for what the heart has felt that the Word has revealed as needful or possible. That means the rest of faith, that looks upward in the assurance that the Word will open up and prove its power in the soul that meekly and patiently gives itself away to it.

The reward of resting for a time from intellectual effort, and cultivating the habit of holy meditation, will be that in course of time the two will be brought into harmony, and all our study be animated by the spirit of a quiet waiting on God and a yielding up of the heart and life to the Word.

Our fellowship with God is meant for all the day. The blessing of securing a habit of true meditation in the morning watch will be that we shall be brought nearer the blessedness of the man of the first Psalm; "Blessed is the man whose delight is in the law of the Lord; and in his law doth he meditate day and night."

Let all workers and leaders of God's people remember that they need this more than others if they are to train them to it, and keep up their own communication unbroken with the only source of strength and blessing.

— *Andrew Murray*

June 25

SO THERE WAS GREAT JOY IN JERUSALEM:
FOR SINCE THE TIME OF SOLOMON ... THERE
WAS NOT THE LIKE. — II Chron. 30: 26

*In the revivals under Hezekiah, Josiah, and Nehemiah
we see that the work was one of recovery and restoration.* The spiritual life of the nation had sunk low; the
people had departed from the commandments of the
Lord and thus were living in disobedience. It was when
these men of God read the Holy Scriptures once again
and saw God's plan and purpose for His people, that
they called the people to repentance and sought a recovery. *It was a revival of the reading of the Word of
God and a revival of the obeying of the Word of God.*
It was the Word applied by the mighty power of the
Holy Ghost that wrought repentance and brought the
back-slidden nation back to God's original pattern of
worship and service, as given to Moses on the mount.
The predominant meaning of the word "revival" in the
Old Testament is "to recover", "to restore", "to return"
to God's original standard for His people.

— *James A. Stewart*

June 26

I AM WITH THEE, AND NO MAN SHALL SET
ON THEE TO HURT THEE. — Acts 18: 10

*So long as the Lord had work for Paul to do in Cor-
inth, the fury of the mob was restrained.* The Jews opposed themselves and blasphemed; but they could neither
stop the preaching of the gospel, nor the conversion of
the hearers. God has power over the most violent minds.
He makes the wrath of man to praise Him when it
breaks forth, but He still more displays His goodness
when He restrains it; and He can restrain it. "By the
greatness of thine arm they shall be as still as a stone,
till thy people pass over, O Lord."

184

Do not, therefore, feel any fear of man when you know that you are doing your duty. Go straight on, as Jesus would have done, and those who oppose shall be as a bruised reed and as smoking flax. Many a time men have had cause to fear because they were themselves afraid; but a dauntless faith in God brushes fear aside like the cobwebs in a giant's path. No man can harm us unless the Lord permits. He who makes the devil himself to flee at a word, can certainly control the devil's agents. Maybe they are already more afraid of you than you are of them. Therefore, go forward, and where you looked to meet with foes you will find friends.

— *C. H. Spurgeon*

> *In heav'nly love abiding,*
> *No change my heart shall fear;*
> *And safe is such confiding,*
> *For nothing changes here.*
> *The storm may roar without me,*
> *My heart may low be laid,*
> *But God is round about me,*
> *And can I be dismayed?*

Hallelujah!

June 27

AND HE TABERNACLED AMONG US, AND WE BEHELD HIS GLORY. — John 1:14, Lit.

THE TABERNACLE AND ITS TEACHING

In looking at the tabernacle we should ever remember the whole, in its varied aspects, presents to us the excellencies of the Lord Jesus Christ; or as we read in Ps. 29: 9, "In His temple every whit of it uttereth His glory." There were fourteen different materials used in its con-

struction and its furniture and vessels. Let us look at them.

1. *Gold.* The divine glory of the Lord Jesus, the Son of God.

2. *Silver.* This was derived from the atonement money of Israel, and presents to us Christ as the Ransom for the sinner.

3. *Brass.* The divine character of Christ as able to sustain the fire of God's holiness.

4. *Blue.* The heavenly colour. Christ as the manifestation of the love and grace and truth of God.

5. *Purple.* The kingly glory of Christ as the Son of Man.

6. *Scarlet.* Christ as the suffering One unto death — the cross the pathway to the glory.

7. *Fine Linen.* Christ as the spotless, righteous Son of Man.

8. *Goat's Hair.* The memorial of Christ as the Sin Offering.

9. *Ram's Skins dyed Red.* Christ as the One who by His blood made an atonement for sin.

10. *Badger's Skins.* The outward aspect of Christ towards the world as the One without form or comeliness, no beauty in Him.

11. *Shittim Wood.* The incorruptible humanity of Christ.

12. *Oil for the Light.* The Spirit's fulness shining forth in Christ.

13. *Spices for Anointing and for Sweet Incense.* The perfect graces and perfumes of the person of Christ to God and to us.

14. *Precious Stones.* The effulgent glories and brightness of Christ.

What precious food for our souls we have here as we are privileged by the Spirit to be feeding on HIM, in thus meditating on the manifold features of His wondrous character and worth.

— *W. H.*

June 28

APPLES OF GOLD IN PICTURES OF SILVER.

— Prov. 25:11

Golden sayings

The Holy Spirit is the One Who makes real in me what Jesus did for me. — *Oswald Chambers*

Fruit comes from the root, therefore abide. "More fruit" comes from the knife, therefore endure. "Much fruit" comes from DEATH, therefore DIE. — *C. A. Fox*

Remember that your Christian perfection does not so much consist in building a tabernacle upon Mount Tabor, to rest and enjoy rare sights there, as in resolutely taking up the cross and following Christ to an ignominious Calvary. — *John Fletcher*

Do what the Spirit prompts. Better offend ten thousand friends than grieve the Spirit of God.

— *Evan Roberts*

A careless reader of the Scripture will not make a close walker with God. — *Robert Chapman*

June 29

He that goeth forth and weepeth, bearing precious seed, shall doubtless come again with rejoicing, bringing his sheaves with him. — Psalm 126:6

Robert Murray McCheyne, one of Scotland's greatest preachers, died at the age of twenty-nine. Everywhere he stepped, Scotland shook. Whenever he opened his mouth

187

a spiritual force swept in every direction. Thousands followed him into God's kingdom. A traveler, eager to see where McCheyne had preached, went to the Scottish town and found the church. An old gray haired sexton agreed to take him through the church. He led the way into McCheyne's study. "Sit in the chair," he ordered. The traveler hesitated a moment, then sat down. On the table before him was an open Bible. "Drop your head on that Book and weep. That is the way our minister always did before he preached," said the old man. He then led the visitor into the pulpit before the open Bible. "Stand there," he said, "and drop your head on your hands and let the tears flow. That is the way our minister always did before he began to preach!" *With such a passion for lost and needy souls, is it any wonder that the Holy Spirit gave McCheyne a magnetic personality which drew many to Christ?*

— *James A. Stewart*

June 30

AND THE LAMB IS THE LIGHT THEREOF.

— Rev. 21: 23

The Grand Sevenfold Consummation

of all the Redemption plan is given in the twenty-second chapter of Revelation:

"And there shall be no more curse" — *Perfect sinlessness.*

"And the throne of God and of the Lamb shall be in it" — *Perfect authority.*

"And His servants shall serve Him" — *Perfect obedience.*

"And they shall see His face" — *Perfect communion.*

"And His Name shall be in their foreheads" — *Perfect consecration.*

"And there shall be no night there" — *Perfect blessedness.*

188

"And they shall reign for ever and ever" — *Perfect glory.*

What visions of such sevenfold perfection are found anywhere outside of the Oracles of God!

— *A. T. Pierson*

> *"Till He come!" Oh, let the words*
> *Linger on the trembling chords;*
> *Let the "little while" between*
> *In their golden light be seen:*
> *Let us think how heaven and home*
> *Lie beyond that "Till He come!"*

July 1

THERE IS NOTHING TOO HARD FOR THEE.

— Jeremiah 32: 17

> *There is nothing too hard for Thee, dear Lord,*
> *No matter how grave things be;*
> *All power belongeth to Thee, dear Lord,*
> *Thus why should we anxious be?*
>
> *There is nothing too hard for Thee, dear Lord,*
> *Thus why should I be dismayed*
> *When those who would fain help me, dear Lord,*
> *Inadequate find their aid.*
>
> *There is nothing too hard for Thee, dear Lord,*
> *No burdens Thou canst not move;*
> *And since Thou carest for me, dear Lord,*
> *I may rest in Thy faithful love.*
>
> *There is nothing too hard for Thee, dear Lord,*
> *I sing it, I will! I will!*
> *And wonders great I may see, dear Lord,*
> *Because of Thy sovereign skill.*

Then sing my soul! — *J. Danson Smith*

July 2

*But ye shall receive power when the Holy Spirit com-
eth upon you, and ye shall be my witnesses both in Jerusalem, and in all Judea and Samaria, and as far as the
uttermost part.* — Acts 1: 8, Rotherham

*Here we see that the Spirit was given on the Day of
Pentecost for the one specific purpose of empowering
the disciples of Christ to take the gospel to every creature.* As William Arthur has said in *The Tongue of Fire,*
"If the preaching of the gospel is to exercise a great power over mankind, it must be either by enlisting extraordinary men, or by the endowing of ordinary men with
extraordinary power." I would go a step further and
boldly assert that even extraordinary men, apart from
the unction of the Spirit, would not be able to accomplish
this. The glory of Christianity and the glory of this book
is that very ordinary men and women, dominated,
possessed and controlled by the Holy Spirit, accomplished
mighty results for God.

*In the Upper Room discourse of our Lord we discover
that the Holy Spirit is the Great Evangelist of the Son
of God:* "He shall glorify Me" (John 10: 14). Strictly
speaking, we may say that the Holy Spirit ought *not* to
be here. The Saviour ought to be here, but the world
despised and rejected Him and so the Spirit came to
represent the absent Christ. This is Peter's explanation
of the Phenomenon of Pentecost. The Father had received
to Himself the Person Whom the world had crucified,
and the Spirit had descended to witness to the crucified
Redeemer:

"Therefore being by the right hand of God exalted, and
having received of the Father the promise of the Holy
Ghost, he hath shed forth this, which ye now see and
hear" (Acts 2: 33).

— *James A. Stewart*

July 3

HINDER ME NOT. — Gen. 24: 56

*Have we learnt that to gather out of the world a bride
for Christ and to lead her home to Him is the supreme
work of the Holy Ghost? If those who are saved have
more heart for the world and for earthly things, than
they have for the Lord and His things, the Holy Ghost
is hindered in His great work.* If we are inclined to
loiter on the homeward way, or if going forth to meet
the Bridegroom is not the all-important thing with us, we
might well hear a grieved Holy Spirit saying to us,
"Hinder Me not." We cannot separate the bright hope
of the coming again of the Lord Jesus from the work
of the Holy Spirit within us; we shall not be eager to
see Him as He is, if we have not ears to hear what the
Spirit has to say to us. He has come to: —

> Speak of Jesus and His love,
> Passing all bounds of human thought.

He has come to unfold the glories of the Son of God
to our souls. He wants our whole hearts for Christ and
is delighted when He gets them; He is grieved and hindered when He does not.

It is remarkable that the last mention of the Holy
Spirit in Holy Scripture is in the last chapter of the
Bible, where we read, "The Spirit and the bride say,
Come." It shows us the end and the climax of the Spirit's
work. Here we have "the unity of the Spirit" in practical
manifestation, for here we see the hearts of the saints
bound together in one great desire for the coming of the
Lord Jesus Christ. For this the Spirit of God is labouring.
*He is taking the things of Christ and showing them to the
saints of God, and in this way He is tuning their hearts
into full unison with His own, so that the Lamb may hear
at last the music of this prayer from the heart of the
bride, "EVEN SO, COME, LORD JESUS."*

— *J. T. Mawson*

191

July 4

IF, YE THEN BE RISEN WITH CHRIST, SEEK
THOSE THINGS WHICH ARE ABOVE, WHERE
CHRIST SITTETH ON THE RIGHT HAND OF
GOD. — Col. 3: 1

*Now Christ's presence at the Father's right hand, and
His ministry in the Holy of Holies above, constitute the
ground of our access there; and this blessed fact of our
privilege to enter into the Holiest by the blood of Jesus
is the truth with which the Epistle to the Hebrews is
especially occupied.* Indeed, Christ's exaltation to the
Father's throne is counted as our presence and residence
there, and we find it so set forth in the Epistles to the
Ephesians, Colossians, and Philippians. But is it not plain
that access carries with it the opposite idea of separation; that drawing near to God involves a withdrawing
from fellowship with an evil world? The fact that Christ
is at the right hand of the Father, and that we are one
with Him in His exaltation, gives us our reckoning-point
by which to fix our relation to this world. The paradox
of Lady Powerscourt that "the Christian is not one who
is looking up from earth to heaven, but one who is
looking down from heaven to earth," can be compre-
hended in this light. If "our citizenship is in heaven," we
are spiritually disfranchised of the world, and are bound
to confess that "we are strangers and pilgrims on the
earth."

— *A. J. Gordon*

July 5

I HAVE SET THEE FOR A SIGN UNTO THE
HOUSE OF ISRAEL. — Ezekiel 12: 6

*Not only has the Spirit, the Lord of the Harvest, bur-
dened many hearts to pray and long for revival in their
midst; He has raised up and sent forth into His vineyard*

fearless prophets with a burning message and call for repentance to the Church today. The message God has given to these holy men and women is an uncomfortable one, which tends to insult the lukewarm Church and infuriate her cold sleeping members. It is a message which will not compromise with the sinful, selfish, fruitless, powerless condition which characterizes God's people. Like the prophet Ezekiel, these special anointed messengers are "for a sign" to a disobedient, rebellious Church. *Having been broken down themselves before the Lord, and having been shown the abominations of Zion, and having literally digested the message of God until it is their very own, they have now become living, vital representatives of the message in their lives* (see Ezek. 12: 11). *"They are men which are for a sign"* (Zech. 3: 8, lit. Heb.). They are crucified with Christ, dead to their own feelings, and fear not the face of a stiff-necked generation (Jer. 1: 8). Their message rudely awakens and disturbs the saints, as the thought of "the Master of the House" coming suddenly and interrupting all their plans is far from welcome, and they rise up in protest. The message of the prophet of revival can never be a popular one, since the Holy God commands, "Cry aloud, spare not, lift up thy voice, like a trumpet, and show my people their transgressions, and the House of Jacob their sins" (Isa. 58: 1).

— *James A. Stewart*

Oh dear reader! ask God now to make thee "a sign Christian".

July 6

MEDITATE ON THESE THINGS. — 1 Tim. 4: 15

Now, worship is just contemplation and adoration of God the Father. But how can we conceive of God Who is Spirit? Only through the medium of revelation; and so, for this holy exercise we must turn to the pages of

Scripture, wherein God is revealed. A single passage will suffice for illustration. When you can be alone and quiet for a while, contemplate the unveiling of the Divine set forth in Revelation 1: 13—16. *There are here nine lines of description, each of which we should worshipfully meditate upon.* The garment to the feet tells of official dignity; the golden-girt breasts, of pure love; the white hair, of perfect holiness, the flaming eyes, of consuming knowledge; the brazen-like feet, of righteous judgment; the voice as the sound of many waters, of absolute authority; the right hand with the stars, of sovereign administration; the sharp two-edged sword, of searching truth; and the countenance as the sun, of transcendent glory.

There are scores of such passages awaiting our contemplation.

— *W. Graham Scroggie*

July 7

FOR THIS CAUSE. — Eph. 5: 31

In Ephesians 5 Paul uses the illustration of Adam and Eve as the type of the Church. As saintly William Gurnell, the Puritan writer, says: "The Church is taken out of dying Jesus' side as Eve out of sleeping Adam's." In Genesis we find a dead man and a lost woman, while in Revelation we have a Risen Man and a Redeemed Woman. In the building of a helpmeet for Adam, there was foreshadowed the great purpose that was in the heart of God for the glory and joy of His beloved Son. In that place of power and glory He must have His helpmeet who shall be more to Him than all the glory, one who shall satisfy His heart forevermore. "For this cause" Christ left the heights of glory, and endured the cross of shame. *Yes, God purposed from all eternity to associate with Christ in a realm of inconceivable glory a unique*

194

and glorious company, out of the redeemed, in order that through them He might make known to the angelic hosts the fullness of Christ, Who filleth all in all.

— James A. Stewart

What a stupendous thought! I bow in adoration at such matchless grace. How great my responsibility.

July 8

HERE I AM; SEND ME. — Isa 6: 8

Lord, the distant lands are needing
All the fulness of Thy grace,
Lost and blind and all unheeding,
Till they see the Saviour's face.

Millions yet abide in darkness,
Bound by sin and fear of death;
Wretched, cruel, base, and hopeless,
Yet — "I love them," Jesus saith.

Oh to share with Christ His yearning
O'er the souls that perish there;
Oh to see those dear lambs turning
To His love and truth and care.

Dead to friends, wealth, reputation,
Worldly joy and devil's snare,
Fearless heralds of salvation,
In Thy travail, Lord, we share

Give us now Thy Spirit's filling,
Make us men of faith and prayer;
In Thy will may we be willing,
Lead us forth to serve and dare.

— Ernest Bacon

GO ... TELL HIS DISCIPLES AND PETER.
— Mark. 16:7

The Seven Steps Upward

First step: *The intercession of Christ* (Luke 22:31, 32). "I have prayed for thee."

Second step: *The look of Christ* (Luke 22:61). Oh, the pity of that look! Oh, the love in it! And oh, the power of it! It did much to restore unhappy Peter. "He went out and wept bitterly."

Third step: *The message from Christ* (Mark 16:7). "Tell His disciples — *and Peter*." He knoweth His own sheep by name — the sick ones as well as the others — and He is of great compassion. He had died for Peter: should He now let him go? He had been delivered for Peter's offences — and doubtless they were many — and He had been raised for Peter's justification: how could He let him go? He could not, and He did not. "And Peter!" What a gracious message for Simon's ears! The joy of it — that message from Christ!

Fourth step: *The interview with Christ* (Luke 24:34; I Cor. 15:3—5). It has to come to this sooner or later in the case of every backslidden saint — and the sooner, the better. There is nothing like a personal "talk with Jesus, to smooth the rugged road."

Fifth step: *Open Confession* (John 21:15—17). This was threefold, and corresponds to the threefold open denial. Peter had begun with a boast that he loved Jesus more than all the other disciples. And now the question must be answered — "Lovest thou Me more than these?" All boasting is excluded from Peter's answers, and fellowship is restored.

Sixth step: *Peter restored to his work* (John 21:15—17). "Feed My lambs ... Tend My sheep ... Feed My sheep."

Seventh step: *Back to the starting point* (John 21:18, 19). "Follow Me." Thus does He perfectly restore. "What a wonderful Saviour!"
— *Selected*

July 10

HEAR ME, OH LORD, HEAR ME. — I Kings 18: 37

Elijah builds his altar, implicitly observing the commands of the Holy Scripture in Leviticus 1: 7, 8 and Exodus 21: 25. He then pours water three times upon the altar in order to prevent any suggestion of concealed fire. *His confidence is exuberent.* He is so sure of God because of His mighty times of wrestling in the secret place. He prays aloud. What an utterance of faith and calm repose! There is no trace of nervousness. There is no panic. There is no strain. There are no theatrics. *There is simply the confident petition of the man who knows his God and is sure that it is very easy for Him to perform the miracle.* Let every Christian worker study this prayer intently. Let him read it alone in his closet upon his knees.

— *James A. Stewart*

July 11

TO AN INHERITANCE. — I Pet. 1: 4

A GREATER INHERITANCE. — I Pet. 1: 1—9

I am begotten to a living hope. There are hopes which are inoperative and ineffective. They create no energy. They impart no power. But the hope of a redeemed soul has in it an overflowing vitality and a superabundant life. It quickens my thought, giving me a glowing and glorious future to engage and stimulate my mind. It enlivens my emotion, for the prospects in front of me are such as to intensify and refine and uplift my feeling. It puts force into my will; how can I but be diligent when I see the sky before me radiant with colour?

I am begotten to an inheritance. However poor in this world's wealth I am, I am an heir of GOD and a joint heir with Christ. Incorruptible my possession is; it is beyond the reach of death, and I shall look in vain for any graveyard in the upper garden of GOD. Undefiled my possession is; it is beyond the taint of sin, and the robes of its citizens are whiter than new-fallen snow. Unfading my possession is, it is beyond the blight of change, and within it I shall dwell and grow and prosper through the ages of the ages.

I am begotten to a salvation ready to be revealed in the last time. Much of this salvation I taste and enjoy now; but much of it remains to be disclosed and imparted by and by. GOD leads me from the preludes and foretastes of to-day to the realisations and fulfilments of tomorrow, And He asks me to live as the child of so great a salvation — with glad looks, with a heart at leisure, with helpful lips and words, with feet shod with the sandals of obedience and alacrity in His blessed service.

— *Alexander Smellie*

July 12

The Lord make you to increase and abound in love one toward another, and toward all men, even as we also do toward you; to the end that He may stabilish your hearts unblameable in holiness. — 1 Thess. 3: 12, 13

What a prayer! That the Lord would make them to abound in love towards each other, even as Paul did towards them: that He would strengthen their hearts to be unblameable in holiness. Without love this was impossible. Their hearts would be strengthened for a life of true holiness through the love of the brethren, by the power of God. Let us use this prayer often, both for ourselves and for those around us. Do you pray for holiness? Then show it by a hearty love to the brethren!

In 2 Thess. 3. 5 we read: "The Lord direct your hearts into the love of God." Yes, that is what the Lord Jesus will do for us, give us a heart always directed to the love of God. *Lord, by Thy great love, grant me a heart of love!*

198

"Always in every prayer of mine for you all making request with joy. I pray that your love may abound yet more and more in knowledge . . . that ye may be filled with the fruits of righteousness" (Phil. 1:4—11). The Apostle, in his constant prayer for those in his charge, makes *Love the chief thing*. Let us do the same.

"I would that ye knew what great conflict I have for you, that your hearts may be comforted, being knit together in love, unto all riches of understanding" (Col. 2:1, 2). Paul considers it indispensable for their growth in the knowledge of God that the hearts of the believers should be knit together in love. God is love — everlasting, endless love. That love can only be experienced when Christians are knit together in love, and live for others, and not only for themselves.

These four prayers of Paul give us abundant matter for meditation and prayer. Take time to let these heavenly thoughts grow in your heart. As the sun freely gives its light and heat to the grass and grain, that they may grow and bring forth fruit, so God is far more willing to give His love to us in ever-increasing measure. O Christian, if you feel as if you cannot pray, take these words of divine love, and ponder them in your heart. You will gain a strong and a joyous assurance of what God is able to do for you. He will make you to abound in love, and strengthen your heart to live before Him in holiness and love of the brethren. Lord, teach me so to pray!

— *Andrew Murray*

July 13

THAT HE SHOULD ADD IT UNTO THE PRAYERS OF THE SAINTS. — Rev. 8:3, Margin

The Believer's Prayers Accepted in Christ Jesus.

The believer comes and brings his poor petitions, but they are not fit for the great God to read over, to consider, nor to look upon; but Jesus Christ examines them,

199

and He mends the petitions, and draws them up fit to be presented to His Father, and delivers them with His own hand, and then they come to be accepted.

"Ye shall be unto Me," says God unto His Church of old, "a kingdom of priests, and an holy nation" (Exod. 19: 6). Now, this is applied unto the Church in New Testament days by Peter, "Ye also, as lively stones, are built up a spiritual house, a holy priesthood, to offer up spiritual sacrifices, acceptable to God by Jesus Christ . . . Ye are a chosen generation, a royal priesthood, a holy nation, a peculiar (or "purchased," see margin) people" (I Pet. 2: 5, 9). Ye are made a holy priesthood to offer up spiritual sacrifices. Ah! but will they be accepted? Yes, through Jesus Christ, acceptable to God by Christ Jesus.

And again in the Book of Revelation it is said, "He hath made us kings and priests unto God and His Father" (Rev. 1: 6); that is, to offer up spiritual sacrifices; but this will not do alone; Jesus Christ stands to receive every offering, and it passes through His refining and cleansing hand, and His perfuming incense, and so it comes unto God, and then it is a valuable sacrifice; then it is a pleasant and delightful sacrifice; He puts it into His golden censer, and offers it up to His Father (Rev. 8: 3). Here is the great mystery of the intercession of Jesus Christ held forth to you, in reference to your spiritual oblations. He had a golden censer, "and there was given unto Him much incense;" He hath enough for all your prayers; there was given Him much incense, "that He should offer it with the prayers of all saints." So we read it; but it might also be read, That He should add it unto the prayers of all saints (see Rev. 8: 3, margin): importing that our prayers are not weighty as they come from us, nor acceptable, but *they have the incense of Christ Jesus added to them, and then they are weighty, and then they are acceptable,* and from hence God the Father comes to be delighted in the supplications of His servants.   — *Robert Asty*

WHOM THE LORD LOVETH HE CHASTENETH.
— Heb. 12: 6

AWAITING HIS PLEASURE

Precious stones are cut and polished
  By the lapidary's skill;
Cruel knife and rasping friction
  Work on each the master's will
Not until the sparkling facets
  With an equal lustre glow,
Does the artist choose a setting
  For the gem perfected so.

Thus I wait the royal pleasure.
  And when trouble comes to me,
Smile to think He may be working
  On the gem, small though it be.
All I ask is strength to bear it,
  Faith and patience to be still:
Held by Him, no knife can slay me,
  Trusting Him, no anguish kill.

— James H. Brookes

OUR OLD MAN WAS CRUCIFIED TOGETHER WITH HIM. — Rom. 6: 6, Rotherham.

Paul tells us to "*reckon* ourselves to be dead" — "dead indeed *unto sin,* but alive unto God through Jesus Christ our Lord" (Rom. 6: 11). We are to *believe* that we died with Christ, simply because God says so, and not because we *feel* dead, or ever will. God tells ut that in His sight it is so, and expects us as simply to believe it as we do that Christ died for our sins. *God reckons our Substi-*

tute's *death as our death*, and the reckonings of faith always agree with His.

Thus our old standing as children of fallen Adam came to an end before God at the cross, or, as Scripture puts it, "*Our old man has been crucified with Christ*" (Rom. 6: 6), and we are now connected in life with the last Adam — the risen Christ, or, as it is expressed in Romans 7: 4 — "Married to another, even to Him who is raised from the dead."

As believers, we have been brought into a new position altogether. He who took our condemnation, being made sin for us upon the cross, is now risen out of death, and God sees us "IN HIM." We are made "The righteousness of God in Christ," and are therefore forever beyond the reach of condemnation.

> *Death and judgment are behind us,*
> *Grace and glory are before;*
> *All the billows rolled o'er Jesus,*
> *There they spent their utmost pow'r.*

> *"First-fruits" of the resurrection,*
> *He is risen from the tomb;*
> *Now we stand in new creation,*
> *"Free," because beyond our doom.*

— *George Cutting*

July 16

. . . CREATED IN CHRIST JESUS UNTO GOOD WORKS WHICH GOD HATH BEFORE ORDAINED, THAT WE SHOULD WALK IN THEM.

— Eph. 2: 10

"*Created in Christ Jesus.*" That means every child of God is a new creation in Christ Jesus. "*Unto good works.*" And that means every such child of God is created anew in Christ Jesus for a life of service. "Which

202

God hath before ordained." That means God has laid the plan for this life of service in Christ Jesus, ages before we came into existence. "That we should walk in them." *"Walk" is a practical word.* And that means God's great purpose of service for the lives of his children is not a mere fancy, but a practical reality, to be known and lived out in our present work-a-day life. Therefore all through this great text runs the one supreme thought that —

✻ ✻ ✻

God has a plan for every life in Christ Jesus.

What a wondrous truth is this! And yet how reasonable a one. Shall the architect draw the plans for his stately palace? Shall the artist sketch the outlines of his masterpiece? Shall the shipbuilder lay down the lines for his colossal ship? And yet shall God have no plan for the immortal soul which He brings into being and puts "in Christ Jesus"? Surely he has. Yet, for every cloud that floats across the summer sky: for every blade of grass that points its tiny spear heavenward: for every dewdrop that gleams in the morning sun: for every beam of light that shoots across the limitless space from sun to earth, *God has a purpose and a plan.* How much more then, for you who are His own, in Christ Jesus, does God have a perfect before-prepared life plan.

— J. H. McConkey

July 17

EVEN SO, FATHER. — Luke 10: 21

A visitor at a school for the deaf and dumb was writing questions on the blackboard for the children. By and by he wrote this sentence: "Why has God made me to hear and speak, and made you deaf and dumb?" The awful sentence fell upon the little ones like a fierce blow in the face. They sat palsied before that dreadful "why."

And then a little girl arose. Her lip was trembling. Her eyes were swimming with tears. Straight to the board she walked, and picking up the crayon wrote with firm hand these precious words: —

"Even so, Father, for so it seemed good in Thy sight!" What a reply! It reaches up and lays hold of an eternal truth upon which the maturest believer as well as the youngest child of God may alike unshakably rest — the truth that *God is your Father. Do you mean that? Do you really and fully believe that?* When you do, then your dove of faith will no longer wander in weary unrest, but will settle down forever in its eternal resting place of peace. *"Your Father!"* Why, that takes in everything! Because He is your Father, how *could* He fail, or forget you? Look into your own father's heart and mark the strength, the tenderness, the unspeakableness of your love for that winsome little one enshrined in your heart of hearts. Then say to yourself, "God's Father love for me infinitely surpasses all this." Your Father! Against that all doubts must at last dash themselves to pieces as the sea-spray beats itself to nothingness upon a rockbound coast. Down upon that your childtrained soul will find a final resting place in untrembling trustfulness. Rear that up before the devil's subtle, hideous, hissing "why" and he will stagger back, the unmasked, baffled, beaten traitor that in truth he is.

— *J. H. McConkey*

July 18

SUPER CONQUERORS! — Rom. 8: 37, Lit.

Ephesians 6 portrays to us the battle arena with the battle drawn, and no quarter given to the enemy. In verses 12, 13 and 18 we read, "Ours is not a conflict with mere flesh and blood, but with the despotisms, the empires, the forces that control and govern this dark world — the spiritual hosts of evil arrayed against us in the heavenly warfare. Therefore put on the complete armour of God, so that you may be able to stand your ground on the day of battle, and having fought to the end, *to remain victors on the field.* . . . Pray with unceasing (unwearied) prayer and entreaty on every fitting occasion in the Spirit, and be always on the alert to seize opportunities for doing so, with unwearied persistence and entreaty on behalf of all God's people" (Weymouth).

The victorious intercessor, having vanquished the foe on the battlefield, must remain standing for further conquests, using the shield of faith, and wielding the sword of the Spirit. The prayer warrior goes on conquering and to conquer, standing on the ground of Christ's victory.

— *James A. Stewart*

> *Stand still! Stand firm!*
> *Stand ever sound —*
> *Stand armour clad,*
> *'Tis fighting ground;*
> *Then stand with victor's grip,*
> *The "foe" to overthrow;*
> *With holy hands, unloose the bands —*
> *'Tis Christ that brought him low.*

— *Evan Roberts*

July 19

THE HOLY CITY. — Rev. 21: 2

THE GLORIES OF HEAVEN

History began in a garden, it ends in a garden city. The first city was built by the first murderer to hide himself therein, the last city is one into which no stain of any kind will find entrance. This garden city is the Home of God and the redeemed, a place of dazzling splendour, of unassailable security, of marvellous accessibility, of impregnable strength, of inconceivable compass, of ravishing beauty, of unparalleled blessedness, of stainless purity, with guarded entrance, and withal, redolent with the memory of the death of the Lamb.

— A. Borland

Reader are you going there? Heaven is a prepared place for a prepared people.

July 20

THE COMMUNION OF THE HOLY SPIRIT.

— 2 Cor. 13:14

Although the prayers in the New Testament are generally addressed to the Father, surely there is no harm in praying to the Son and the Spirit. I know of several hymn books of worship, where almost half the number are addressed to the Son and not the Father. There is just as much Scriptural authority to pray to the Spirit as there is to pray to the Son. Just as there are a few Scriptures where prayer is addressed to the Lord Jesus, so there are just a few where prayer is addressed to the Holy Spirit. For example, the Lord Jesus exhorts His disciples, "Pray ye, therefore, the Lord of the harvest, that He will send forth labourers into His harvest" (Matt. 9:38). In the Acts of the Apostles, we find that the Holy Spirit is the Lord of the harvest, and that He is the One Who calls and thrusts forth the labourers. "The Spirit of the Lord caught away Philip" (Acts 8:39). Paul invoked the Spirit for the believers at Thessalonica: "And the Lord direct your hearts into the love of God and into the patient waiting for Christ" (II Thess. 3:5).

The Moravians have left a rich legacy to the Church in some beautiful hymns invoking the Spirit, such as this:

> *To Thee, God the Holy Ghost, we pray,*
> *Who lead'st us in the Gospel way,*
> *Those precious gifts on us bestow,*
> *Which from our Saviour's merits flow.*

— James A. Stewart

206

July 21

AS A PRINCE HAST THOU PREVAILED.
— Gen. 32: 28, Margin.

WANTED — INTERCESSORS

Vision, Compassion, Intercession — these are three great links in the golden chain of redemptive service. How clearly you can see them in the saving ministry and life service of our Lord Jesus Himself. He saw the multitudes as sheep without a shepherd — scattered, torn, bruised and bleeding — and if that was the vision before His eyes when He looked on a multitude from the quiet religious villages of Galilee, where the people were moral in their habits of life, and not soaked with drink and manifold vice, what would be the vision before Him if He looked on the great cities of to-day? With that vision His heart was moved with compassion, agitated with deep feeling — agonised within Him, would be a better word. He had compassion on them, taking their pain and sorrow up into His Own Heart of Love; and with that love-swept spirit He turns to His disciples and says, "Pray ye" and on every possible occasion slips off Himself to the lonely mountain side to spend the night or early morning hours in prayer.

Beloved, how few of us have the Master's vision, and hence how few of us have the compassion-filled heart, and the consequent ministry of intercession!
— *John Harper*

Vision — Compassion — Intercession.

July 22

PRESENT YOUR BODIES . . . UNTO GOD, WHICH IS YOUR REASONABLE SERVICE.
— Rom. 12: 1

Full consecration may in one sense be the act of a moment, and in another the work of a lifetime. It must be complete to be real, and yet, if real, it is always incomplete; a point of rest, and yet a perpetual progression. Suppose you make over a piece of ground to another person. From the moment of giving the title-deed, it is no longer your possession; it is entirely his. But his practical occupation of it may not appear all at once. There may be waste land which he will take into cultivation only by degrees... Just so it is with our lives. The transaction of, so to speak, making them over to God is definite and complete. But then begins the practical development of consecration.

— *Frances Ridley Havergal*

July 23

I AM NOT RESPONSIBLE FOR THE RUIN OF ANY ONE OF YOU: FOR I HAVE NOT SHRUNK FROM DECLARING TO YOU GOD'S WHOLE TRUTH. — Acts 20: 27, Weymouth.

It is our sincere and profound conviction that one of the main contributing factors to the low standard of spirituality in our churches today is the failure of the Church to preach and teach a full salvation to the lost and dying.

Somewhere down the years we have lost the knowledge of God's plan and purpose in and through the redemptive work of His beloved Son. Today the Holy Saviour is offered on God's terms of free grace, to all and sundry, irrespective of their attitude to God's holiness and to the regal claims of the majestic Christ. He is offered, may I say kindly, as One who will deliver from the penalty of sin, and yet allow the sinner to remain in love with his sins. He is presented as the Saviour of sinners, while His royal claims are ignored. *The full implications of the Christian Gospel and the Christian life are entirely forgotten.* The inevitable consequence of such teaching and preaching is that we have many "converts" struggling to live the Christian life who have never been born again. They have accepted the literal truth of the Gospel, but not in its living power. Their intellect has apprehended certain facts, while the heart has remained untouched. *The free grace of the Gospel has been preached to them, but the standard of discipleship has been omitted.* At the same time, we also have true converts who are poor examples of the redemptive power of the Gospel of the Lord Jesus.

— James A. Stewart

July 24

TENDERHEARTED, FORGIVING ONE ANOTHER.
— Eph. 4: 32

One cause of the leakage of divine power is allowing a root of bitterness to spring up in our hearts because of a wrong inflicted upon us. An unforgiving spirit will blight spiritual fruit, and also cause a deep shadow to come between you and your Lord. We must remember that at all times it is the reaction to the incident or source of conflict that matters more than the incident itself. The incident will soon pass away, but the effect upon our spiritual life does not. *The most important question is not whether we are right or wrong, but whether we have been kept from resentment and have an inward sweetness. Do we genuinely love those who have wronged us?*

Hudson Taylor, commenting on the blessed adversity of Job, wrote as follows: "Even Satan did not presume to ask God to be allowed himself to afflict Job. In the first chapter and the eleventh verse he says: 'Put forth Thine hand and touch his bone and his flesh, and he will curse Thee to Thy face.' Satan knew that none but God could touch Job; and when Satan was permitted to afflict him, Job was quite right in recognizing the Lord Himself as the Doer of these things which He permitted to be done. Oft-times we should be helped and blessed if we would bear in mind that Satan is servant and not master, and that he and wicked men incited are only permitted to do that which God by His determinate counsel and foreknowledge has before determined shall be done. Come joy or come sorrow, we may always take it from the hand of God."

How the tendency to wrong feeling and resentment would be removed, could we take an injury from the hand of a loving Father, instead of looking chiefly at the agent through which it comes! It matters not who is the messenger — it is with God that His children have to do. Yes, we must refuse to look at second causes.

— *James A. Stewart*

> *Do you 'neath injustice smart?*
> *Do wrongs rankle in your heart?*
> *Ponder this, and cease to fret,*
>   *"I forgave thee all that debt!"*

July 25

BEHOLD I GIVE UNTO YOU POWER . . . OVER ALL THE POWER OF THE ENEMY.

— *Luke 10: 19*

Once the believer gets the fact of this power fixed in his mind and heart and begins to act on it, then, indeed, he becomes more than conqueror. He no longer quails before the enemy. Like David before the giant Philistine who had defied Israel's hosts and, blaspheming her Lord, had made her army tremble, he says: "I come to thee in the name of the Lord of hosts, the God of the armies of Israel, whom thou hast defied . . . This day will the Lord deliver thee into mine hand; and I will smite thee."

Once a little cat that was being madly chased by a big dog, suddenly stopped and, turning on the dog, bristled defiance and arched as if to strike. The result was that the dog fell back, cowed, and slunk away defeated. The believer, who would be victorious in all the circumstances of life, must no longer cower before Satan. He must realize that the enemy is a defeated foe. *He must once and for all settle it that according to God's Holy Word, the Devil's rights have all been annulled.* Taking his stand firmly on such a text as, for example, Hebrews 2: 14, where we read that through death the Redeemer destroyed him that had the power of death, that is the Devil, he exercises authority in the Name of his all triumphant Lord. If, in the hour of conflict with the powers of darkness, he does this, he will find that he is able to move mountains — mountains of Satanic oppression. He finds that as he withstands in the evil day according to Ephesians 6: 13, and having done all stands, he comes off the field of battle more than conqueror.

— *F. J. Huegel*

July 26

BEING JUSTIFIED FREELY BY HIS GRACE.

— Rom. 3: 24

In this epistle we have the Gospel defined. The Epistle to the Romans is a treatise on "JUSTIFICATION" by the greatest evangelist of all times. It is the most powerful Gospel presentation in all the world. No book in the Bible has been so used of God to the salvation of souls as has this book. It may be truly said that the teachings of this book have laid the foundation for every true spiritual awakening since the Day of Pentecost. It was the message of this book that opened the eyes of Martin Luther and John Wesley, thus bringing about the Reformation and the great Methodist revival. I am often astonished as I read Robert Haldane's exposition on this Epistle to remember that, as he gave these expositions in a small Bible class in his own home, in the city of Geneva, through this study large numbers of university students were saved. These young converts became the foremost evangelists, pastors, and Bible expositors of their day. A new Reformation came to some parts of Switzerland and France through these messages from the book of Romans.

The Roman Epistle is written in the language of a lawcourt. The theme is *"How can a holy God truly justify a guilty man righteously, when he deserves nothing but eternal death."* Man is a sinner. God is a holy God. He will by no means clear the guilty (Exod. 23:7). God's righteousness must be maintained at all cost. How can a holy God offer salvation to guilty sinners, and yet His righteousness be fully vindicated?

In the opening chapters, the pagan Gentile and the religious Jew are both found equally guilty before God. The verdict is summed up in verses 22 and 23 of the 3rd chapter: "For there is no difference (or distinction); for ALL have sinned and come short of the glory of God."

Now God's verdict is true. He never makes a mistake. God is a holy judge and also an omniscient judge, and no sinner can deceive Him. I read some time ago of a colored man who was arrested and charged with stealing a gold watch and chain. After all the evidence of the complaining witness had been heard, the judge looked down at the prisoner and announced. "The sentence of this court is ACQUITTAL!"

The man leaned forward and said, "What was that you said, Judge?"

"I said, the sentence of this court is acquittal."

The colored man looked puzzled and said to the judge, "Judge, I don't understand what that means."

"Well," the judge explained, "you are acquitted."

"Well, Judge, does that mean I've got to give the watch back?"

Yes, an earthly judge may make a mistake, or be deceived, but the Judge of heaven never!

— *James A. Stewart*

Come dear reader just now as a guilty sinner and trust Christ as your Saviour.

July 27

AND HE REQUESTED FOR HIMSELF THAT HE MIGHT DIE. — 1 Kings 19: 4

Juniper Tree Prayers

Elijah was mighty in prayer. God answered all his prayers but one, and that was the prayer that he might die. He was under the juniper tree, suffering from mental and physical reaction. Yesterday had been a great day. He had stood alone as God's champion: strong, defiant, triumphant. The next day was the day after! At the threat of a woman he fled. His nerves were unstrung. Fear, despondency, and despair took hold of him. In the fret and frenzy of depression he prayed that he might die. The disease is still with us, and is so multiplied that there are not enough juniper trees to go round. There are morbid Christians who have built tabernacles under them. Nerve collapse is more spiritual than physical, though it is usually both. There is no despondency in faith. What a mercy God does not always take us at our word. Nothing dishonours God more than the fretful despondency of the saints. *Juniper trees make poor sanctuaries.*

— *Samuel Chadwick*

July 28

MY HEART'S DESIRE. — Rom. 10: 1

"It is about fifteen years since I last saw you, so I appreciated your letter all the more. I have had a heavy cross to carry, but I am glad to tell you that His grace has been sufficient for me at every step of the way. At first I was somewhat rebellious, for I had great plans for the future. Many souls were turning to the Lord in all parts of the field, and I looked forward to the time when I should have the privilege of baptising thousands.

"I had said, 'Lord, let me be Thy servant, filled with Thy Spirit, giving all my thought, all my energy and my life for Thee.' And He answered me. But instead of letting me serve Him as I had planned to do, He suddenly took me away from the work for ever. As I lay in the hospital in England, when the first horror of the final outcome was upon me, I thought sometimes that the Lord had forgotten and forsaken me, that He had hidden His face from me. But it was not so. The more sorrow I have had to bear, the easier it has become, and now I am rejoicing in my Saviour every hour. I know the time cannot now be long before I shall be with Him, but while I am in the body I cannot keep still. I must testify; I must tell of His great love for me, and I have written a paper to be read at the Missionary Conference in India, on 'Filling full our place in life.'

"You ask how I am. I have lost my eyesight now and my voice; I have no feet or ankles; no arms; but my heart is far from dead. *I still feel, and long, and sympathise, I still yearn for the extension of Christ's Kingdom.*"

The writer was a most succesful missionary in the Telegu country. His letter was written to a fellow missionary after fifteen years of slowly dying of leprosy.

Oh God! give me such a passion for souls.

July 29

TEACHING THEM. — Math. 28: 30

The great channel of His authority, and quickening and renewing power, was the Word.

The apostles continued the ministry of the Word. Remember Peter's preaching on the day of Pentecost. How easy would it have been for him to assume authority, and to dispense with teaching! How easy would it have been for him to point to the miraculous manifestations, and to claim obedience to the accredited messengers of the Messiah, and thus use the excitement of the astonished

214

multitude to bring them under the sway of priestly domination! Instead of this, instead of any assertion of authority and power of the keys, the Apostle Peter teaches, and reminding his countrymen, to whom pertained the Divine oracles, of the Prophecy of Joel, of the 16th Psalm, which testifies of the Holy One of God conquering death and the grave; of the 110th Psalm, in which, by the Holy Ghost, David calls his Son Lord, and beholds Him at the right hand of God — he declares the mystery of Christ's cross and resurrection, and the outpouring of the Holy Ghost. *He taught the Scriptures.* He first analysed the prophecies, and having brought before his brethren, as it were, the syllables into which the great Word, the all-comprehensive message, had been divided, he gathers them up in the full announcement of the great salvation. *Thus was the Church founded through the teaching of Scripture. Men believed by the Holy Ghost the testimony of truth, the apostolic teaching of God's revealed and fulfilled promises.* How different from the self-styled successors of Peter, who keep the Word of God from the people, and with "blind mouths" usurp authority over God's heritage!

Look at the Bereans. They are commended in that they received the Word with all readiness of mind, and searched the Scriptures daily whether these things were so. *The apostles preached; the people examined. They did not believe the gospel on the authority of the apostles; no such authority or mediatorial position was claimed by the messengers of Christ.* They declared the Word of God, and the people of Berea are commended for their earnestness, activity, independence of mind, or rather dependence on God, in that they searched the Scriptures to convince themselves of the truth and reality of the glad tidings declared to them.

— *Adolph Saphir*

July 30

THIS DAY. — Luke 4: 21

When the anointed Lord preached His first sermon in the synagogue at Nazareth, we read that the people all wondered at the gracious words which proceeded out of His mouth. Wherein above all things lay the grace? Was it not that He said: "This day is this Scripture fulfilled in your ears"? For many decades these words had been read and heard, but on this memorable day came the fulfillment.

Christ's message was: "To-day" — here and now; there is no need to wait; the Saviour is at hand to-day; at this very moment all that was foretold of Him is to be fulfilled. When General Booth was once asked the secret of his life, he replied: "I can give it in three letters, *N-o-w.*" He believed that the Holy Ghost said "To-day." He decided *now;* he acted *now;* He sought God *now;* and above all he believed *now.*

— *Paget Wilkes*

It shall be NOW, Lord from my heart I say it,
No longer will I wait;
No longer will I slight Thy love and patience,
So wonderfully great.

It shall be NOW, that I will yield unto Thee
The last unyielded thing;
Here I renounce my right to His dominion,
And now I crown Thee King.

It shall be NOW, and Thou wilt gladly take me
In spite of all my sin;
NOW that Thou wilt unto Thyself receive me,
And cleanse my heart within.

July 31

EVERY PLACE THAT THE SOLE OF YOUR FOOT SHALL TREAD UPON, THAT HAVE I GIVEN UNTO YOU. — Joshua 1:3

We sing lustily in our gatherings, "Standing on the Promises of Christ, my King," but, my dear brother and sister, we cannot stand on the promises until we have fallen on our knees and claimed them before God's face. And once we have claimed them at the Throne of Grace for ourselves, and asked God to make them real in our experience, we must arise and virtually walk over all the unoccupied, unclaimed, untrodden territory of God's promises until they are truly performed in us. Remember the Word of the Lord to Joshua: *"Every place that the sole of your foot shall tread upon, that have I given unto you"* (Joshua 1:3). Before the Land of Promise could become theirs, the Children of Israel had to walk through the length and breadth of it and measure it off foot by foot (by their own feet). It is interesting to note that they only measured off one-third of the territory God had given them, and consequently they never possessed more than that. *They possessed only that which they measured off, and no more.* How glorious are the precious promises of God to His people! They are as true in these apostate days as they were in the days in which they were spoken. *How very few of us have ever conceived the wealth and extent of the land, and how very few of us have ever taken possession of the promises of God in the all-conquering Name of the Lord Jesus!*

— *James A. Stewart*

HE THAT ABIDETH IN ME, AND I IN HIM, THE SAME BEARETH MUCH FRUIT. — John 15:5

THE VINE AND THE BRANCHES

In this parable we see what the new life is, which the Lord promised His disciples for the work of the Holy Spirit. It clearly mirrors the life of faith.

1. "Not fruit," "more fruit," "much fruit," "fruit that abides" (vs. 2, 8, 16): The one object of the life of faith is to bear much fruit to the glory of God the Father.

2. Cleansing: v. 2. The indispensable cleansing through the Word that is sharper than a two-edged sword.

3. "Abide in Me": Intimate, continuous fellowship.

4. "I in you": Divine indwelling through the Spirit.

5. "Apart from Me ye can do nothing": Complete impotence, deep humility, constant dependence.

6. "My words abide in you," "If ye keep My commandments ye shall abide in My love," "Ye are My friends, if ye do the things I command you": Indispensable obedience.

7. "If My words abide in you, ye shall ask whatsoever ye will": Limitless confidence of faith.

8. "It shall be done unto you": Powerful answer to prayer.

9. "Even as the Father hath loved Me, I also have loved you; abide ye in My love": Life through faith in Him that loved Me.

10. "These things have I spoken unto you that My joy may be in you and that your joy may be fulfilled": Joy full and abiding.

11. "This is My commandment, that ye love one another, even as I have loved you": The new commandment kept through the power of Christ's love in our hearts.

12. "I appointed you that your fruit should abide, that whatsoever ye shall ask of the Father in My name, He will give it you": The all-prevailing Name of Christ.

This is the life Christ makes possible for us and works in us through the Holy Spirit. This is the life so sadly wanting in the Church and yet so indispensable. This is the life assured to childlike faith and obedience.

— *Andrew Murray*

August 2

SPEAK; FOR THY SERVANT HEARETH.

1 Sam. 3:10

Master, speak! Thy servant heareth,
Longing for Thy gracious word,
Longing for Thy voice that cheereth,
Master, let it now be heard.
I am listening, Lord, for Thee;
What hast Thou to say to me?

Often through my heart is pealing
Many another voice than Thine,
Many an unwilled echo stealing
From the walls of this Thy shrine.
Let Thy longed-for accents fall;
Master, speak! and silence all.

Master, speak! though least and lowest,
Let me not unheard depart;
Master, speak! for oh, Thou knowest
All the yearning of my heart.
Knowest all its truest need:
Speak! and make me blest indeed.

Master, speak! and make me ready,
When Thy voice is truly heard,
With obedience glad and steady,
Still to follow every word.
I am listening, Lord, for Thee:
Master, speak, oh speak to me!

Speak to me by name, O Master,
Let me know it is to me;
Speak, that I may follow faster,
With a step more firm and free,
Where the Shepherd leads the flock,
In the shadow of the Rock!

— F. R. Havergal

August 3

HE SHALL HIDE ME IN HIS PAVILION.

— Psalm 27: 5

In the "secret of God's tabernacle" no enemy can find us, and no troubles can reach us. The "pride of man" and the "strife of tongues" find no entrance into the "pavilion" of God. The "secret of his presence" is a more secure refuge than a thousand Gibraltars. I do not mean that no trials will come. They may come in abundance, but they cannot penetrate into the sanctuary of the soul, and we may dwell in perfect peace even in the midst of life's fiercest storms.   — *Hannah Whitall Smith*

In the secret of His presence
I am kept from strife of tongues;
His pavilion is around me,
And within are ceaseless songs!
Stormy winds, His word fulfilling,
Beat without, but cannot harm,
For the Master's voice is stilling
Storm and tempest to a calm.

— H. Burton

220

August 4

THAT THEY MAY ADORN THE DOCTRINE OF GOD OUR SAVIOUR IN ALL THINGS.
— Tit. 2: 10

In a city in the north of Scotland where I spent my school and university days we had a minister, the principal of a theological college, who was a very great man of God. His name was Dr. Brown. There lived next door to him another man of exactly the same name, but a medical doctor. One night a man was ushered into the minister's study, very hastily, and began describing the symptoms of the trouble at home. The minister, who loved a little bit of a joke, with a twinkle in his eye said to this man that he was afraid he had come to the wrong Dr. Brown. The man in his anxiety burst out, *"The Dr. Brown I want is not the Dr. Brown that preaches but the Dr. Brown that practises."*

I want that story to sink into your hearts and memories. That is exactly what the world is saying to-day: "We are not much taken up with the Doctor Browns who preach, we want the Doctor Browns who practise what they preach." That is the walker and not the talker. The most eloquent talker is the man who follows the Lamb whithersoever he goes. The most successful worker for God is the man who will give obedience to the Lamb up to the last glimmer of light that is given to him.
— *Gordon Watt*

August 5

CHRIST . . . SHALL APPEAR. — Heb. 9: 28

HIS COMING IS TYPIFIED IN SCRIPTURE

In Lev. 16: 11 we read: "Aaron shall bring the bullock of the sin offering, which is for himself, and shall make an atonement for himself, and for his house, and shall kill the bullock of the sin offering which is for himself."

221

Lev. 16: 12 (a): "He shall take a censer full of burning coals of fire from off the altar before the Lord, and his hands full of sweet incense beaten small."

Lev. 16: 12 (b), "and bring it within the vail."

Ex. 28: 35: "And it shall be upon Aaron to minister; and his sound shall be heard when he goeth into the holy place before the Lord, and when he cometh out."

You will notice that in the first passage we have the High Priest's work at the Brazen Altar; in the second, in the Holy Place; in the third, in the Holiest of All; and in the fourth, his return to the waiting people without: that is, Sacrifice, Service, Supplication, and final Salvation.

Turn now to the Epistle to the Hebrews, where these truths again appear:

Ch. 9: 14: *"Christ . . . offered Himself without spot to God."*

Ch. 4: 6: *". . . the priests went always into the first tabernacle, accomplishing the service of God."*

Ch. 9: 24: *"Christ is . . . entered into heaven itself, now to appear in the presence of God for us."*

Ch. 9: 28: *"Christ . . . shall appear the second time without sin unto salvation."*

Thus all the previous four passages have their counterpart in Christ; but with this notable difference that, in the antitype, service comes before sacrifice; for Christ had no need of sacrifice for Himself as had the High Priests of old; so His life's work is set forth before His atoning death, though, in our experience, we must know the value of His death before we can follow the pattern of His life: He lived to die, but we die to live. He served during those wonderful years which preceded Calvary; then He was sacrificed, rising from the dead, He ascended up to the Father's presence to make supplication for His people, and very soon He is coming out from that presence to bring to us full salvation.

— *Selected*

August 6

BEHOLD, I HAVE GRAVEN THEE UPON THE PALMS OF MY HANDS; THY WALLS ARE CONTINUALLY BEFORE ME. — Isaiah 49: 16

This is the Lord's reply to the complaint of Zion, "The Lord hath forsaken me, and my Lord hath forgotten me." Jehovah answers by an appeal to the highest and tenderest human love, "Can a woman forget her sucking child, that she should not have compassion on the son of her womb? yea, they may forget, yet will I not forget thee. Behold, I have graven thee upon the palms of my hands; thy walls are continually before me."

This beautiful figure expresses, first, God's personal knowledge of each one of us. He addresses us in the second person, "Thee", and this implies that He knows and records our own individual name. God knows each of us personally. We are not lost in the great mass, or loved in the aggregate, or dashed in the vast billows of humanity upon the shores of destiny; but each of us, singly and alone, is recognized by our Father and personally cared for with a definiteness that human love cannot know; for He tells us, the very hairs of our head are all numbered, and we are of more value than many sparrows. The shepherd knoweth His sheep, and calleth them by name. The Master speaks to each of His disciples the old personal word that He spoke to Mary, and each fills a place in His thought that is all his own. *Oh, let us hear Him say to us today, with a more grateful appreciation of all that it means,* "I have graven *thee* upon the palms of my hands."

— *A. B. Simpson*

I will go forth to-day in the strength of this blessed truth.

August 7

AND THUS SHALL YE EAT IT; WITH YOUR LOINS GIRDED, YOUR SHOES ON YOUR FEET, AND YOUR STAFF IN YOUR HAND.

— Exodus. 12 : 11

When Shackleton, the great explorer, was planning what proved to be his last expedition to the Arctic seas an interesting incident is said to have occurred. Shackleton was seated in an office in London, speaking to a friend about his forth-coming expedition. The friend said "I am surprised at the publicity you are giving to your new venture. It is rather unlike you."

Shackleton replied, "I have a purpose in doing so. I want my colleague, Mr Wild, to hear about my plans. He has buried himself in the heart of Africa, and has left no address, but I thought that if I would broadcast the news that I was going, it might filter through into the very center of Africa, and if Wild knows I am going, he will come." . . .

They both turned and saw, standing in the doorway, Mr. Wild. It was a dramatic moment as Shackleton and Mr. Wild shook hands — the handshake of loyalty.

"I heard you were going," said Wild; "the news found its way into the heart of Africa, and when I knew, I dropped my gun, picked up a bit of baggage, and made straight for home, and here I am. What are your orders?"

Would you do as much for Jesus Christ? Are your loins girded for action? Would you go to the ends of the earth for Him? God needs men today who are ready at any cost to follow implicitly at a moment's notice.

We are the eleventh-hour laborers and thus must toil hard in the Lord's vineyard. Every idle hour will be taken out of our wages when the day of reckoning comes.   — *James A. Stewart*

> *He was not willing that any should perish,*
> *Am I His follower and can I live*
> *Longer at ease with a soul going downward*
> *Lost for the lack of the help I might give?*

224

August 8

IF TWO OF YOU SHALL AGREE . . . Math. 18:19

If two harp-strings are in perfect tune, you cannot smite the one without causing the other to vibrate; and if one Christian is touched and agitated by the Spirit of God, think it not strange that all who are like-minded in the Church are moved by the same divine impulse. Not for ourselves, and that we may enjoy the holy luxury of communion with God, are we to seek for the times of refreshing. If so, doubtless we shall fail of them, for even spiritual blessings we may ask and receive not, if we only ask that we may consume them upon ourselves.

— *A. J. Gordon*

God loves unity, and so He loves a united cry; a petition signed by more than one.

— *Andrew Bonar*

August 9

THOU WILT KEEP HIM IN PERFECT PEACE WHOSE MIND IS STAYED ON THEE: BECAUSE HE TRUSTETH IN THEE. — Isa. 26:3

It adds immensely to the meaning of Isaiah 26:3 to read it in its free translation: "Thou wilt keep him in perfect peace whose mind *stops at God.*" In other words the mind that reckons on God in everything, and refuses to go beyond Him; the heart that is satisfied to lean hard on Him, and leave all its affairs to His almighty wisdom, love and care; the heart that is stayed upon God — is kept "in perfect peace."

Art thou so right with God that thou canst "stay" upon Him; that thou canst "stop at God," unloading every care, and leaving all in His all-loving hands?

— *B. Mc Call Barbour*

Faith came singing into my room,
And other guests took flight;
Fear and anxiety, grief and gloom,
Sped out into the night.
I wondered that such peace could be,
But faith said gently, "Don't you see
They really cannot live with me?"

— Elizabeth Cheney

August 10

CHRIST LIVETH IN ME. — Gal. 2:20

HIS VICTORY IS OUR VICTORY

You remember the great cry of triumph in Colossians?
He stripped them of their armour and triumphed over
them openly by means of His cross. Christ has conquered
Satan once for all, and the Satan whom He has conquered is practically your vassal and mine for ever. I am
not afraid of the Devil. Don't *you* get scared. "Whom
resist." "Resist the Devil and he will flee from you."
We need to have our armour on, we need to be on the
watch, but never for a moment need we have any fear.
The victory is ours. Our living Christ, whose Life dwells
within us, has conquered all the power of hell on Calvary, and that was the Life that broke the barriers of
the grave. *You must never disconnect the death from
the resurrection.* If He had not risen again the death
would not have availed anything; we should have been
all dead together. Death would have been the last word.
But on the morning of the third day — Life came.

Oh, that wonderful morning! Has death been able to
conquer this atoning Jesus, this Jesus Who has laid down
His life for the sin of the world! Can He rise again? All
the universe was waiting for the morning of the third
day. The destiny of all creation depended upon the morning of the third day. If He had not risen there would

have been a black pall upon the throne of the eternal God and the universe would have collapsed in fire and ruin. "But now is Christ risen from the dead." That is the great trumpet peal in the 15th chapter of 1 Corinthians. "Now is Christ risen from the dead" — and *this is the Life that enters into His redeemed people!* Do you realize that? *The life that made atonement for the guilt of humanity, the life that broke Satan to pieces on the cross, the life that smashed death for ever — that has got into me! That is the victory!* What in the wide world can conquer that? Christ liveth in me, His risen life, His all-conquering life is the centre and soul in me. The great powers of God are all His. It is a wonderful conception. You see a poor little child of faith. No notable of the world, not known to anybody except God; and in that poor little worshipping life there is all the glorious power of the conquering Son of God, just within that little tenement.

— *John Thomas*

August 11

CHRIST LIVETH IN ME. — Gal. 2: 20

But how does it happen? How does Christ get into us? He gets us into Him first. We get into Him *by faith.* Faith is the centre word of the Bible. "This is the victory that overcometh the world, even your faith." Faith and victory must go together. There is a very simple way of getting Jesus into us. *By faith. Only believe.* It is easy, is it not? Of course it is, the difficult work was done by Him. All the store of His power is ready, you have only to touch the button — a child can do that — and all the glory blazes. If I may but touch the hem of His garment — that is all — I shall be whole. Oh, touch the hem of His garment and thou too shalt be free.

And then we know that Christ has entered into us. His life supercedes everything else. *He has come in and*

227

taken possession and He is all in all. I live, but no longer I — not the old I, not the little insignificant, impotent I — Oh, no, He has not annihilated me, He has *made me* — I am a personality now. I am somebody. What do you mean, Paul? "I am another I." What is it like? "Oh, *I can do all things through* Christ which strengtheneth me." What a big *I* you are Paul! "Yes, but it is *Christ* — Christ in me.*" There is a new "me" with a larger responsibility. Christian people used to sing "There is nothing left for me to do, Hallelujah." It is *all* left for you to do, a great deal more than ever you thought you had to do. Once you live the Christ life, you have wonderful things to do, if you are to be worthy of the Christ life. *"In me!"* Oh, no, I am not annihilated. He makes me preach, pray, serve, He gives me vision, He shows me glories pending, He makes me travel for dear life, and He makes me young for ever! How can you grow old when your life is Christ in you? He does not grow old. Jesus Christ is the same yesterday, to-day, and for ever. There's everlasting youth for you!

Ah, but it means "crucified with Christ." There on the cross was nailed the law of sin and death, and now I belong to the law of the spirit of life in Christ Jesus, and every day I am being enabled to put to death the deeds of the body.

LIVING BY CHRIST'S FAITH

Only realize that you are to live the Christ life; not to be passive. There is a doctrine of passivity which is dangerous beyond telling. You are not to lie before Him as an empty vessel in that sense. When once He has filled you you must be *full*, not empty. Full of His energy, full of His life, full of His power, full of the enthusiasm of His glory, and every nerve in you must be given to live for Christ and to die for Him. Do not listen to the cult of passivity. You remember our Saviour's condemnation of it — the empty house, garnished, furnished well, but no tenant. If that house had been filled with father and

228

mother and children and life, the devils could not have come back. If you want all holy power to come in, you must have a life full of the activity of Jesus, not a thing that is empty, meaning nothing. *After Christ comes in your house is full, and all your powers must be given to live out by faith the life of Christ, putting to death all the while the deeds of the body, and remembering that your "old man" has been nailed to the cross.* Faith is the grand key to all the reserves of God. "I live by the faith of the Son of God, Who loved me and gave Himself for me." I am His and He is mine for ever and for ever.

— *John Thomas*

August 12

THE FULNESS OF HIM THAT FILLETH ALL IN ALL. — Eph. 1: 23

THE MISSION OF THE CHURCH

The Church is the visible part of the invisible Christ to an ungodly world. As the wife is the glory of the husband, so the Church is the glory of Christ, Who is her Head. The Church is His body, the fulness of Him who filleth all in all. (Eph. 1: 23). Therefore the Church is the complement or fullness of Christ. (Col. 2: 10). The Church is the representation or continuation of Christ. The Church which is His body, is the theatre where God displays to Heaven and Hell His manifold wisdom (Eph. 3: 10). The Head triumphed over the Devil, who had the power of death, and stripped him of that power, so that all who constitute His body share in His triumph. *Yes, this matchless new creation is God's masterpiece.* The purpose of a body is to express the character of the person who inhabits the body. The peculiar mission of the Church is to manifest the character and life of the Son of God. *The purpose of the Church is thus to gather, through her testimony of truth and love, a people who,*

229

saved by grace and separated by the Holy Ghost from
the world, are serving the Lord and waiting for His
coming.   — James A. Stewart

Oh, Heavenly Father! help me to be a true member
of Thy Church.

August 13

THE FELLOWSHIP OF HIS SUFFERINGS.
                                        — Phil. 3: 10

*Oh brethren, this is no time to be cold and indifferent!
This is no time to be occupied with social and financial
prestige here on earth. These are the last days of a dying
dispensation of Grace, and we must sacrifice and suffer
with our blessed Lord until the last soul is gathered in.
Let us not shrink from sharing His suffering, no matter
the cost.*

John Henry Jowett entered into the significance of
the words of the battle-scarred warrior when he said:

" 'I fill up that which is behind of the sufferings of
Christ,' wrote Paul. That is not the presumptious boast
of perilous pride; it is the quiet, awed aspiration of privileged fellowship with the Lord. Here then, is a principle.
*The gospel of a broken heart demands the ministry of
bleeding hearts.* If that succession be broken, we lose our
fellowship with the King. As soon as we cease to bleed
we cease to bless. When our sympathy loses its pang we
can no longer be the servants of passion. We no longer
'fill up the sufferings of Christ.' And not to 'fill up' is
to paralyze and to 'make the cross of none effect.' "

"The ministers of Calvary must supplicate in bloody
sweat, and their intercession must touch the point of
agony. If we pray in cold blood, we are no longer the
ministers of the Cross. True intercession is a sacrifice, a
bleeding sacrifice, a perpetuation of Calvary, a filling
up of the sufferings of Christ.

"My brethren, this is the ministry which the Master

owns, the agonized yearnings which perfect the sufferings of His own intercession. Are we in His succession? Do our prayers bleed? Have we felt the painful fellowship of the pierced hand? I am so often ashamed of my prayers. They so frequently cost me nothing; they shed no blood. I am amazed at the grace and condescension of my Lord that He confers any fruitfulness upon my superficial pains."

May God help us to be living exponents of the truth of this verse. Let us pray fervently, in closing, with the apostle: THAT I MAY KNOW HIM AND THE POWER OF HIS RESURRECTION, AND THE FELLOWSHIP OF HIS SUFFERING, BEING MADE CONFORMABLE UNTO HIS DEATH.

— *James A. Stewart*

August 14

I HAVE FOUND MY SHEEP WHICH WAS LOST.
— Luke 15: 6

I was a wand'ring sheep,
I did not love the fold,
I did not love my Saviour's voice,
I would not be controlled;

I was a wayward child,
I did not love my home,
I did not love my Father's voice,
I loved afar to roam.

The Shepherd loved His sheep,
The Father sought His child;
He followed me o'er vale and hill,
O'er deserts waste and wild.

He found me nigh to death,
Famished and faint and lone;
He bound me with the bands of love,
He saved the wand'ring one.

I was a wayward child,
I once preferred to roam;
But now I love my Father's voice,
I love, I love His home!

— H. Bonar

August 15

BALAAM AND BALAK. — Numbers 12

As the wilderness journey drew near to its close, another enemy advanced to meet the pilgrim host. This was Balak, the King of Moab, assisted by Balaam, the covetous prophet. We cannot here enter into the details of this extraordinary compact, or trace the devices of this accomplished servant of Satan. Suffice to say, his object was to curse the host of God, and to exterminate the people of Jehovah's choice. The time chosen was at the close of their wanderings, after forty long years of provocation and unfaithfulness to God. Balaam supposed that he would readily incite Jehovah to curse the people for their long continued failures. But in this he was mistaken. Instead of pronouncing His curse, God filled the prophet's mouth with blessings. Instead of giving him a solemn indictment against His people, He poured forth, in language grand and lofty, such as He had never used before, His delight in His redeemed, their glorious standing in His grace, their present calling, and their glory to come.

But another device of the enemy had yet to be revealed. If he cannot destroy the people of the Lord, by cursing, he will try and seduce them by craft and wile. When the devil fails to overcome the saints as "the roaring lion," he seeks to seduce them as "the subtle serpent," and alas! this wile of his too often succeeds. It is written concerning this second device of Balaam, that "he taught Balak to cast a stumblingblock before the children of Israel" (Rev. 2: 4), and by this he succeeded in

232

allying the chosen and separated people with the unclean. *The reference to this as "the doctrine of Balaam" in New Testament times, in the midst of the church at Thyatira, warns us, that the same tactic will be used to drag the church of God into unholy alliance with the world.* And has it not succeeded? Full well the devil knows, that a corrupted church, intermingled with the ungodly, unequally yoked with unbelievers, will bring down the judgement of God, as the iniquity at Baal-peor did in days gone by. Let the saints of God be fully awake to this. *Already there are many anti-Christs.* The mystery of iniquity doth already work. The chief part of Satan's business among the saints is to seduce them into alliance and spiritual whoredom with the world, and thus blot out their testimony as a redeemed and separated people, unto the Lord.

— *John Ritchie*

August 16

SING UNTO HIM A NEW SONG. — Psalm 33: 3

The basis of faith is where you begin, the fight of faith is where you win, and the rest of faith is where you rejoice. The battle is now over, the victory now won, and Faith sings! The song of Faith has no minor key. The song of Mary followed the declaration of her faith. "Be it unto me according to thy word." "My soul doth magnify the Lord, and my spirit hath rejoiced in God my Saviour." *You can never sing until you believe.* Habakkuk's circumstances were adverse, but he had the rest of Faith, and sang, "Although the fig tree shall not blossom, neither shall fruit be in the vines; the labour of the olive shall fail, and the fields shall yield no meat; the flocks shall be cut off from the fold, and there shall be no herd in the stalls: YET I will rejoice in the Lord, I will joy in the God of my salvation."

— *Paget Wilkes*

August 17

AND THE LORD TURNED, AND LOOKED ON PETER. — Luke 22:61

Peter, by the look of his Master, is wholly dissolved in grief and humiliation. As if he were unworthy to appear before God or man, he begins to "weep bitterly."

It is said that a tear glistened in Peter's eye as long as he lived. If this is any thing but a legend, it was not a tear of sorrow only, but of joy at the mercy experienced. The remembrance of his fall never left him for a moment; and in the degree in which it kept him low, it sharpened his spiritual vision for the mystery of the cross and of salvation by grace. This is abundantly evident, especially in his first epistle. He there comforts believers with the cheering assurance that they are "kept by the power of God through faith unto salvation." He calls upon them to "hope to the end for the grace that shall be revealed." He impressively reminds them of the weakness and evanescent nature of every thing human, while calling to their recollection the words of the prophet: "All flesh is grass, and all the glory of man as the flower of grass. The grass withereth, and the flower thereof falleth away." *He speaks of "the precious blood of Christ as of a Lamb without spot," with a fervor which immediately indicates him as one who had deeply experienced its healing power. It is he who addresses the warning to us, "Be sober, be vigilant; for your adversary the devil goeth about as a roaring lion, seeking whom he may devour."*

— *Krummacker*

I would humble myself this day and seek the power of Christ.

AND THEY WERE ALL FILLED WITH THE HOLY GHOST. — Acts. 4:31

The premise of this book is that the normal condition of the Church is not revival but rather the state resulting from revival. However, we must recognize the fact that the Christian life is one of constant renewings of the Holy Spirit. As Dr. D. M. McIntyre reasons, "If we could imagine an unbroken progress of the Church, in faith and obedience, we might still suppose that she would be called to pass, at recurrent intervals, through a climacteric experience. There is always the emergence of new truths, the acceptance of fresh obligations and the realization of a richer and more elevated experience which inevitably impart an added splendour to the glory of the Bride of Christ."

It might appear on the surface that there is nothing to induce spiritual decay in the Church, but as we are too sorrowfully aware, the spiritual energy of the Church of God has ebbed and flowed like tides since the beginning. There is always a tendency to degeneration which belongs to every Christian life. Individual Christians are apt to decline from their first fervour of devotion and sacrifice to Christ, at which time the fire burns low on the altar of their heart.

We see in the Acts of the Apostles that even the members of the early Church needed fresh renewings. In chapter two we find that the believers were filled with the Holy Ghost in the Upper Room. Yet in chapter four we read of their being filled once again: "And when they had prayed, the place was shaken where they were assembled together; and they were all filled with the Holy Ghost, and they spake the Word of God with boldness." This does not mean that they had been living in sin and had followed the Lord afar off, but that they needed a fresh infilling for a fresh emergency that arose in their aggressive evangelism for their Blessed Redeemer.

Those that were endowed *habitually* with the power of the Spirit had yet occasion for fresh supplies of the Spirit, according to the various experiences in their ministry. *As John Bunyan says, "The apostles had now used up their spending money and needed to go back to the bank of heaven for more."* Had these disciples not waited on the Lord for a fresh anointing, they would have been living on a fast diminishing capital which would have ended in spiritual bankruptcy.

— *James A. Stewart*

IF ANY MAN... BRING AN OFFERING UNTO THE LORD. — Lev. 1: 2

Leviticus is the Book of the Worship of a redeemed people. Exodus sets forth their redemption, but Leviticus sees them gathered around the Tabernacle in goodly order, drawing near to God in worship.

The book opens with *the Five Great Levitical Offerings,* which differ from those in Exodus in two great particulars. In the great Exodus type (the Passover) there is *no priest* and *no laying on of hands,* teaching that the offering was for those not yet brought to God; but in Leviticus seeing it is a redeemed people, there is both priest and substitution, things pertaining only to the Saints of God. So we have teaching here, not for the unsaved, but for believers. The five great Levitical offerings are:

(1) *The Burnt Offering* (Ch. 1); (2) the *Meat* (or Meal, R. V.) *Offering* (Ch. 2); (3) *the Peace Offering* (Ch. 3); (4) *the Sin Offering* (Ch. 2); and (5) *the Trespass Offering* (Ch. 5).

Three of these are called *Sweet Savour Offerings:* the last two are *Judgment Offerings.* In the first three is typified the acceptableness to God of the Work and Person of Christ; in the last two, the wrath that fell on Him for our sin and sins.

236

Each of the Five Offerings tells of Substitution, symbolised by the laying on of hands of the offerer, thus identifying himself with his offering that it may be accepted for him. They may be easily remembered thus:

(1) The Burnt Offering — Christ our Substitute for what we *should have done* (the will of God).

(2) The Meat Offering — Christ for what we *should have been* (sinless).

(3) The Peace Offering — Christ for what *we should have had* or enjoyed (peace).

(4) The Sin Offering — Christ for what *we have been* (sinners — guilty).

(5) The Trespass Offering — Christ for what *we have done* (sinned).

The distinctive feature of the Burnt Offering was that it was all burnt on the brazen altar, wholly consumed, and ascended as a sweet substitutionary savour to God. It spoke of Christ in His perfect and wholehearted obedience to the Father, delighting to do His will, even to the sacrifice of Himself on Calvary. Heb. 10: 7—10, is the New Testament equivalent.

— *George Goodman*

August 20

SIMON, SIMON, BEHOLD, SATAN HATH DESIRED TO HAVE YOU, THAT HE MAY SIFT YOU AS WHEAT. — Luke 22: 31

What language is this, rendered doubly appalling by the darkness, and the circumstances under which it is uttered! At the very moment when the disciples are to be deprived of their only help and shield, they are informed of the approach of the most dreadful of enemies. The Lord expresses Himself strangely, and in a manner calculated to excite the greatest astonishment. "Satan", says He, "hath desired to have you" — that is, he has challenged you, laid claim to you, and begged to have you, that he might manifest his power in you, in order to prove that your goodness is naught, and your conversion only specious and deceptive.

The Lord occasionally permits the wicked one to try his power to tempt the redeemed to a certain point. He does so, in order to prove to the infernal spirits the invincibility of those who confide themselves to Him, and thereby to glorify His name; and also, that He may purify His children as gold in such a furnace of temptation, and draw those, who live no longer to themselves, deeper into the fellowship of His life.

— *Krummacker*

August 21

FOR GOD SO LOVED... THAT HE GAVE HIS ONLY BEGOTTEN SON. — John 3: 16

Who loved? The Monarch of the universe. Oh, it was a rare love, that of the great God, when, passing by the nature of angels, He came to us in the person of Jesus Christ, treading along the aisles of heaven, past Seraphim and Cherubim, past all the celestial intelligences who crowd around the throne of the Eternal, right down from the glory to the suffering and the shame, the sorrow and the agony of life; down to be a man among men, a sufferer with sufferers, a rejected Saviour in a God-dishonouring world; down to Gethsemane's awful agony, and Calvary's cruel cross; down to the silent grave, *that He might afterwards lift us poor rebels up to the heights of glory*. It would almost seem as though the great God were resolute to fill up those seats in heaven, vacant through the fall of rebel angels in millenniums long gone by, determined to recreate by love out of the foul ruins of a polluted humanity a race of beings who would reflect His glory, discharge His will, and everlastingly adore His grace. Do we believe it, brethren, that it was God, your Creator and mine, who *Himself* took this mighty task in hand, and, manifest in human flesh, died upon Calvary's cross to ransom sinners? If so, surely a mighty Hallelujah anthem should ascend from every heart in this vast gathering.

— *Hugh D. Brown*

August 22

A NEW CREATION IN CHRIST JESUS.
— 2 Cor. 5: 17

The eternal Son of God came into the world, only for the sake of this new birth, to give God the glory of restoring it to all the dead sons of fallen Adam. All the mysteries of this incarnate, suffering, dying Son of God, all the price that He paid for our redemption, all the washings that we have from His all-cleansing blood poured out for us, all the life that we receive from eating His flesh, and drinking His blood, have their infinite value, their high glory, and amazing greatness in this, because nothing less than these supernatural mysteries of a God-man, could raise that new creature out of Adam's death, which could be again a living temple, and deified habitation of the Spirit of God.

That this new birth of the Spirit, or the divine life in man, was the truth, the substance, and sole end of His miraculous mysteries, is plainly told us by Christ Himself, who at the end of all His process on earth, tells His disciples, what was to be the blessed, and full effect of it, namely, that the Holy Spirit, the Comforter (being now fully purchased for them) *should after His ascension, come in the stead of a Christ in the flesh.* "If I go not away," says He, "the Comforter will not come; but if I go away, I will send Him unto you, and He shall guide you into all truth." Therefore all that Christ was, did, suffered, dying in the flesh, and ascending into heaven, was for the sole end, to purchase for all His followers a new birth, new life, and new light, in and by the Spirit

239

of God restored to them, and living in them, as their support, Comforter, and Guide into all truth. And this was His, *"Lo, I am with you alway, even unto the end of the world."*

— *W. M. Law*

August 23

Christ loved the church, and gave himself for it; that he might sanctify and cleanse it . . . that he might present it to himself a glorious church, not having spot, or wrinkle, or any such thing; but that it should be holy and without blemish." — Eph. 5: 25—27

God desires a starting point from which to do His work on earth. The world has departed from God and He cannot work through the world; therefore, He must take out of the world a group through which He can work. *And this group is the church. But for the church to maintain its position as a church and be a separated people, it must practice church discipline, and if it does not exercise church discipline the church will become the world.* The world will come into the church and the church will go out into the world. The boundary will be eliminated and the Christian church will no longer be a church; it will no longer represent a separated people, but be like the world. And then it would be simply a parody to call it the church of God.

We know that much has been done during the passing of the years to eliminate the boundary between the Christian church and the world. But when a real revival comes, it is always significant that the people of God separate themselves from the world.

— *Lewi Pethrus*

240

August 24

THEY ... WERE AMAZED. — Acts 2:6

This is a glorious day of triumph for our blessed Lord! No longer is He straitened. In the Spirit of Pentecost, the risen Redeemer finds an enlarged opportunity. As the covenant head of the church, the victorious Saviour equips the members of His Church with the power of the Spirit.

As we prayerfully consider this enduement of Pentecost, we are driven to our knees to cry out in despair and humiliation, "O, God, why can we not see the likes of these happenings today?" In these last days of a dying dispensation of grace, we see very little of the manifestation of the phenomena of Pentecost.

Where is the mystery and the marvel of the Spirit-possessed church?

Where is the mystery and the marvel of transformed disciples?

Where is the mystery and the marvel of dynamic Christianity?

Where is the mystery and the marvel of the miraculous in the church of God today?

No longer do we find the crowds greatly wondering.

No longer do we find the crowds greatly perplexed.

No longer do we hear the cry of awakened, disturbed multitudes.

No longer do we see the Spirit of God fall upon our congregations.

No longer do we leave our evangelistic campaigns and prayer meetings with the fragrance of the Rose of Sharon upon our gatherings and the glory of God upon our faces.

No longer is there the awed and mesmeric rumor being breathed through the streets of our cities concerning the miraculous taking place inside our churches today.

Alas! The Shekinah glory of the Lord has departed.

16 - Still waters

241

Alas! We need a fresh Pentecostal experience to revital-
ize our lives and ministry. Our churches today are mere
caricatures of the real thing. We have substituted and
offered up strange fire in the place of the fire of God.

— *James A. Stewart*

August 25

I WILL NEVER LEAVE THEE, NOR FORSAKE
THEE. — Heb. 13:5

Forty-six years ago Walker Iyer told me that "forsake", in Hebrews 13:5 is in the Greek a compound of
three words — "leave behind in". It conveys the idea
of leaving comrades exposed to peril in the conflict, or
forsaking them in some crisis of danger. And Westcott
translates the verse, *"I will in no wise desert you or
leave you alone in the field of contest, or in a position
of suffering. I will in no wise let go — loose hold — my
sustaining grasp."*

This promise cannot fail. Come now, let us stand upon
it and rejoice in it. Let us show to all who observe us that
those words are for ever true: Christ our Lord is with us.
He Who reigned from the Tree is our Leader. *The shout
of a King is among us.* Alleluia.

— *Amy Carmichael*

August 26

GOD IS LOVE. — 1 John 4:16

UNCHANGING LOVE

The Old Farmer had a weathervane with the words
"God is Love" painted in discernible letters on the indi-
cator. His agnostic friend called and remarked how sorry
he was that God's love was as changeable as the wind.
"Not so," said the farmer, "you've got it wrong. The
message of the weathervane is — WHICHEVER WAY
THE WIND SHALL BLOW GOD IS LOVE."

Whichever way the wind shall blow
God is Love.
Warming sun or chilling snow
God is Love.
His the love that never changes
Though the storm around me rages.
I am safe within His keeping
In the hour of doubt and weeping.

When I feel the stab of pain
God is Love.
The Hand that chastens doth sustain
God is Love.
Though the mountains move and quake
And my heart is near to break,
I can feel His love so tender
Who of all things is the sender.

Whether it be dark or fair
God is Love.
He is always standing there
God is Love.
Though my heart be filled with sorrow
God has yet a bright tomorrow.
Knowing this I can prevail.
Though the enemy assail.

I can never doubt His favour
God is Love.
Calvary provides a Saviour
God is Love.
Though my path be steep and rough
The grace of God is e'er enough.
And I lay me down to sleep
Safe within my Saviour's keep.

— David B. Stewart

August 27

BY FAITH MOSES . . . — Heb. 11:24

God never hurries over the training of His servants. It took forty years to find out how strong he was, and another forty ere he knew his own weakness and God's grace to be sufficient for him and his life work. You cannot educate a natural man into a spiritual one. If so, Moses might have been so, for he was grown, educated, and mighty in word and deed.

— *Taylor Smith*

August 28

Remember . . . repent . . . return, or else I will come to visit thee, and when I find thee still unrepentant will *remove thy candlestick from its place.* — Rev. 2:5

Here is no idle threat. Here is judgment swift and sure. The message is urgent. There is no time for delay. We need not wait until the judgment seat of Christ to have judgment come upon us. The wrath of God can come upon us now. God can write "Ichabod" (the glory of the Lord has departed, I Sam. 4:21) over our churches now. "Behold your house is left unto you desolate" (Matt. 23:38), is not true of Jewish temples alone. Oh how many stone buildings adorn our cities today from which the candlestick has already been removed. Their history is known to Him Who walks among the golden candlesticks. "They have a name that they are living, but they are dead" (Rev. 3:1).

Along with the warning comes a word for the "Overcomer." The trouble with these local churches was that the "shortcomers" were in the majority. In these last dark days of a dying dispensation of grace, the Holy Spirit is calling out a select company from the saints of every kindred, tongue, people and nation, who will be red-hot in their devotion to Him. God is purging His

Church and preparing it for revival and the coming of the Lord. Have you returned to your first love? Are you standing triumphantly as an overcomer?

In closing, let us notice that the message the Spirit has for the churches is addressed primarily to the "angel" or "messenger" of each local church. This places the pastors and Christian leaders in a very impotant place of responsibility. Much of the coldness and indifference in our churches today can be attributed directly to the pulpit. "Like people, like priest . . ." (Hosea 4: 9).

— *James A. Stewart*

August 29

THE GOD OF PEACE SHALL BRUISE SATAN UNDER YOUR FEET SHORTLY. — Rom. 16: 20

God is in you, possessing and filling you with power that makes it possible for you to tread upon satan.

— Moule

The shield of faith is that which the hand of faith grasps and presents to meet the fiery darts of Satan. That shield is none other than the blood of Jesus. . . . By this means alone can we quench the darts of fire, burning, stinging, poisoning all the secret springs of hope and faith and assurance.

— *A. Paget Wilkes*

August 30

NOT A SOUL FROM THE OUTSIDE DARED TO JOIN THEM. — Acts 5: 13, Free translation.

We dwell much upon the attractions of Christanity, but rarely stop to think that it may also have repulsions, which are vitally necessary to its purity and permanence. If the Church of Christ draws to herself that which she

245

cannot assimilate to herself, her life is at once imperilled; for the body of believers must be at one with itself, though it be at war with the world. Its purity and its power depend, first of all, upon its unity. So that if perchance the Church shall attract without at the same time transforming them; if she shall attach them to her membership without assimilating them to her life — she has only weakened herself by her increase, and diminished herself by her additions. Such is the lesson that is impressed upon us by the text "and of the rest durst no man join himself to them."

— A. J. Gordon

August 31

I WILL LEAD THEM. — Isaiah 42: 16

THE FOOTPRINTS

He led me to the way of pain,
A barren and a starless place,
(I didn't know His eyes were wet,
He would not let me see His face).

He left me like a frightened child,
Unshielded in a night of storm
(How should I dream He was so near?
The rain-swept darkness hid His form).

But when the clouds were driven back
And dawn was breaking into day,
I knew Whose feet had walked with mine,
I saw the footprints all the way.

— George Goodman

This poignant poem was written during great days of pain and suffering by our beloved brother.

246

September 1

I AM FILLED WITH COMFORT, I OVERFLOW WITH JOY IN ALL OUR AFFLICTION.

— 2 Cor. 7: 4, R.V.

Mrs Boardman relates an experience she had after her husband had died. The Lord said to her: "I want you to praise Me for the way in which I have taken your loved one." "How can I, Lord?" she asked. She repeated the word "Praise," but her heart gave no response. Then she said, "Lord, I will accept the spirit of praise if Thou dost give it" and in a moment she was filled with praise.

Sing my soul!

September 2

HE EVER LIVETH TO MAKE INTERCESSION FOR THEM. — Hebrews 7: 25

The believer liveth upon the earth, and Christ liveth at the right hand of the majesty on high; and between these two there is a vital bond; Christ liveth there for the Christian, and the Christian liveth here for Christ. There was a time when believers were indebted to the daily sacrifice for their daily confidence; now they are indebted to the inviolable life of the risen Christ for an ever-enduring confidence. If there be a copartnery betwixt you and the King's Son, and you know assuredly that his unrejected solicitations are continually offered in your behalf, then should you walk in a path of ever augmenting wealth. You are embarked upon the true stream of prosperity, and daily, as you are borne onward, its banks look down upon you with more and more of sublimity and beauty. If the Beloved intercedes for you, then the exuberance of the treasury of heaven must be ever for you. Are you as careful to keep open that door of your house which looks Christward, as Christ is to keep open that door of heaven which looks towards you?

I fear that often, too often, there come processions of gift-bearers to your door, and wait some time, and are at length constrained to go back, wondering, sorrowing; while at another door you stand, saying to the passers-by, "Give a trifle," and in return receive but insults.

Christ lives to-day, to-morrow, and every day, making intercession for you; this means, by interpretation, that Christ lives to perfect you day by day in wisdom, knowledge of the word, spiritual power, patience, self-denial, love, faith, humility, beneficence, purity, and submission.

— *George Bowen*

September 3

THUS YE SHALL EAT IT. — Ex. 12: 11

THE FEAST OF THE REDEEMED

The Redeemed were gathered around a table, each one girded for a journey, a staff in every hand.

Meanwhile they were fully occupied feeding on the lamb during the hours of that eventful night. It was not spent in cool indifference, nor unconscious slumber.

Blessed lesson for us. We have been left in this dark world for a little while, to hold communion with the Son of God. This is the highest privilege of all the Lord's redeemed.

Dear young believer, you have known the meaning of the blood-stained lintel. What do you know of the table spread? Is it your daily habit to live in communion with God? Do you spend your ransomed moments feeding on Christ? God has given the blood of Christ to answer the claims of your awakened conscience, and now it is at rest, perfect rest. He has also given the *Person of Christ* to satisfy your longing heart. How truly happy is the heart that delights itself in the Lord. It needs no other cheer. It wants no other joy.

— *John Ritchie*

Let us keep the Feast. — I Cor. 5: 8

September 4

Ye shall eat the flesh on that night, roast with fire, and with bitter herbs ye shall eat it. Eat not of it raw nor sodden at all with water, but roast with fire; his head with his legs, and the purtenance thereof.

— Exodus 12: 8—9

Jesus is the Lamb of God. Roasting with fire shows the suffering He endured from the hand of God. We feed upon a suffering Christ. We have fellowship with Jesus as the suffering One. And what a feast this is! How tender it makes the conscience! How it moves and fills the heart with tenderest love to Him! Thinking of His dying agony — His anguish of soul upon the tree, His deep and mighty love that many waters could not quench, nor floods drown, we love Him in return. The heart is won, the affections are engaged, and Jesus —. Jesus only — becomes the object of the saint's admiration, and worship, the theme of his sweetest song. All else grows dim, the world loses its hold, the soul recoils from its pleasures, once so truly loved, for it has got a better *portion,* and it is satisfied, yea abundantly satisfied.

— *John Ritchie*

Thou Precious Lamb of God I would feed on Thee today!

September 5

WITH BITTER HERBS THEY SHALL EAT IT.

— Exodus 12: 8

The Lamb was eaten with bitter herbs. Eaten by themselves they are an unsavoury morsel. Not so eaten with the roast lamb. The "bitter herbs" have been spoken of as sorrow for sin. And surely at no time does sin appear so exceedingly sinful, as when in communion with the Lord. There the mask is dropped, and sin is seen in its true character in the light of the Cross. We remember *whose* sins they were that brought the blessed Sufferer there, and beneath whose load He died. The heart melts, the tears flow — tears of true love, too — a tribute of affection to the One who died. Grace alone can work true repentance, love alone can win the rebel sinner's heart, and where that grace and love are truly known, such sorrow for sin and hatred of it too, will not be found wanting. Many seeking souls have put the "bitter herbs" in the place of the sprinkled blood. They have sought to find peace with God by being sorry for the past, instead of in the blood of Christ alone; and in this condition they have gone on for years, *hoping* their hard hearts would melt, and that they would *feel* love to God begotten in them. Such love is foreign to the revolted heart of fallen man, nor can he ever put it there. Love to God can only be begotten by believing His love for us.

> *Then a sense of blood bought pardon*
> *Soon dissolves a heart of stone.*

> — *John Ritchie*

September 6

A FOREIGNER AND A HIRED SERVANT SHALL NOT EAT. — Exodus 12: 45

The Lord's Supper is not for the unconverted, whose condition is that of "strangers and foreigners" (Eph. 2: 19). *No unconverted communicant was at the Feast when is was instituted by the Lord.* Judas Iscariot went out before it *began* (compare Matt. 26 with John 13), and we read in the Acts of the Apostles that the disciples "continued in the breaking of bread," and "of the rest (*i.e.*, the unconverted), durst no man join himself to them" (Acts 2: 42; 5: 13).

250

Things are changed now. The unconverted "parishioner" claims his seat at "the sacrament" as he does his stance on the market, and even in most of the churches and chapels in Christendom the unconverted crowd to "the sacrament" expecting to get salvation, or in some way to be made ready for heaven by this "means of grace." The ministers and office-bearers of many of the so-called churches do not even ask the young communicant if he has been "born again." "Hired servants" truly they are too; poor souls, working hard to earn the salvation that God says is a gift, and this "sacrament taking" helps them on in the sad delusion. *Some of God's people are mixed up with this sham, and by giving it their patronage and support, they help on the ruin of souls.*

— *John Ritchie*

September 7

THY WAY IS IN THE SEA, AND THY PATH IN THE GREAT WATERS, AND THY FOOTSTEPS ARE NOT KNOWN. — Ps. 77:19

THEY WANDERED IN THE WILDERNESS IN A SOLITARY WAY; THEY FOUND NO CITY TO DWELL IN. — Ps. 107:4

HE HATH DONE ALL THINGS WELL.

— Mark 7:37

OH BAFFLED SOUL, BESET BY FEARS,
Blind, groping through thy mist of tears
Look up to God to see you through,
And know His ways are just toward you.

Although thy way be hedged with thorn,
Thy feet on stony ground be torn,
God's hand marks out the path you tread,
And safely 'long it you are led.

251

He loves thee still, thou fainting heart
In all thy griefs has major part,
He bore sin's sorrows once for thee,
Can He not now thy succourer be?

He holds thee strongly by the hand,
Across each plain of burning sand,
And at the end will surely prove,
That all His judgments were in love.

His eye can see the landscape far,
A sky all studded bright with star,
When to your heart will then be known
The meaning of thy pathway lone.

To you a brighter day shall dawn,
When all your sorrows will have gone,
And to thy soul God's peace be given
And on thee rest the calm of heaven.

There's meaning in God's plan for thee,
Although thou findest not the key,
His "dealings strange" will yet appear,
The perfect answer to thy prayer.

So let thy soul contented dwell,
On this one fact, "God doeth well,"
He locks the mysteries of His grace
Within the "hiding of His face."

— *David B. Stewart*

September 8

The hand of the Lord was upon me, and carried me out in the Spirit of the Lord, and set me down in the midst of the valley which was full of bones . . . and he said unto me, Son of man, can these bones live? And I answered, O Lord God, Thou knowest. Again He said unto me, Prophesy upon these bones, and say unto them, Oh ye dry bones, hear the word of the Lord." (Ezekiel 37: 1, 3, 4).

The Lord set Ezekiel down in the midst of the valley of dry bones. Many Christian workers believe that the Lord has also done this same thing for them! He has given them a drybone ministry in the valley of death. They have been called to be the Lord's messengers to dry bones. How many dear pastors are preaching to congregations Sunday after Sunday with no apparent sign of life, whether among the professing Christians or sinners under the wrath of God.

When challenged by Jehovah to believe that this great valley of dry bones could come to life, the prophet of God answered, "Oh, Lord God, Thou knowest". I do not know exactly what Ezekiel meant by this reply, but I can only give you my experience. How many times we have preached our hearts out, fasted and prayed, without any sign of spiritual movement whatsoever in our congregation or in our mission field of dry bones. Heartbroken and discouraged, we have fallen to our knees, and with tears streaming down our faces, we have cried, "Oh God, Thou knowest we have preached our heart out. Oh God, Thou knowest we have travailed in spritual childbirth. Oh God, Thou knowest that we have sounded the alarm faithfully, Yet, we see no sign of life. Oh! Lord, Thou knowest we can do no more."

Possibly the prophet referred the question back to God for an answer. "Oh Lord God, Thou alone knowest. If these are ever made to live, Thou wilt have to tell us how." In this chapter God proceeds to give the answer as to how dry bones in all places may be made to live.

One commissioned to raise dry bones must have a special preparation. This preparation is two-fold: he must see a vision of God and must feel the touch of God upon his life. In the first chapter we are told that Ezekiel saw visions of God. (1: 1). In the vision under consideration, Ezekiel feels the touch of God: "The hand of the Lord being upon me" (Rotherham). The hand of the Lord symbolizes His power, and to be under His hand is to be endued with His power. *The Spirit of God is in every Christian for life, but every Christian is not under God's hand for power.* The prophet responds to the touch of God and follows where He leads: "The hand of the Lord was upon me, and carried me out in the Spirit of the Lord, and set me down in the midst of the valley which was full of bones". He was willing to be led by the Lord's hand, even into a valley of dry bones. The temptation for every Christian worker is to seek a fruitful vineyard and shun a valley of death. How blessed it is to labor under the Spirit's control.

— James A. Stewart

September 9

AND CAUSED ME TO PASS BY THEM.

— Ezek. 37: 2

A DRY BONE MINISTRY

The Prophet also responds when God's hand sets him down in the midst of the bones. He was made to feel the mighty impact of death. "And he caused me to pass near them round about on every side" (Rotherham). Ezekiel was not allowed to look at them from a distance. Dwelling with bones is more trying than just going to them on a visit. To have bones for neighbors and companions may not be very pleasant. We love rather to live with a company of living people. But unless we are ready to respond to the hand of God which would lead us to the bones and make us dwell among them, we are not prepared for the work of raising them to life. *The work cannot be done from a distance.* The Holy Ghost would never have used General and Mrs William Booth, the early Salvationists, had they not been willing to settle down in the midst of those whom they were called to help.

The Lord said to Ezekiel, "Go round about these bones and take in the scene". By taking in the scene he received a mighty burden for his congregation. *My brother and my sister, until you feel the burden upon your heart concerning the spiritual desolation of the people whom you serve, you are not ready for the resurrection ministry.*

— *James A. Stewart*

September 10

REST IN THE LORD AND WAIT PATIENTLY FOR HIM. — Psalm 37:7

George Müller was once consulted by a man who had a business offered to him that promised great profits. "I have to give an answer within an hour," said the man. Mr. Müller replied: "Then the answer is "No, for that cannot be right that leaves a man no time for prayer." The praying man discovers disguises, for prayer clears the vision (see Josh. 9).

— *James A. Stewart*

September 11

I WILL POUR . . . FLOODS ON DRY GROUND.
— Isa. 44:3

That is revival blessing. Floods, where you don't expect it, floods where till now there has been little or nothing of the working of God's Holy Spirit, nothing but dryness and desert land and wilderness. "I will pour floods upon the dry ground."

When God has poured water on him that is thirsty that one is a fountain of blessing to those around him. From him flow forth rivers of living water and there are floods upon the dry ground. We could tell you story after story from Japan of the same thing. *One Spirit-filled soul will bring revival blessing around.* How generous God is! How He loves to open the riches of His grace! See the word He uses, floods. God is not content with just a little shower of grace; He loves to give so that all are filled. "Floods upon the dry ground." *Lay hold of that word "floods." That is God's measure.*

— *Barclay Buxton*

Lord fulfill Thy promise now I pray!

September 12

IF THOU SHALT CONFESS WITH THY MOUTH THAT JESUS IS LORD. — Rom. 10: 9 A.R.V.

In our evangelical preaching of today there is a by-passing of the emphasis on the Lordship of Christ. In so doing, we have given the impression that the acceptance of the Lordship of Christ is a second experience of grace or a sort of optional after-choice in the Christian life. *Actually, many messages addressed to Christians at a holiness convention should be in reality a part of the gospel message addressed to sinners.* In one of his gospel messages, Peter declares "Him hath God exalted ... to be a Prince and a Saviour" (Acts 5: 31). Today we have reversed the gospel message by stating Him to be a Saviour first and then a Prince! We do not deny that it is possible for a time to come in the believer's life when he will recognize more clearly what is involved in the Lordship of Christ, but this does not alter the fact that a person cannot receive Christ as Saviour without having in some manner recognized Him as Lord. Romans 10: 9 declares "That if thou shalt confess that Jesus is Lord and in thine heart believe that God has raised Him from the dead, thou shalt be saved." (B. R. V.) *The Word of God makes it perfectly clear that the objective of all true evangelism is the control of the sovereign Lord over the lives of those He has redeemed.*

How can we have revival when the vital note of the Lordship of Christ is omitted from our present-day evangelism? As one has truly reasoned, "What is the gospel of God's grace but the gospel of His sovereignty? Wherein lies the vital efficacy of the gospel of grace unless it relates to His kingdom and leads the individual soul to an acknowledgement of His sovereignty?"

— *James A. Stewart*

September 13

FOR BY ONE SPIRIT ARE WE ALL BAPTIZED INTO ONE BODY. — I. Cor. 12:13

This is a day when men like to magnify their denominations. Many evangelistic efforts seem to be conducted for the sole glory of the denomination. How often in evangelistic campaigns is a good gospel message offset by an invitation which implies that denominational membership is equivalent to membership in the supernatural body of Christ! Denominational membership can never be a substitute for the new birth.

In our special love and loyalty for our denomination, we must be careful not to ignore the whole mystical body of Christ which is composed of all true born-again, bloodwashed souls. How tragic it is to see many lovely believers who never glory in the oneness of the body of Christ! The Holy Spirit has very little concern for any special denominaion or group, as such. He is seeking to break down the denominational barriers that divide the saints of God. The barriers that we so carefully erect now will be destroyed suddenly at the coming of the Lord.

There are no denominations in heaven. Why should we not seek to prepare for glory now! No wonder George Whitefield cried out in his day:

"I wish all names among the saints of God were swallowed up in that one name of Christian! Are you Christ's? If so, I love you with all my heart!"

The time has now come for us to preach this trans-
forming truth of the oneness of the body of Christ as
expounded by Paul in such letters as Colossians and
Ephesians. It was this precious truth that brought revival
to the churches in Hungary under my ministry. God cares
little for numerical increase in church membership but
rather for all true additions to the mystical body of
Christ. To such, the Holy Spirit alone can make any real
additions.

— *James A. Stewart*

September 14

RISE UP, AND GET YE FORTH. — Exodus 12:31

Closely connected with the people's salvation from
the destroying angel's sword was their separation and
departure from the land of Egypt. The same night on
which the blood of the Paschal lamb was sprinkled on
their lintels and door-posts, they turned their backs on
Egypt, its people, and its gods, and bade farewell to the
scenes of their idolatry and slavery, for ever. Every link
that had bound them was snapped, and they went free
to serve the living and true God.

How solemn and how real their departure from that
doomed country must have been! At the dead hour of
midnight, amid the shrieks of the Egyptians bewailing
their first-born dead, they silently hurried forth!

"Egypt was glad when they departed" (Psa. 105:38),
and Pharaoh urged them forth from among his people.
Truly might they say, "By strength of hand, the Lord
brought us forth from Egypt, from the house of bondage" (Exod. 13:14); and He who led them out, could
never lead them back again.

The believer's separation from the world is closely
linked with his salvation. *We read of "Jesus Christ,*
who gave Himself for our sins, that He might deliver
us from this present evil world, according to the will of

God and our Father" (Gal. 1: 3—4). *The Cross of Christ is the door of escape from a doomed world, as well as the place of refuge for a guilty sinner. By the Cross the believer is crucified to the world, and separated unto God.*

Many do not see this, or do not want to see it. They boast of the Cross as their deliverance from the wrath to come, but ignore its power to separate them from the world. They live at home in Egypt — the ungodly are their associates; and although they speak of being in heaven at last, they grasp as much of the world as they can, or, to use a popular phrase, they try *"to make the best of both worlds."* It is not the will of God that His children should be mixed up in unhallowed alliance with the world.

— *John Ritchie*

September 15

There were Prophets who earnestly inquired about that salvation and closely searched into it — even those who spoke beforehand of the grace which was to come to you. They were eager to know the time when the Spirit of Christ within them kept indicating, or the characteristics of that time, when they solemnly made known beforehand the sufferings that were to come upon Christ and the glories which would follow. To them it was revealed that they were serving not themselves but you, when they foretold the very things which now have been openly declared to you by those who, having been taught by the Holy Spirit which had been sent from Heaven, brought you the Good News. The angels longed to stoop and look into these things". (I Peter 1: 10—12, free translation).

The glory and magnitude of our salvation is so wonderful that with holy zeal and solemnity the prophets earnestly inquired and searched diligently into the very truths they were foretelling. They rejoiced in the testi-

259

mony of the Spirit within them, but they were not free from the necessity to search — and search diligently — if they would for themselves derive the benefit from their revelation. That the searching was intense in character is proved by the Greek word which describes it. They "scrutinized with care" the revelations made to them in order that they might understand what was implied. The words *inquired* and *searched diligently* are strong and emphatic, alluding to miners who dig to the bottom and break through, not only the earth, but the rock in order to come to the ore.

Not only were the prophets earnest in their inquiry, but so also were the angels. Peter says they "desired to look into" the matter. To *look into* in the original means *to bend over and see to the bottom of a thing; to bend over in order to examine minutely,* as the cherubims stood bending over the Mercy Seat, the emblem of redemption by blood.

— *James A. Stewart*

September 16

THE ANGELS DESIRED TO LOOK INTO.

— I. Pet. 1:12

Oh God, make us likewise dead in earnest! No man can be dead in earnest for the salvation of others who has not been dead earnest in contemplating and evaluating the glory of his own salvation. How pathetic that many professed Christians never ponder or meditate deeply into the wonders of sovereign grace.

> *He plucked me as a brand from hell,*
> *My Jesus hath done all things well*

Duncan Mathieson, that fiery Scottish evangelist who labored in the Highlands, was a man filled with the wonder of redeeming grace and thus was in earnest for the salvation of the lost. Often he cried out in the midst of his message, "Eternity is stamped on my eyeballs. I have seen a sight which has dimmed the glory of all else!"

While stricken at Aberdeen of a painful internal malady, he spoke in a solemn manner to a gathering in a house he visited. Upon reaching his own home he became very ill and in his fevered condition his mind began to wander. He imagined he was addressing a group of theological students at Edinburgh. Rising from bed, he cried, "Up young men, souls are perishing! Up, and aim at sinners!"

James Turner, another fellow Scot, a fisherman by profession and a mighty revivalist, was also dead in earnest. Those who saw him tell us that his intenseness was awe-inspiring. He knew that he was dying of consumption and that his days were numbered, and so he travelled all over the towns of the Scottish east coast, sounding the alarm for sinners to escape from the wrath of God. At the close of his life, spent and ill in health, he cried on his sick bed, "Oh to live at Jesus' feet and to gather in souls in armfuls for our blessed Master!"

— *James A. Stewart*

September 17

GIRD UP THE LOINS OF YOUR MIND.

— I Pet. 1: 13

What a crime then it must be if we have allowed the loins of our minds to become ungirded so that we do not show the same enthusiasm for our salvation as did the prophets and the angels! Think you, if these glorious spirits who needed not to be redeemed intently gazed upon our glorious Redeemer, should not we also be earnest in our desire to look into and get to the bottom of the meaning of His redemptive sacrifice?

"Methinks," says Spurgeon, "If I saw an angel gazing intently on any object, if I were a passerby I should stop and look, too"

These seraphic beings, who dwelt in the unsullied light of the Throne for ages, had peered into the mysteries of the Cross as the Spirit of God in holy men testified beforehand. They understood that it was for us fallen men and women, who deserve nothing but the damnation of God, that the blessed Son suffered such unutterable anguish. I can well imagine as the angels look upon us, as the objects of the great redemption, purchased at such a price, they stand in holy wonder at our apathy and indifference.

"Surely," they cry, "these redeemed souls should be burning with devotion to their sovereign Lord and in dead earnest for the salvation of their fellowmen."

Alas, what do they see? Let the lukewarmness, the selfishness, the lack of practical holiness, the undedicated gold, time and talents of the professed disciples of Christ be the answer; and the angels, if such they could do in that bright world, would add weeping to their wonder and denounce us before high Heaven as the most ungracious creatures in all the universe of the Most High! *How we do stand condemned in the light of the earnestness and enthusiasm of the prophets and angels!*

— *James A. Stewart*

September 18

WEEPING MAY ENDURE FOR A NIGHT, BUT JOY COMETH IN THE MORNING. — Psalm 30:5

A missionary's faith.

THE SOWER

Far among rocks and hills,
Have I planted my seed.
In the dust and drought under sun-baked clod
Where the foot of a sower never trod;
In the crumbled furrows where birds of prey
Hidden in clefts in the heat of the day,

Swoop at even to snatch the shoot
Of the living seed that has cast its root
Where crackling creeper and leafless thorn
Strangle the life of a blade new born,
And the sower's labour is laughed to scorn
I have planted my seed.

Unto the Spirit of life
I commit my seed.
Now will I rise and go my way
To stars by night and the sun by day,
To the cold of winter and autumn rain
I yield my treasure of gathered grain.
With empty hands and a trembling faith.
I leave my seed to the wastes of death.
Scattered so far, I shall never know
How much may die and how much may grow
Nor of secret stirrings neath frost and snow
In the buried seed.

Power of a risen life
Shall quicken my seed.
Life that is born of God's own breath
Stronger than winter or drought or death
Scattered, stunted, blighted at birth,
Yet each living seedling of matchless worth
To the Lord Who shall lift them from fields of time
And transplant them far in a sweeter clime
Where in love's own soil they shall cast
           their root
And His life shall quicken the shrivelled shoot
And each branch abiding shall bear its fruit
Through the life of God.

—Patricia St. John

Moslem Morocco

263

September 19

GOD DID TEST ABRAHAM. — Gen. 22:1, Margin
THE TRIAL OF YOUR FAITH. — 1 Pet. 1:7

God "*did tempt Abraham*", and the context proves that the word "*tempt*" has the underlying meaning of purifying: God had to lift Abraham's faith into an understanding of Himself. The life of Abraham is a life of faith, and faith in its actual working out has to go through spells of unsyllabled isolation (cf. Romans 8: 26). Temptations in the life of faith are not accidents, each temptation is part of a plan, a step in the progress of faith. Faith is not logical, it works on the line of life and by its very nature must be tried. Never confound the trial of faith with the ordinary discipline of life. Much that we call the trial of our faith is the inevitable result of being alive. The problem lies in the clearing of God's character with regard to what He allows. Faith according to the Bible is confidence in God when He is inscrutable and apparently contradictory in His providences.

— Oswald Chambers

Let no man think that sudden in a minute
All is accomplished and the work is done;
Though with thine earliest dawn thou shouldst begin it,
Scarce were it ended in thy setting sun.
How have I knelt with arms of my aspiring
Lifted all night in irresponsive air,
Dazed and amazed with overmuch desiring,
Blank with the utter agony of prayer!

— Myers

I HAVE BEEN CRUCIFIED WITH CHRIST.

— Gal. 2: 20

That old capital "I" has great respect for itself; it has a great sense of its own importance. It has an overwhelming estimate of its own abilities. It gets upset and almost has a brain storm if its importance is not recognized: if its gifts are not valued, and if its rights are not granted: if it isn't shown proper consideration; all because it came to be ministered unto instead of to minister.

That old capital "I" knows a great deal about the Bible, but it knows nothing about the part that says "In honour preferring one another", or of "not seeking its own" nor of "rejoicing with those that rejoice." So it gives way to jealousy and to envy, even to unforgiveness in resentment and hatred, because "it came to be ministered unto, instead of to minister." It finally gets around to doing a kindness for somebody, and it does a kindness, and then it nearly has a nervous breakdown because it wasn't sufficiently appreciated. *A great enough fuss* wasn't made over it. The thanks were not profuse enough. It almost wishes it hadn't done the kindness because it didn't pay, for it even did the kindness for the sake of "it came to be ministered unto and not to minister."

It prides itself on its sound judgment and its wise counsel. It loves to be consulted, and considers itelf a final authority on all matters. Then people seem to get along quite nicely without its advice. Or if its advice is given, it is ignored, or even the very opposite thing is done, and then its reputation has suffered a severe loss — "It came to be ministered unto."

— *Ruth Paxson*

September 21

CHRIST WHO IS OUR LIFE. — Col. 3:4

There are two schools of doctrine among professing Christians as to the offices and relations of the Lord. The first speaks thus: Any work or office, held by Christ, cannot be held by us; it usurps His right if we pretend to share them. The other, which is the old doctrine, answers thus: If the Incarnation means anything, if Christ and His Church are really one body, all Christ's offices first held and exercised by Him on behalf of men must likewise be held and shared by His members, because He lives in them just as they apprehend that for which they were apprehended. The former view, which I feel assured is a mistake, arises from a misconception of the first great truth of *Christ for us,* to the denial of the greather truth of *Christ in us,* and we His members. The latter opens the riches of the glory of the mystery, which is now revealed, which is *Christ in us,* the hope of glory. The latter is the Church's faith which, however caricatured and abused, cannot be denied without sore loss to the deniers. For this faith confesses the Incarnation, that the Lord still dwells in flesh and blood, and that because He dwells in us, though in ourselves we can do nothing, we can yet do all things through Christ, who is the power in us; and because He is 'the same yesterday, to-day, and for ever,' if He lives in us, He will yet do His proper works, in and through those who grow up out of self to live in Him.

— *Andrew Jukes*

September 22

I WILL NOT LEAVE YOU DESOLATE.
— John 14: 8, A.R.V.

I have written and preached much on the Holy Spirit, for the knowledge of Him has been the most vital fact in my experience. I owe everything to the Gift of Pentecost . . . I came across a prophet, heard a testimony, and set out to seek I knew not what. I knew that it was a bigger thing and a deeper need than I had ever known. It came along the line of duty, and I entered in through a crisis of obedience. When it came, I could not explain what had happened, but I was aware of things unspeakable and full of glory.

Some results were immediate. There came into my soul a deep peace, a thrilling joy, and a new sense of power. My mind was quickened. I felt that I had received a new faculty of understanding. Every power was alert. Either illumination took the place of logic, or reason became intuitive. My bodily powers also were quickened. There was a new sense of spring and vitality, a new power of endurance, a strong man's exhilaration in big things. Things began to happen. What we had failed to do by strenuous endeavor came to pass without labour. It was as when the Lord Jesus stepped into the boat that with all their rowing had made no progress. Immediately the ship was at the land whither they went. *It was gloriously wonderful.*

— *Samuel Chadwick*

September 23

We have a more sure word of prophecy: whereunto ye do well that ye take heed, as unto a light that shineth in a dark place, until the day dawn and the day star arise in your hearts. — 1 Pet. 1: 19

That is the optimistic outlook for Christians. We see the ominous darkness, but we look for the dawn of a better day. We are pilgrims of the night, with our faces to the sunrising. Travellers in foreign lands patiently endure discomfort with the knowledge that it is but for a time; soon they will be home. The mariner bravely faces the storm and tempest, knowing that every mile brings him nearer to the harbour. There are heavy clouds upon the church and the world, but the earnest believer sees the silver lining, and rejoices with the Psalmist (Ps. 112: 4), "Unto the upright there ariseth light in the darkness."

Prophecy, says the inspired apostle, is as a light shining in a dark place. And surely we have reached a dark place in the history of mankind. There is much talk of the desire for peace, but there is at the same time a speeding up of preparation for war, and politicians talk of the danger of the smashing up of civilization. The amazing thing is that there is almost a universal ignorance of the fact that *only* One can bring peace to the world, He who is the Prince of Peace, He who stood on deck amid the storm and said, "Peace, be still!" Thank God for the light of His Word! Prophecy is a beacon light across the dark waves. There is warfare, sorrow and tears, but it is not for ever. We may hear the voice of Christ on the waters, "It is I, be not afraid!" "I will come again."

Have you noticed that near the close of the Old Testament Scriptures we are told of the rising of the Sun of Righteousness with healing in His wings, a picture of the Millennial Dawn when "He whose right it is," will reign in righteousness and peace. Then the New Testament in its closing scene has this message, "I am the Bright and Morning Star," reminding us of the "blessed hope" and the day star arising in our hearts. It is at the darkest hour when the morning star appears, as the signal of the coming dawn. "The night is far spent, the day is at hand." "Ye are not children of the night, but of the day." It was at midnight when the call was heard. "Behold, the Bridegroom cometh!" Let us take heed of the warning. The Day Star will arise. "I am the Bright and Morning Star." *The Great I Am* — Jehovah-Jesus — He is coming. The day-star shall arise in your heart — the star of the Blessed Hope of His appearing. The hidden mystery is revealed to His saved ones — "Christ in you the hope of glory." *And when He comes, the Christ in the heart will recognise the Christ in the air.* Let us be true to the vision and walk as "children of the Light."

"The Lord is my light and my salvation, whom shall I fear." "Maranatha!"

— *Selected*

September 24

HE LOOKED FOR A CITY. — Heb. 11:10

The Christian is a man who can see afar off; he is a far-sighted man, he is the only far-sighted man the world contains. Hence the Master speaks — if we may paraphrase another figure employed by Him — "He that hath eyes to see, let him look." Look, look, look! I look above, and what do I see? I see Christ Himself sitting on the right hand of God the Father interceding for me; for "He ever liveth to make intercession." I see Him preparing for the coming day. I see Him watching over His Church; and whenever that Church is, as it were, in weakness and despondency, He cheers her with the word from the throne of God, "Behold, I come quickly."

— *Horatius Bonar*

September 25

AND HE SAID, CERTAINLY I WILL BE WITH THEE. — Exod. 3:12

Of course, if the Lord sent Moses on an errand, He would not let him go alone. The tremendous risk which it would involve, and the great power it would require, would render it ridiculous for God to send a poor lone Hebrew to confront the mightiest king in all the world, and then leave him to himself. It could not be imagined that a wise God would match poor Moses with Pharaoh and the enormous forces of Egypt. Hence He says, "Certainly I will be with thee," as if it were out of the question that He would send him alone.

In my case, also the same rule will hold good. If I go upon the Lord's errand, with a simple reliance upon His power, and a single eye to His glory, it is certain that He will be with me. His sending me binds Him to back me up. Is not this enough? What more can I want? If all the angels and archangels were with me, I might fail; but if HE is with me, I must succeed. Only let me take care that I act worthily toward this promise. Let me not go timidly, halfheartedly, carelessly, presumptuously. What manner of person ought he to be who has God with him! In such company it behoveth me to play the man, and like Moses go in unto Pharaoh without fear.

— *C. H. Spurgeon*

September 26

THE SON OF GOD WHO LOVED ME.

— Gal. 2: 20

Charles Wesley, John Newton, and other such men of God to their dying breath could never get over the wonder of the Christ of God dying for them. Writes the sweet singer of Methodism:

> *And can it be that I should gain*
> *An interest in the Saviour's blood?*
> *Died He for me, who caused His pain?*
> *For me, who Him to death pursued?*
> *Amazing love! How can it be*
> *That Thou, my God, shouldst die for me?*
>
> *'Tis mystery all! Th' Immortal dies!*
> *Who can explore His strange design?*
> *In vain the first-born seraph tries*
> *To sound the depths of love divine*
> *'Tis mercy all! Let earth adore!*
> *Let angel minds inquire no more!*

— *Charles Wesley*

270

In like manner the former slave-trader who became a flaming evangelist writes of his first gaze at redeeming grace:

Sure, never, till my latest breath,
Can I forget that look:
It seemed to charge me with His death,
Though not a word He spoke.

— *John Newton*

I hold in my hand, as I write, John Calvin's exposition of Galatians. As I seek for his exposition of Galatians 2: 20, I am at first disappointed, for the mighty expositor and giant of God has little to say. *Then, as I continue to meditate over the page, I soon discover that the awe of God is upon the soul of the Prince of Geneva.* Methinks he has laid down his pen as he writes in his study and sits overwhelmed at the thought of such redeeming grace! "The Son of God, Who loved me and gave Himself for me!"

— *James A. Stewart*

September 27

AND GREAT FEAR CAME UPON ALL THE CHURCH. — Acts 5: 11

The tragic death of Ananias and Sapphira has struck terror into the hearts of the saints down the ages. We verily tremble every time we read the story. Here is the Nadab and Abihu incident in the New Testament. Ananias and Sapphira offer up to God the "strange fire" of an insincere consecration believing that their fraud will go unnoticed. It was given to Peter on this occasion supernaturally by the Spirit to read their hearts, just as it was given to Elisha to detect Gehazi's fraudulent act. (II Kings 5: 25—27). *This instance is only one among many which reveal the pure spiritual atmosphere which*

271

the early church breathed; that a lie to the apostles was a lie to the Holy Ghost! The Spirit of Pentecost so lived in the church inspiring and controlling her every movement that when one lied before men he lied to God.

What are the spiritual lessons for us today from this incident? We would affirm that the Holy Spirit must maintain still the purity of the spiritual atmosphere of the church. All Christian work must be carried out on a spiritual basis.

No carnal hand should dare to touch the work of God. Every pastor, elder, deacon, choir member, Sunday school teacher and every member of the assembly should be filled with the Spirit. In the early church there was no line of demarcation between the secular and the spiritual. Even to "serve tables" the deacons had to be "full of the Spirit" (Acts 6: 3).

The Holy Spirit is the leader of the affairs of the assembly. All acts in the Christian life must be inspired by Him. We must recognize His personality, deity, and authority. When we give offerings for the Lord's work, we are giving to God and not to our human leaders. There must be no giving for show or for the praise of man.

How many lie today and play the hypocrite in the things of God! They sing lustily, "I surrender all" and yet hold tightly to their checkbooks while the lonely sentinels of the Cross of Christ in heathen mission fields desperately need financial help. How many profess to be fully surrendered to the Lord during the invitations given in our public gatherings, while deep down in their hearts they know it is only a sham. One of the greatest hindrances to God's blessing sweeping through the church to a dying world is the sin of insincerity. How many broken covenants and vows there are that only the eye of God can see! "Speaking lies in hypocrisy; having their conscience seared with a hot iron" (I Tim. 4: 2).

— *James A. Stewart*

272

September 28

AND WHEN I SAW HIM, I FELL AT HIS FEET AS DEAD. — Rev. 1: 17

It is the devil's business to rob the Church of its reverence for the great God of wonders.

More than seventy-five years ago that keen evangelical scholar, Bishop Wescott of Durham Cathedral, wrote, "Every day makes me tremble at the daring with which people speak of spiritual things. This is an age of an impoverished conception of the God of the Bible. This is an age of blasphemy and irreverence inside the church of Jesus Christ. How often our worship and service are as a loud and irreverent tramp in the ears of the Almighty! I believe God is crying to us today in these solemn words:

"When ye come to appear before me, who hath required this at your hand, to trample my courts?' " (Isa. 1: 12).

What would the good man say today? Much of our so-called worship and singing is an abomination to the Lord. *By all means let us sing cheerfully and joyfully, but never let us forget the majesty and holiness of the God Whom we adore.* This is the age of "The good Lord bless and keep you." This is the age of "The Man Upstairs." This is the age when everyone seems to be on good terms with God, and yet never was there so much sin and iniquity in this fair land of ours. Dishonesty, greed, lying, sensuality and blasphemy have struck at the very foundation of our nation. This is the day when we are trying to humanize God and bring Him down to the popular level of a "good pal" to everyone.

There can never be a mighty movement of the Holy Spirit inside the church until we clothe ourselves in sackcloth and ashes and repent of this sin of irreverence. Jowett kindly lets us in on a most distressing incident during his ministry. He says, "Once I preached a sermon on the bitter cup which was drunk by our Lord and Saviour Jesus Christ. Later I noticed that one of the papers, in reference to the sermon, had said that I had spoken on the sufferings of Christ "with charming effect.' These words sent me to my knees in humiliation and fear. Soul of mine! What had I said, or what had I left unsaid, or through what perverted medium had I been interpreted?"

No one can shut himself up in his closet in communion with God without receiving the reverential awe of God upon his soul. *Oh, for deliverance from an impoverished conception of God!*

— *James A. Stewart*

September 29

THE DEVIL ... TAKETH AWAY THE WORD OUT OF THEIR HEARTS, LEST THEY SHOULD BE-LIEVE. — Luke 8:12

In this remarkable message it is clearly stated that if only Satan can take away "the implanted Word," then faith collapses. It is strange but true that faith, when sorely pressed, at any rate, cannot rest upon generalities, however clear. True conceptions even of the power and love and work of God are not sufficient basis for faith. *Faith demands the written Word — the letter no less than the spirit — on which to stand.*

"Give me a promise," cried a young man under the deepest conviction for inward holiness. He knew the truth that God was able to sanctify; he knew the depravity of his own nature, and that Christ had shed His precious blood to cleanse it; he knew that the Holy Ghost was ready to occupy and transform his earthly temple, and yet faith could find no resting-place. "Give me a promise," he repeated.

His friend, who was kneeling by his side,, silently lifting up his heart to God, repeated slowly: "He is able to save to the uttermost them that come unto God by Him." *It was enough; victory was assured; faith could rest there.* At once the seeking soul laid hold of the written promise and entered into rest. It is through the "exceeding great and precious promises" that we are blessed.

This is God's wonderful way! The foundation of faith is the written Word of the living God. Again and again is this borne out in the Gospels. The most distressed and storm-tossed souls found immediate peace when Jesus spoke the word which was spirit and life.

— *Paget Wilkes*

September 30

Therefore I say unto you, What things soever ye desire, when ye pray, believe that ye have received them, and ye shall have them. — Mark 11: 24, R.V.

Prayer in faith is not faith in prayer. "The prayer of faith shall save"; or, as the Japanese version has it: "The prayer that proceedeth forth from faith." There is a great difference between the prayer of desire and the prayer of faith, and though earnest desire is a true element of prayer, yet the prayer of desire itself will produce nothing. It is not until the prayer of desire passes into the prayer of faith that we shall obtain what we seek. "The soul of the sluggard desireth and hath nothing!" is a solemn warning indeed.

It is moreover a solemn fact of experience that if the prayer of desire does not pass into the prayer of faith, the very desire to pray slowly but surely ebbs away. *Prayer is a blessed stimulus to faith. Solitary prayer and united prayer with real believing and expectant souls tend to create an atmosphere of faith within.* Alas, how many of our prayer-meetings are destitute of that holy expectancy of faith! And so nothing is accomplished, nothing done!

It is as we wait upon God, using the little faith we have, that He will enable us to renew our strength; we shall gradually mount up on the wings of faith as eagles, and find, not only all the world and its vanity, but also all inward doubt, and fear, and darkness, and *uncertainty beneath our feet.*   — *Paget Wilkes*

October 1

AND THE HOUSE WAS FILLED WITH THE ODOUR OF OINTMENT. — John 12:3

The Lord has just placed Himself at the table, when Mary approaches, deeply affected by gratitude, veneration, love, and with a foreboding of what is about to befall Him. She feels impelled to display to Him her inmost soul once more, and to manifest her reverential and devout attachment to Him. But how is she to do this? Words seem to her too poor. Presents she has none to make. *But what she has that is valuable — possibly a legacy left by her mother — is an alabaster vessel of pure oil of spikenard, much valued in the East, and used only on peculiarly festive occasions.* She brings it with her. *She does not intend to pour out a few drops only, but that it should be wholly an emblem of her profound devotion to the Lord of Glory.* With the utmost reverence she approaches her divine Friend, breaks unobservedly behind Him the well-closed vessel, sheds the spikenard upon His head and feet, then humbly bends herself down and wipes the latter with her loosened tresses.

"And the whole house was filled with the ointment." Yes, we may well believe that this odor ascended up even into the throne-room of heaven, and was inhaled with delight by the holy angels. *In this affectionate and symbolical act, a degree of devotedness was manifested such as is rarely exhibited. Mary desires to belong to Christ for time and eternity; to cleave to Him by faith, like the ivy to the tree, round which it entwines itself.* She wishes to live in His light, like a dark planet in the beams of the sun which lends it its radiance. Mary knows no anchor of hope, no ground of consolation, no way to heaven, except through His mediation; and were she to imagine existence without Him, she could only think of herself as in the jaws of despair, and irrecoverably lost. He is her last resource, but at the same time all-sufficient for her eternal salvation. Hence she cleaves to Him with all her soul, and nothing is able to divide her from Him. He is always in her thoughts her sole delight, and the supreme object of her affections — all this she expresses in the anointing. — *Krummacker*

October 2
I THIRST! — John 19: 28

There, unseen, He was surrounded by the bands of Belial. There the powers of darkness aimed at Him their most dangerous missile. From this appalling host of adversaries, from this horrible desert, from this "pit in which there was no water," and in which He could only believe that God was His God, without feeling Him to be so, rose, like the prayer of the lost man to send Lazarus, the cry, "I thirst!" To spare us sinners the thirst of an infinite absence of comfort. He submitted to such torment in His mediatorial capacity! O what a well of consolation has He opened for us by His thirst!

"I thirst!" For what did He thirst? I think the answer now is plain. It was not only for earthly water that He languished, but for something greater, higher, and more essential. He longed for the termination of His redeeming toil, and the completion of His great work of mediation. When this object was attained. He would again be restored to the full beautifying fellowship of His heavenly Father. He would not then have laboriously to struggle for the consciousness that God was kindly and paternally inclined toward Him, but would again taste it, for He would then rest as formerly in His Father's bosom, and instead of the horrible images of sin, the curse, and death, the radiance of a spotless purity and holiness would beam upon Him anew from every side. Peace and joy would then return. The viperous hissing of the powers of darkness around Him would be silenced. He would hear only the hallelujahs of angels and the blest above. Every discord would be dissolved in blissful harmony, and the atmosphere which He breathed would again be love, entirely love. — *Krummacker*

October 3

IT IS FINISHED. — John 19: 30

Two thousand years ago,
My Lord was crucified,
Bowing His kindly head in rest,
" 'its finished" Jesus cried.
And that strange cry of peace
That rent the earth that day
Shall echo through the centuries
Till time has past away.

Two thousand years ago,
He finished all my quest
His dying shout of victory,
The dying on which I rest.
No problem unresolved,
No trespass unforgiven
No foe unconquered, fear unmet
No barrier to Heaven.

Alone He struggled on
Through sins' infernal night
Through bleakest wastes of deepest we
Alone he waged His fight.
He braved the floods of death,
Forsaken and undone,
And struggled to that shore of rest
His victory fought and won.

Beyond that boundary
No questing feet need stray
However steep and long the path
His footsteps marked the way.
And we who love His Cross
And die where Jesus died,
Shall live to share the rest of God
At peace and satisfied.

— Patricia St. John

October 4

And they were all filled with the Holy Ghost and began to speak in other tongues, as the Spirit gave them utterance. — Acts 2: 4

These utterances were the result of the advent and incarnation of the Spirit. What happened when the disciples were filled with the Holy Spirit? Precisely the thing that would happen today if all of us were filled! "They began to speak as the Spirit gave them utterance." The moment they were filled they were empowered to witness for Christ. How glorious and awesome it is to talk as the Spirit gives us utterance! If we know anything of the mighty work of the Spirit in our lives, we shall know the miracle of Spirit controlled utterances.

Immediately they began to witness in Jerusalem and unto the uttermost parts of the earth, because the uttermost parts of the earth were right in Jerusalem at that moment. And so they fulfilled Acts 1: 8 that same day in miniature! What happened? We find that there were 3000 souls saved. Think of it! The church then had only 120 members, yet had 3000 additions. Today if a church of 3000 members had 120 souls saved they would think they were having revival! Yes, a New Testament church is a soul-saving church. If an assembly is not winning souls for the Lord Jesus, it is deceiving itself.

— *James A. Stewart*

Oh, that I may speak as the Blessed Spirit gives me utterance! Amen!

October 5

Let your loins be girded about, and your lights burning; And ye yourselves like unto men that wait for their lord, when he will return from the wedding; that when he cometh and knocketh, they may open unto him immediately. Blessed are those servants, whom the Lord when he cometh shall find watching. — Luke 12: 35—37

The picture here also is oriental. A nobleman has gone to the wedding of a friend. The festivites are spread over many days. Day after day the faithful servants watch and wait for the return of their absent lord, while the day passes into evening and the evening shades into night. The faithful servants keep watch with their loose robes taken up, with their lamps all trimmed and burning, patiently waiting to receive their lord. They never dream of relaxing their vigilance though he may tarry long.

The word translated *watching* is rendered also *wake* and *vigilant* (I Thess. 5: 10; I Peter 5: 8). May we not then read these words as indicating a three-fold attitude regarding our Lord's return?

a) We are to be "vigilant" in His service.

b) We are to be "awake" in using every talent of opportunity and in trading with the "pound" of the gospel.

c) We are to "watch" for His return with the ardent affection of love, with the longing expectation of hope and with alert eyes of watchfulness and faithfulness.

How often was the word watch upon our Lord's lips! The apostles took it up in their epistles and in the Apocalypse the Lord resumes it: "Blessed is he that watcheth."

Oh, my soul! let my lamps be trimmed and burning.

— *James A. Stewart*

October 6

MARAN-ATHA. — I Cor. 16: 22

The atmosphere of earth seems to be loaded with slumberous vapors. Satan, the prince of the power of the air, does all he can to lull us to sleep. What a high value, then, our Lord places upon our attitude of expectancy and watchfulness. He receives it as the expression of the heart's attachment to His own Person.

The apostolic watchword, *Maranatha* (Our Lord cometh) expresses the love of Christ's appearing which possessed the Christians of the first ages. As the early church carried on a guerilla warfare against the powers of darkness they had to meet under cover of night. They needed some token by which to recognize each other as brothers and sisters in Christ. The very fact that *Maranatha* became their password indicates the prominent place which the great truth of Christ's second coming occupied in the thought and life of primitive believers — (I Cor. 16: 22).

The coming of Christ forms the keynote for the warnings and exhortations of the New Testament. It is mentioned no fewer than three hundred and eighteen times in the New Testament, a ratio of one verse in every twenty-five.

The doctrine of the Lord's second coming as it appears in the New Testament is like a lofty mountain which dominates the entire landscape. No matter which road you take, no matter what pass you tread, you will find that mountain bursting in upon your vision at every turning of the way and at every parting of the hills.

The period of the church's pilgrimage in the world is nearing its end. The long night of our Lord's absence is drawing to a close. Soon we shall see His face and soon shall we hear His voice. What a blessed meeting that will be. What raptures of delight shall fill every watchful soul. What bursts of everlasting praise shall fill the heavens as that vast redeemed multitude of every nation and tribe shall rise to meet the Lord in the air! (I Thess. 4: 16—17).

To our Laodicean age Christ is speaking loudly today. Oh Christians! lulled to sleep by worldly compromise, stupefied by luxury and self-indulgence, the Son of God cries, "Behold, I come as a thief."

Up! therefore, Christian, gird up the loins of your mind. Trim your lamp! Let us, with girded loins, with busy hands, with uplifted eyes and with radiant faces be alert for the coming of our blessed Lord!

— *James A. Stewart*

WHO IS ON THE LORD'S SIDE? — Exodus 32: 26

It was not a question now of who were Israelites — that had been made clear on the night of their exodus from Egypt; but now it was — Who is for Jehovah? "And all the sons of Levi gathered themselves together unto him." They took their place on Jehovah's side, openly and definitely, and for this they received the Lord's approval, and His "covenant of life and peace" (see Deut. 33: 8—9; Malachi 2: 5). They shunned not to execute the judgment of the Lord, even upon their brethren, for the fear of the Lord and the honour of His Name was before them. *In this day of a defiled camp, an apostate church, in which the Name of God is dishonoured, the Lordship of Christ ignored, and His Word rendered of none effect, the call is again heard — Who is on the Lord's side?* It is not a question of who are Christians, but of who are willing to give the Lord His place and take their stand with Him, even should they have to leave their kindred and dearest earthly treasures, in order to obey the will of God, and purge themselves from association where He has been dishonoured. This may sever many a link, and cleave asunder many a life-long bond. It will be sure to cost us something, yea, more than flesh and blood can bear, but to those who set the Lord before them, and by grace determine to be on His side, *strength will be given* to go forth "without the camp," and to use "the sword of the Spirit, which is the Word of God," to accomplish whatever He has commanded. "And Moses took the Tabernacle and pitched it without the camp, and called it the Tabernacle of the congregation," or the "Tent of appointed meeting." And it came to pass that every one which *sought the Lord,* went out unto the Tabernacle of the congregation (Tent of appointed meeting) which was without the camp" (Exod. 33: 7). And thus it is, that all who seek the Lord, and hear the call of a rejected Christ, whose Name and claims have been dishonoured in what professes to be the church must "Go forth unto Him without the camp" gathering unto His Name alone, to hear His voice as the one shepherd of his flock, to own His claims over them individually and His authority and rule in the true assembly of God.

— *John Ritchie*

October 8

THEY ARE NOT OF THE WORLD, EVEN AS I AM NOT OF THE WORLD. — John 17: 16

The same words are found in v. 14, but in a different connection: there He was stating the chief reason why the world hated them; here He is advancing a reason *why* He asked the Father to keep them from evil — because "they are not of the world." *The truth of this verse applies in a sevenfold way: First,* Christians have a different *standing* from those who belong to the world: their standing is in Adam, ours in Christ; they are under condemnation, we "accepted in the beloved." *Second,* we possess a different *nature:* theirs is born of the flesh, ours "of the Spirit;" theirs is evil and corrupt, ours holy and Divine. *Third,* we serve a different *Master:* they are of their father the Devil, and the desires of their father they do; we serve the Lord Christ. *Fourth,* we have a different *aim:* theirs is to please self, ours to glorify God. *Fifth,* we have a different *citizenship:* theirs is on earth; ours in heaven. *Sixth,* we have a different *life:* far below the standard set before us it is true: nevertheless, no Christian (in the general tenor of his conduct) goes to the same excess of sin as does the worldling. *Seventh,* we have a different *destiny:* theirs is the Lake of Fire, ours is the Father's House on High. The "world" is a system built up away from God, and from it we have been taken, delivered, separated. *The Lord grant needed grace to us all that we may manifest this in our daily walk.*

— *A. W. Pink*

October 9

HE LEADETH ME IN THE RIGHT PATHS.
— Psalm 23: 3

James McConkey tells how he was once crossing a great glacier while on a sight-seeing trip in Switzerland. The path was extremely narrow and winding and seemingly filled with unnecessary detours. At one place especially it appeared as if the guide should have proceeded straight ahead, but instead he turned sharply and began to take a roundabout course. One man, evidently annoyed, resolved to take a shortcut, so he went straight ahead instead of following the leader. Immediately the guide rushed back, grasped him by the collar, and with no gentle hand dragged him back. Then he pointed to a patch of snow upon which the man had intended to walk. Instead of being a sure foothold, it was a mere crust of ice covering a great crevasse opening into the deep recesses of the glacier. *The shortcut would have ended in disaster.* Says McConkey, "A similar peril besets the believer's walk. Sometimes our Guide seems too slow for us ... and indeed seems to lead us by devious paths; but it pays us far better to take the detours *with* Him, than to take the shortcuts *without Him!*"

— *James A. Stewart*

October 10

COME! — Ezekiel 37: 9

Come, coals of fire, from altar flames
And purge a church in Satan's grip;
Come now as when in days of yore
You came and purged Isaiah's lip.

Bring us the prophet's glorious dream
Fulfilled in Zion clothed with pow'r
A church that dons her royal garb
To reign with Christ this glorious hour.

284

Come, breath of God, and breath on us,
Thy Church, a valley of dry bones
That needs must learn from Christ, her Head,
That she is more than builder's stones.

Come, oil of Heaven, that filled the lamps
Of those five virgins that were wise,
And give Thy church (while still she may)
The clarion call "Arise! Arise!"

— *Tucker A. Littleton*

October 11

I HAVE GLORIFIED THEE ON THE EARTH.
— John 17: 4

I conceive that these were the greatest words ever spoken here below, even by the Lord Jesus himself; and I am sure if we could enter into *all their fullness we should be convinced that this is true. Who can express them in their height, and depth, and length, and breadth?* "I have glorified Thee on the earth, My Father; I have, according to the good pleasure of Thy will, according to the riches of the glory of Thy grace, and according to the covenant engagements between Me and Thee, performed all that was in Thine heart, and all that Thou didst require of Me for the accomplishing of the salvation of Thy people given to Me. I have opened all Thine heart, I have expressed Thine eternal and everlasting love to poor sinners; I have manifested Thy faithfulness to Thy promises; I have displayed the riches of the grace Thou didst bestow on a lost world. I have come down from heaven to make known the holiness of Thy nature and Thine unspeakable gift; I have magnified the perfection of Thy law by descending from heaven to obey it. I have demonstrated Thy justice and Thine abhorrence of sin to the uttermost, for I am about to lay down My life upon

285

the cross to expiate it; I have revealed and displayed Thine infinite love, for Thou didst so love the world that Thou didst give Thine only begotten Son, that Thou mightest be just and the justifier of him that believeth in Jesus. This I have done; and all that remains to be done I am prepared to do and to fulfill to the uttermost. Look upon the Son of Thy right hand; upon the Son of Man whom Thou hast made strong for Thyself. Thou knowest Me, Father, that I am Thy fellow, Thou God of Hosts; Thou King of Saints; Thou knowest the honor I have done to Thy law by being born under it, and by My obedience unto death to expiate the guilt of those who transgressed against it; Thou knowest the preciousness of My blood — Thou knowest its eternal efficacy to put away sin; Thou knowest that I have more than vindicated the dishonor done to Thy name, Thy character, Thine attributes, and Thy will. I have glorified Thee on the earth; that earth so long a land of darkness to Thee — that earth so long in the hands of the usurper — that earth which has been so long arrayed in arms against Thee; I have glorified Thee here, and I will glorify Thee again."

— *Marcus Rainsford*

Oh heavenly Father! we thank Thee for the glorious way Thy dear Son glorified Thee here on earth. Help us also to glorify Thee in our lives. Amen!

October 12

AND THOU SHALT ANOINT AARON AND HIS SONS AND CONSECRATE THEM. — Exod. 30: 30

Aaron is a type of Christ and therefore Aaron's sons are types of believers. Aaron's sons were virtually anointed in the anointing of Aaron, and each member of the mystical body receives from the fullness of the Head HIS anointing.

286

All Levites descended from Aaron were priests by *birth;* but it was only after their consecration, as here set forth, that they could enter on the performance of the priestly office. So, all the children of God by faith in Christ are priests by birth, but do all as a royal priest-hood recognize and enjoy the privilege? Are we all a consecrated priesthood?

As "holy priests" we go inside the veil for sanctuary ministry. If there ever was a time in the history of the church of God when holy priests were needed, it is today. Oh, that God would give us praying Hydes once again!

Dr. Wilbur Chapman wrote to a friend, "I have learn-ed some great lessons concerning prayer. At one of our missions in England the audience was exceedingly small; but I received a note saying that an American missionary was going to pray God's blessing down upon our work. He was known as 'Praying Hyde.' Almost instantly the tide turned. The hall became packed and upon my first invitation, fifty men accepted Christ as Saviour.

"As we were leaving, I said, 'Mr. Hyde, I want you to pray for me.' He came into my room, turned the key in the door and dropped on his knees and waited five minutes without a single syllable coming from his lips. I could hear my own heart thumping and his beating. I felt the hot tears running down my face. I knew I was with God.

"Then, with upturned face, down which the tears were streaming, he said, 'Oh, God!' Then for five minutes at least he was still again; and then when he knew that he was talking with God there came up from the depths of his heart such petitions for men as I had never heard before. I arose from my knees to know what real prayer was. We believe that prayer is mighty and we believe it as we never did before."

I am sure that those of us who have witnessed revival in our ministry will agree that the sweetest and most pre-cious manifestations of God's power have been through the ministry of the "holy priests." How many of such priests have you in your church? If I saw 300,000 people at an evangelistic service in your city, I would not be so confident that revival was coming as I would be if I saw 5.000 believers at an early morning prayer meeting. Revival does not come by mass meetings; revival begins in the sanctuary.

— *James A. Stewart*

October 13

UPON MAN'S FLESH SHALL IT NOT BE POURED.

— Exodus 30: 32

It is a false gospel that promises sanctification and power for service apart from regeneration. The "stranger" in a typical sense is one who is unsaved — a stranger to God. A person must be born anew before he can receive the Holy Spirit. Only a true believer can be anointed with the heavenly oil.

"But the natural, non-spiritual man does not accept, or welcome, or admit into his heart the gifts and teachings and revelations of the Spirit of God, for they are folly (meaningless, nonsense) to him; and he is incapable of knowing them — of progressively recognizing, understanding and becoming better acquainted with them — because they are spiritually discerned and estimated and appreciated" (2 Cor. 2: 14, Amplified).

The Holy Spirit is never poured out upon man's nature. Much preaching which passes for the gospel is nothing more than good advice concerning the cultivation and improvement of the "old man." Much of the preaching today is only psychology propounded, completely ignoring the dark background of man's ruin. This is a false gospel. Calvary forever condemned the old Adamic nature lock-stock-and-barrel.

"For what was impossible by the law, in that it was weak through the flesh, God, sending His own Son in the likeness of sinful flesh, and concerning sin, *condemned sin in the flesh,* in order that the righteous requirements of the law might be fulfilled in us, who not according to the flesh (the old nature) we walk, but according to the Spirit" (Romans 8: 3—4, Rotherham).

No fruit of the Spirit has ever been produced on the barren soil of human nature.

— *James A. Stewart*

October 14

WHOSOEVER COMPOUNDETH ANYTHING LIKE IT... SHALL EVEN BE CUT OFF FROM HIS PEOPLE. — Exodus 30:33

God abhors imitations. When man in the energy of the flesh tries to imitate or substitute the human for the divine, it comes very near the sin of blasphemy against the Holy Spirit. *There is no substitute for the unction of the Spirit.* A person was immediately put to death under the old economy who sought to counterfeit or imitate the holy oil. God said "It shall be holy unto you."

In the Old Testament false prophets sought to imitate the true prophets of God, while in the New Testament false spirits seek to imitate the precious Holy Spirit.

Substituting human energy for the Spirit's might is one illustration of this sin. Even unknowingly a worker can labor in the energy of the flesh instead of under the anointing of the Spirit. How many times we have listened to a brother begin his message in the Spirit and finish in the flesh! How many times the whole spiritual atmosphere of a gathering has been changed through the soulish singing of a quartet or a choir! Many in their earnestness to win souls for Christ are ministering in the power of a soulish nature. Their ministry is eminating from the soul. That is why there are so many sham converts and false professions in our evangelistic meetings. THERE HAS BEEN A LARGE NUMBER OF PSYCHOLOGICAL CONVERSIONS.

The natural, unregenerated man cannot be argued, fascinated or enthused into accepting Christ as his Lord and Saviour. How dangerous, then, it is to move upon the people's emotions by our own emotions! *One of the easiest things in evangelistic meetings is to get people to make a decision for Christ without the convicting power of the Holy Ghost to regenerate.* Many are moved to "accept Chist" through the personality of the preacher or the moving strains of the music. I have known many audiences to weep over a death bed story who would not weep over the sufferings of Christ. How dangerous it is, then, for a Christian worker to "fling about" his personality! It is true that God puts "this treasure in earthen vessels" and uses sanctified instruments, but in the last analysis it is only the Holy Spirit Who can accomplish the miraculous work of God in regeneration.

— *James A. Stewart*

October 15

NEITHER GIVE PLACE TO THE DEVIL.
— Eph. 4: 27

Giving place to the Devil gives Satan headquarters in Christ's camp. It provides him a base from which to conduct his campaign. *Giving place to the devil* makes a part of Christ's army an ally of His arch-enemy, for the devil will not wrestle against himself. *Giving place to the devil* lessens the man power of the Lord's host and surrenders to Satan spiritual resources which belong only to the captain of our salvation. It compels Christ to go out to war handicapped. It weakens the warring powers of omnipotence. It diminishes the working force of the supernatural. *Giving place to the devil* divides allegiance and puts traitors and deserters into the army of the Lord.

So the devil is ceaselessly busy seeking to gain some place in the life of every Christian wrestler. He will start with a very small place, anything so long as he gains a foothold. He knows our weak spot. He comes up on our blind side. He breaks through where the crust is thinnest. He bides his time until he can take us unawares. He tempts at our most susceptible points. He works wilily, arch-deceiver that he is, to beguile us into making a league with him. To the truly spiritual warrior he comes most often as a veritable angel of light, even ensnaring some by claiming to be an envoy from God. He uses any method, however clever or cruel, to gain access and does his best to disguise his approach. What he seeks to gain is a "place" to begin his activities, that he may undermine the Christian warrior's morale and render him incapable of fighting.

— *Ruth Paxson*

October 16

OUR LIGHT AFFLICTION, WHICH IS BUT FOR A MOMENT, WORKETH FOR US A FAR MORE EXCEEDING AND ETERNAL WEIGHT OF GLORY.
— 2 Cor. 4: 17

Now the Apostle turns from the darker to the brighter side of the picture, from the debit to the credit side of the balance-sheet. Having mentioned the things that are *against* us, he comes to those that are *for* us.

First of all, in apposition to that grim word *affliction,* he sets down this alluring word *glory,* saying: "Affiction ... glory." HERE it is the sorrow, the trial, and the tears; THERE it is only *glory* transcending human conception. For "eye hath not seen, nor ear heard, neither have entered into the heart of man, the things which God hath prepared for them that love Him."

Glory! Who can define the full content of such a word? Approach it from any side and its grandeur overwhelms us; view it from any angle and its splendor dazzles us. Have we HERE tasted that the Lord is gracious? THERE His grace will be our food and drink! Have we HERE known His love even amid the trials, THERE we bask in its unclouded blaze, where trials cannot come! "NOW we see through a glass darkly" — that is grace; "but THEN, face to face" — that will be glory.

Again, Paul writes a second word qualifying glory. Says he — "a *weight* of glory," in marked contrast to the *light affliction.* Therefore, in describing the *glory,* he resorts to the very word which men are wont to apply to their afflictions. We speak of a *weight* of sorrow, of a *heavy* trial. But it is all reversed by the Apostle; the affliction is *light,* the glory *weighty.* To indicate something of that glory, he is driven to the antithesis of language, and what we predicate of our present burdens he predicts of our future glory. But still the idea is not forceful enough. While one epithet sufficed to measure the affliction, one alone fails to compute the glory. So he adds another phrase, saying — "a *far more exceeding* weight of glory." This is compound of two others he uses elsewhere — one rendered *out of measure* (2 Cor. 1: 8) and *more excellent* (12: 31); the other translated as *excellence* (4: 7) — which give us the word *hyperbole,* literally, "a throwing beyond." There is not merely "a weight of glory"; there is a *"more excellent excellence of weight,"* an *"unmeasured excellence* of weight." But is not that redundance of language? True, for there is abundance of glory! Its very immensity defies expression and beggars speech. It is being prepared "more and more exceedingly" (R. V.), "beyond all proportion" (Weymouth), "past all comparision" (Moffatt).

— R. D. Johnson

October 17

AND ETERNAL WEIGHT OF GLORY.

— 2 Cor. 4: 17

But now we reach another word — eternal. Concerning the affliction, the writer has declared that it is *but for a moment.* Bounds are set to the trial, limits appointed to what we are called to endure. Then are we to suppose the glory to be similarly limited? We rejoice that the affliction will end; we fear lest the glory ever should. But this new word is reassuring, for says Paul — "an *eternal* weight of glory." Ages will never exhaust it, enjoyment never wither it. It is boundless, inexhaustible, coextensive with Him Who declares: "I am the Lord; I change not." And that was what set J. H. Brown asinging when she wrote —

> One little hour for watching with the Master,
> Eternal years to walk with Him in white;
> One little hour to bravely meet disaster,
> Eternal years to reign with Him in light.
>
> One little hour to suffer scorn and losses,
> Eternal years beyond earth's cruel frowns;
> One little hour to carry heavy crosses,
> Eternal years to wear unfading crowns.
>
> One little hour for weary toils and trials,
> Eternal years for calm and peaceful rest;
> One little hour for patient self-denials,
> Eternal years of life where life is blest.

> — *R. D. Johnson*

October 18

AND CALL UPON ME IN THE DAY OF TROUBLE: I WILL DELIVER THEE, AND THOU SHALT GLORIFY ME. — Psalm 50: 15

Naturally we connect this verse with the closing words of the Psalm, "Whoso offereth praise glorifieth Me: and to him that ordereth his conversation aright will I shew the salvation of God." Or according to its other renderings; in the Variorum Version, "Whoso offereth praise glorifieth Me, and prepareth a way by which I will shew him the salvation of God;" and in Spurrell's translation "And such will I shew the way of God's salvation," while the Septuagint Version is "The sacrifice of praise will glorify Me, and that is the way wherein I will shew to him the salvation of God."

Each of these Versions agree in shewing that the praise here mentioned as glorifying God is not praise after the deliverance has been wrought, but praise beforehand; praise while we are yet in the day of trouble, and while yet there is no sign of deliverance from it. For it is "the *sacrifice* of praise" (Sept.); Spurrell also renders it "Whoso sacrificeth praise." And out of about sixteen Hebrew words translated *offer* in the Authorized Version this special word means to *slaughter or offer sacrifice.*

And so God knows that the praise costs, and in order to show us that He appreciates the full cost, in the law concerning the animal sacrificed for any man's burnt offering, the Lord spake unto Moses, saying, "the priest shall have to himself the skin of the burnt offering which he hath offered"; and thus would be made aware of the size of the animal offered and of its consequent cost to the offerer. Teaching us that our great High Priest fully knows all the cost of the praise which is offered to Him; and that He understands all that the day of trouble means to us, and all the suffering of waiting.

— *Alpha White*

October 19

THOU SHALT GLORIFY ME. — Psalm 50: 15

But there is another meaning hidden in the words "Thou shalt glorify Me;" something beside offering God praise. The Lord Jesus explained it when He said, "Herein is My Father glorified that ye bear much fruit." For the day of trouble has been permitted, or as it is in Hebrew "the day of straitness or distress," not only that we might praise God beforehand for deliverance, but that through our straitness and through our distress God might have much fruit. And so shall He be glorified. For just as abundant and choice fruit from the owner's vine must bring credit and satisfaction to himself and to the vine-dresser, so also much fruit from our lips and through our lives will bring glory to our Father who is the husbandman.

Fruit has a twofold meaning not only throughout the Word of God, but also in Greek where the word signifies both fruit and offspring. Then how wonderful is God's promise to us, "Thou shalt glorify Me;" glorify Him by bringing forth the fruit of the Spirit ourselves, as well as by the spiritual offspring of others blessed through our instrumentality; and not only fruit and offspring, but "much" fruit and "much" offspring!

So that the further meaning of *profit* or *gain* (which Souter gives for the Greek word *fruit)* comes to pass, and we bring our Master much gain. And lest we should doubt the possibility of our day of straitness and distress glorifying Him by bringing Him much profit, He Himself gives to us the promise, *"And thou shalt glorify Me."*

— *Alpha White*

October 20

I HEARD THE VOICE OF THE LORD SAYING, WHOM SHALL I SEND, AND WHO WILL GO FOR US? THEN SAID I, HERE AM I; SEND ME.

— Isaiah 6: 8

Life for Christ's missionary should be the continual providence of Christ. His love and His supply went with the Twelve when they were away from His side, and He accomplished as much for them as if He had been present. He guides my affairs. I do not see Him, but He is at the heart of things. With most familiar knowledge and most unerring love He reigns over me.

Life for Christ's missionary should be the explicit commandment of Christ. He sent the Twelve, as a Master does, as a King does. He was their absolute Owner. When He sends me, may I not loiter, or object, or question, but make haste. It is the one way to infuse unity into my history, to win peace for it, to clothe it with power.

Life for Christ's missionary should be the testing discipline of Christ. That excursion into the unknown without purse or scrip or shoes was not a path of roses. There was mystery in it. There was trial. It was a hazard. It was a sacrifice. So He trains me. Into the humility that is profound. Into the faith without abatement. Into the confidence that is certain of Him.

Life for Christ's missionary should be the enlarging knowledge of Christ. The disciples are being apprenticed for greater enterprises, and their experience will beget the assurance that theirs is an illimitable Lord. He has done vast things for me; and these are foretaste that He has still more to do. "And so, through all the length of days, Thy goodness faileth never."

— *Alexander Smellie*

October 21

THE WORD OF THE LORD CAME UNTO JONAH THE SECOND TIME. — Jonah 3: 1

I find comfort in the story of Jonah.

It speaks of the habit of GOD'S government. Men do not easily believe in me again, if I have disappointed them. "Do not let him come back to us," they say: "there will be doubt, hesitation, and pain." But GOD bears and forbears with David, Elijah, John the Baptist, Peter, John, Mark, Jonah. He commits to me anew the work I have abandoned cravenly and sinfully.

It speaks of the wideness of GOD'S mercy. He is aware of Jonah's sin, and hates it altogether. Therefore it is mercy, pure, undeserved, extraordinary, divine, which restores him to the ranks of the spokesmen of the Lord. He knows the worst of me. He abhors my unfaithfulness as no angel and no saint abhors it. It is marvellous that He forgives me.

It speaks of the abundance of GOD'S faith. He does not despair of the recreant's recovery. He does not dismiss me from His service. So, while there is to be godly sorrow on my part, there should be no despondency. "If thou wilt truly grieve for thy sin," said Luther, "have a care that thou thinkest far more on thy future life than on thy past." It is what GOD does, and I am wise when I follow His example.

It speaks of the riches of GOD'S power. By and by He will enable Jonah to rise above his natural fears, and to combat every difficulty, and to endure to the end. By the infilling of His Own Spirit, GOD changes my feebleness into His fortitude, my folly into His wisdom, and my sin into His holiness. He raises me up, He keeps me strong, as I accept and rejoice in His power.

— *Alexander Smellie*

October 22

AND THEY WERE ALL AMAZED AND MARVELLED. — Acts 2: 7

The church always fails at the point of self-confidence. When the church is run on the lines of a circus, there may be crowds; but there can be no Shekinah. Miracles are the direct work of His power and without miracles the church cannot survive. *The root trouble in the present distress is that the church has more faith in the carnal methods of the world than in the power of Pentecost.* Our great church programs and mass evangelistic campaigns are usually along the lines of sound business organization and promotion. Hollywood evangelism and Madison Avenue advertising were entirely absent from the ministry of the apostles Peter and Paul. *All worldly methods of promotion and propaganda are a direct insult to the Spirit of God Himself.* As Samuel Chadwick has stated so eloquently: "Worship is idolatry until He inspires. Preaching is powerless if it be not a demonstration of His power. Prayer is vain unless He energizes it. Human resources of learning, organization, wealth, and enthusiasm are less than useless if there be no Holy Spirit in them."

It was the miraculous inside the church that aroused the interest of the unsaved without.

Oh, my brother, my sister, never forget that the natural can never accomplish the supernatural. Only spiritual people can be the stones of a spiritual house and only Spirit-filled people its priests (1 Pet. 2: 9).

Having been so long used to the natural, one wonders if we are prepared for the supernatural. I am convinced that the average evangelical church would feel that it had been hit by a spiritual cyclone if the Holy Spirit were allowed to come in to perform His mighty works. How easy it is to pray and talk glibly about revival, but it is another matter to be prepared for the consequences of such a visitation.

— *James A. Stewart*

October 23

HE THAT SPARED NOT HIS OWN SON, BUT DELIVERED HIM UP FOR US ALL, HOW SHALL HE NOT WITH HIM ALSO FREELY GIVE US ALL THINGS? — Rom. 8: 32

If this is not a promise in form, it is in fact. Indeed, it is more than one promise, it is a conglomerate of promises. It is a mass of rubies, and emeralds, and diamonds, with a nugget of gold for their setting. It is a question which can never be answered so as to cause us any anxiety of heart. What can the Lord deny us after giving us Jesus? If we need all things in Heaven and earth, He

298

will grant them to us: for if there had been a limit any-where, He would have kept back His own Son.

What do I want today? I have only to ask for it. I may seek earnestly, but not as if I had to use pressure, and extort an unwilling gift from the Lord's hand; for He will give *freely.* Of His own will, He gave us His own Son. Certainly no one would have proposed such a gift to Him. No one would have ventured to ask for it. It would have been too presumptuus. He freely gave His Only-begotten; and, *O my soul, canst thou not trust thy heavenly Father to give thee anything, to give thee everything?* Thy poor prayer would have no force with Omnipotence if force were needed; but His love, like a spring, rises of itself, and overflows for the supply of all thy needs.

— *C. H. Spurgeon*

Oh the boundless love of my heavenly Father!

October 24

SPEAK; FOR THY SERVANT HEARETH.
— 1 Samuel 3: 10

Speak, Lord, in the stillness,
While I wait on Thee;
Hush'd my heart to listen,
In expectancy.

Speak, O blessed Master,
In this quiet hour;
Let me see Thy face, Lord,
Feel Thy touch of power.

For the words Thou speakest,
They are life indeed;
Living bread from heaven,
Now my spirit feed!

All to Thee is yielded,
I am not my own;
Blissful, glad surrender,
I am Thine alone.

Speak, Thy servant heareth,
Be not silent, Lord;
Waits my soul upon Thee
For the quickening word.

Fill me with the knowledge
Of Thy glorious will;
All Thine own good pleasure
In Thy child fulfil.

Like a watered garden,
Full of fragrance rare,
Lingering in Thy presence,
Let my life appear.

— *E. M. Grimes*

October 25

HAVING LOVED HIS OWN WHICH WERE IN THE WORLD, HE LOVED THEM TO THE UTTERMOST. — John 13: 1, Margin

But do we love the breathren to the uttermost? Do we love them to the very end? Love never takes up an attitude of isolation. Love cannot isolate itself. Love must include everybody. The Lord Jesus taught us to say: "Our Father, which art in heaven, hallowed be Thy name." He did not say: "My Father" but "Our Father." We who have been redeemed by the precious blood of the Lord Jesus may not belong to the same denomination, but let us love one another.

It is so easy to profess holiness without manifesting love. According to God's Word, holiness is the most beautiful thing on earth. Christ said: "Be ye holy, for I am holy." Holiness is of the Lord.

Two hermits lived in the desert so that they might get away from man and worship the Lord. They loved only each other and the Lord. One day, one of the hermits said: "Let's have some fun! Let's start quarrelling with each other the way the world does, and the way the other Christian people do!" The other hermit agreed and picked up a stone, saying: "That's my stone!" The first brother said: "No, no, that's my stone!" Then his companion said: "No, I said, that's my stone!" And so the other hermit answered back: "Oh, well, you can take it!" They loved each other so much that they could not quarrel. Would to God that we had that spirit today!

There is a story of an early Christian who was going to the scaffold to die for his faith in the Lord Jesus. A poor brother came weeping and pleading for his forgiveness, saying: "Please forgive me, my brother! I have wronged you, I know, but please forgive me!" The martyr brushed his poor brother to one side and went to the scaffold and died. *But the early Church refused to inscribe his name among the heroes and the martyrs because he was so unloving.* Of what use is it today if we are great and mighty and yet have not love? Oh, may God give us that wonderful love of His toward each other, for the fruit of the Spirit is love.

— *James A. Stewart*

October 26

BEING THEN MADE FREE FROM SIN.

— Rom. 6: 18

The expression *"in Christ"* refers sometimes to what *we are to be practically.* There is the "in Christ" of standing, and the "in Christ" of fellowship. The second springs out of the first. When our Lord says, "Abide in

Me," He plainly refers to the practical aspect of the truth. To be "in Christ" in this sense is not only security, acceptance, completeness; it is power, the secret of victory over sin, of joy and gladness of heart, as well as of fruitfulness.

The duty and privilege of the believer is to enter into God's reckoning in reference to his present relation to his old master sin. Perhaps there is no chapter in the whole Bible that he should prayerfully meditate upon more than the sixth of Romans. It is there that he sees the truth brought out by the two prepositions, "with" and "in," in connection with the death and resurrection of the Lord Jesus Christ. In the fifth chapter the prominent thought is justification, — Christ *for* us, but in the sixth we have that which is the groundwork and true starting-point of sanctification—IDENTIFICATION AND UNION WITH CHRIST.

"Sin shall not have dominion over you." The believer may confidently expect this to be realised in his daily life, as one of the fruits of Christ's death. Every foe that can possibly assail him, Christ has already met and vanquished. It is a grand step in the service of God when we see this. Expectation of victory is the true attitude of those who belong to the Risen Christ. "He is *able to save* them to the *uttermost* that come unto God by Him, seeing He ever liveth to make intercession for them."

As the believer is taught in God's Word that sin is not only a debt which needs to be discharged, but a master from whom he must be set free, so he is taught that through Christ's death there is secured, not only the payment of the one, but also the deliverance from the other. And it is *"being* made free from sin" — not from its guilt alone, but from its power, as the context clearly shows (Rom. 6: 18) — that the believer becomes the servant of righteousness. He leaves the service of the old master — sin — and enters into the new service of righteousness. This was one of the great designs of Christ's death, and of the crucifixion of "our old man with Him, that *henceforth*," from this time forward, "we should not serve sin." And by faith the believer receiving this blessing, blesses God that the law of the Spirit of life in Christ Jesus *hath* made him *free* from the law of sin and death. *Deliverance from the dominion of sin, then, is not the end of holiness, but the true commencement of a life of progressive sanctification.*

— *A. J. Gordon*

October 27

BELIEVE ON THE LORD JESUS CHRIST AND THOU SHALT BE SAVED. — Acts 16: 31

Why You Should Believe

There are lots of things you don't understand that you nevertheless believe.

Supposing I could transform this audience into a clinic and I had a dead body on the table for my subject. I bring on the scalpel; I make an incision and remove two pinkish threads and hold them up. They are just alike in form, shape and colour, and the most powerful magnifying glass could not distinguish one iota of difference. One is the nerve of sight and the other the nerve of hearing.

Can you explain how it is that one nerve will take up the sounds of everyday life and through your ears portray them upon your brain, notes of harmony and discord, so that you can tell whether it is the barking of a dog, the blow of a whistle, the cry of a child? Can you explain how it is that the other nerve will take up that which is absolutely imperceptible to the former nerve and through the retina of the eyes paint on your brain the picture of nature so that you can revel in its beauties? Do you understand it? No. Do you believe it? You have to, or acknowledge that you are a fool. *Yes, there are lots of things you believe but you don't understand. Then don't go to hell because you haven't sense enough to understand all there is in the Bible. There are lots of things you don't understand.* — *Billy Sunday*

October 28

IT IS EXPEDIENT FOR YOU THAT I GO AWAY.

— John 16: 7

"But why should the Saviour go away?" was surely the thought in the hearts of His disciples, "Why could He not stay with us and do these things for us?" Seeing them still perplexed, their Lord says to them, "It is expedient for you that I go away." How startling and strange must these words have seemed as they fell upon the ears of the already baffled disciples. How could it be expedient or profitable for them? What could be more glorious than the actual earthly presence of their Master?

> My Saviour, can it ever be
> That I should gain by losing Thee?

"It is to your advantage that I go away" (Weymouth), said the Saviour. The Lord Jesus Christ, in human flesh, could only be in one place at a time. We remember how the beloved sister cried in sorrow, "Lord, if thou hadst been here, my brother had not died." But now, by the Spirit, the Lord Jesus Christ is present everywhere. "For where two or three are gathered together in My Name, there am I in the midst of them." Christ, in outward companionship, could not be so much to them, nor do so much for them, as He would through intimate communion with them by the Spirit, after His saving work was accomplished.

It was not only to their advantage that the Saviour should go back to the Father, via Calvary, but it was also necessary. In this connection the words of John 7: 39 are illuminating, "The Holy Ghost was not yet given; because that Jesus was not yet glorified."

Until Christ's earthly work had been accomplished, the Spirit's work could not begin. The office of the Spirit is to communicate Christ to us in His entireness. Without the expiatory work of Christ for us, the sanctifying work

304

of the Spirit in us would be impossible. The redemptive work of Christ is the basis of all the operations of the Spirit. There could be no Pentecost had there been no Calvary.

— *James A. Stewart*

October 29

HUSBANDS LOVE YOUR WIVES.

— Eph. 5: 25

If we are truly crucified; redeemed from the tyranny of our own life, and from the ground of sin, it will go on in concentrated circles from victory to victory, and from glory to glory. The closest sphere is that of the family; in the relation of man and wife, parent and child. These are domains where one can see clearly how dominon and love dovetail one into the other; I can only love where I can rule, overcoming evil with good. In course of time every husband will see in his wife, and every wife will see in her husband, something which must be overcome. First of all, then, the husband has to rule; but this rule consists in his being grounded in exactly the opposite from what is generally considered to be his prerogative. True Divine rule is such as Jesus, the Head of the Church, exercises. He has given His life for the Church, that He may kindle in her a reciprocal love, which yields to Him. When, therefore — to begin with the nearest, most intimate circle — a husband discovers in his wife that which is not Divine, it is for him to overcome it, in so far that his love for her is in no way lessened by it, but, on the contrary, stronger and more intense. True love sacrifices itself, and thereby the ties between the husband who rules in love, and the wife who obeys in love, become sanctified, and the Christ-like house becomes a centre from which love shines out beyond.

— *Stockmayer*

True Christianity begins in the home.

HE ALSO DID PREDESTINATE TO BE CONFORMED TO THE IMAGE OF HIS SON.

— Rom. 8: 29

Why delivered? That, as redeemed, we may be able to stand still in the sanctuary, to study the traits of Christ's character until those old traits in our character disappear, and the glory of the image of Christ becomes more and more clearly apparent in us. For this purpose we are here on earth, that from thousands of individuals the image of Christ should be reflected. In these thousands, and ten thousands, nothing must be left which does not bear the impress of Christ, for whatsoever does not bear this mark is displeasing to God, and cannot become His sanctuary.

You know how in Rom. 8: 29, God by an eternal calling, has foreordained such as are to be conformed to the image of His Son. One to whom this Scripture has been enlightened can never forget it again, and in comparison with this marvellous thing, "My God has foreordained me to be conformed to the image of His Son," all else is worthless. If God makes the image of Christ become living to us, we see in this calling a citizenship, a right of privilege. *If thy heart is drawn out to the Crucified One, if this Man of the Cross awakens something in thee, KNOW that this is the best proof that God has predestinated thee from eternity to be conformed to the image of His Son.* This is the practical explanation of predestination.

— *Stockmayer*

HE PERFORMETH THE THING THAT IS APPOINTED FOR ME. — Job 23:14

"Disappointment—His *appointment*,"
  Change one letter, then I see
That the thwarting of my purpose
  Is God's better choice for me.
His appointment must be blessing,
  Tho' it may come in disguise,
For the end from the beginning
  Open to His wisdom lies.

"Disappointment—His *appointment*,"
  Whose? The Lord, who loves me best,
Understands and knows me fully,
  Who my faith and love would test;
For, like loving earthly parent,
  He rejoices when He knows
That His child accepts, UNQUESTIONED,
  All that from His wisdom flows.

"Disappointment—His *appointment*,"
  "No good thing will He withhold,"
From denials oft we gather
  Treasures of His love untold.
Well He knows each broken purpose
  Leads to fuller, deeper trust,
And the end of all His dealings
  Proves our God is wise and just.

"Disappointment—His *appointment*,"
  Lord, I take it, then, as such.
Like the clay in hands of potter,
  Yielding wholly to Thy touch.
All my life's plan is Thy moulding,
  Not one single choice be mine;
Let me answer, unrepining—
  Father, "Not my will, but Thine."

                              — *Edith Lillian Young*

November 1

I DO ALWAYS THOSE THINGS WHICH PLEASE THE FATHER. — John 8: 29

"I do always the things that please Him," our Lord said on one occasion, *laying bare for a moment all His life. It is only by an effort that we can realise the tremendous avowal which breathes in these words.* Thought and imagination, emotion and desire, impulse and purpose, all are wrapped up in this overwhelming affirmation: in every pulse, in every breath that sinless nature maintained *an undisturbed correspondence with God.* It was our Saviour's meat and drink to do His Father's will; it was His rest and home, His joy and heaven. The accomplishment of the divine purpose was the exhilaration of that humble and patient spirit which moved with unhesitating progress from the waters of repentance to the baptism of blood.

This, apparently, is the meaning of our Saviour's words: "I sanctify Myself." In the eternal life of the Godhead the Father had sanctified Him, setting Him apart and appointing Him to His mission of mercy (John 10. 36); and in the fulness of the time He came to sanctify Himself for His baptism of fire, and to learn obedience by the things which He suffered.

We must not for one moment think that there was any stain of sin in Him. He was holy, harmless, undefiled, separate from sinners. And although it behoved Him to be made in all things like unto His brethren, there was between Him and us the absolute distinction of sinlessness as opposed to inbred and indulged sin.

— *D. M. Mc Intyre*

May I follow my Lord's example and sanctify myself to do the Father's will!

November 2

NOW MINE EYE SEETH THEE. — Job 42: 5

*When we hold ourselves in the light of the divine
countenance, we are judged. We sist ourselves before the
tribunal of the Holy One, we examine our actions, we
try our motives, we scrutinise our purposes in that solemn
splendour which fills the judgment throne.* It was a
frequent interrogation which Bernard of Clairvaux was
accustomed to address to himself, "Bernard, what doest
thou here?" The useful practice of self-examination has
sometimes been carried to a hurtful excess, but it is
almost a necessity of the Christian life. If we cease to
practise it, we shall find that our walk with God will
become insensibly less intimate. Sin will be undetected
and therefore indulged; prayer will be restrained and
grace be hindered.

*The continual elevation of our mind to God will
reveal to our astonished view a multitude of hitherto
unsuspected sins, and will display to our own deep
consternation the plague of our own hearts.* Thomas
Shepard notes in his "Meditations and Experiences," "I
had no sense of sin, because I had no sense of God."
It was when Isaiah saw the Lord sitting upon a throne,
high and lifted up, that he confessed and bewailed the
uncleanness of his lips. It was when Abraham drew
near to God in intercession that he exclaimed, "I . . . am
but dust and ashes." It was when Job saw the glory of
his Redeemer that he cried, "Now mine eye seeth Thee,
wherefore I abhor myself and repent." It was when
the beloved disciple saw the risen Saviour in his kingly
beauty that he fell at His feet as dead.

— D. M. McIntyre

November 3

THOU ART MY BELOVED SON. — Luke 3: 22

When our Lord began to be about thirty years of age, He received the investiture of priesthood, and was anointed with the Holy Ghost. As He was praying, the Spirit fell upon Him — "And lo, a voice out of the heavens, saying, This is my beloved Son, in whom I am well pleased." The thirty years of silence during which our Lord had kept Himself unspotted from the world and had succoured the fatherless and widows in their affliction were accepted. The divine scrutiny, which pierced to the dividing asunder of soul and spirit, searched in all His years of childhood, youth, and manhood, and found no thought, no desire, no utterance, no act that had been stained in the tincture of sin. *In the blameless Lamb of God there was found neither spot nor blemish.*

After six days of prayer in the neighbourhood of Cæsarea Philippi, our Saviour climbed one of the spurs of Hermon, and there anew affirmed in loving obedience His will to die. For months, perhaps for years, the cross had been in sight, and the Divine Sacrifice now said, "Lo, I am come! . . . I delight to do Thy will, O my God." The disciples prayed, then fell asleep, but the Lord watched hour after hour beneath the stars. As He bowed in intercession, the glory of the Presence clothed Him as with a garment, and the eternal light laid bare the inmost recesses of His spirit. Not now the thirty years of seclusion alone, but also the days of His public ministry, pressed and full with saving words and healing acts, were discovered and approved. *And while the Lamb of God offered Himself to be a sacrifice, the Father, as High Priest of the Passion, affixed the broad seal of acceptance on a life without a flaw, on words of truth without admixture, on gracious deeds without rebuke* (John 6: 27; Matt. 17: 5). — *D. M. Mc Intyre*

Wonder of wonders. We are accepted in Him.

— Eph. 1: 5.

310

November 4

PUT OFF ... Eph. 4: 22
PUT ON ... Eph. 4: 22

The initial act of our baptism into the death of Christ (Rom. 6: 3) introduces us into a state which must be sedulously maintained. Watchfulness, prayer, and self-denial are the means by which this persistence in death with Christ may be secured. The main efficiency, however, is renunciation. This is sometimes called, though with an inexact use of terms, "dying to self."

The will of God to which "self" opposes itself is love. The direction of our self-discipline, therefore, is to be the strengthening of love, in thought and word and act. No injurious suspicion is to be admitted into the mind, no ungenerous word may pass the lips, no inconsiderate act is to be allowed. All "touchiness" or morbid sensitiveness, all vanity and vain-glory, arrogance and self-elation, un-Christlike ambition, emulation and pride, are to be put away. "A new commandment I give unto you, that ye love one another; even as I have loved you, that ye also love one another" (John 13: 34).

Christianity is positive; its negations lead to attainment. Detachment implies attachment; restraint secures enlargement; renunciation involves possession. When we put off the old man with his affections and desires, we put on Christ with all His excellences — "a heart of compassion, kindness, humility, meeknees, long-suffering." The secure way by which we shall accomplish the denial of the self-life is, that we dwell in the love of God.

— *D. M. Mc Intyre*

November 5

BE YE HOLY. — 1 Pet. 1: 16

The earliest historical reference to holiness is in the 3rd chapter of Exodus. The uncreated fire glows in a thorn bush and the Midianitish shepherd who draws near to see that great sight is startled to hear the voice

311

of God calling him across the desert heath. "Draw not nigh thither; put off thy shoes from off thy feet, for the place whereon thou standest is holy ground." A patch of coarse sand, thinly sprinkled with acacia shrubs, becomes a place of holiness by reason of the presence of the holy One of Israel.

And from that first hint of the covenant relation so soon to be established between Jehovah and the people of His holiness, the broad arrow of the King is stamped on everything which is brought near to Him in worship or in sacrifice. The tabernacle is holy, the priesthood is holy, the altar is most holy, whatsoever toucheth the altar shall be holiness. The covenant appellation of Jehovah is "the Holy One of Israel," the official title of the promised Messiah is "the Holy One of God." The "thrice holy" of the seraphim (Isa. 6: 3) awakens the response of the covenant song with its triple refrain, "Holy is He" (Ps. 49). And the birth of the Forerunner is greeted with the *Benedictus,* charged with the recollection of holy prophets, the holy covenant, and the holy people (Luke 1: 70, 72, 75).

In the New Testament, as in the Old, the people of God are "called to be saints." The covenant engagement is as before, though now with a deeper significance, "Be ye holy, for I am holy" (1 Pet. 1: 16). "Holy Father ... make them holy" is the prayer of the great High Priest (John 17: 11, 17). *The whole work of redemption has this for its end, that they who believe "may be sanctified in truth."* The will of God is the sanctification of His people, and all the energies of grace are designed "to the end He may establish your hearts unblameable in holiness before our God and Father, at the coming of our Lord Jesus with all His saints" (1 Thess. 3: 13). And almost the last words of that book, which for us seals the canon of Scripture, are, "He that is holy, let him be holy still" — holy yet more and more, for ever (Rev. 22: 11). — *Evan Hopkins*

Take the shoes from off thy feet!

312

November 6

THAT MY JOY MIGHT REMAIN IN YOU.

— John 15: 11

On that "dark betrayal night" our Saviour said to His disciples, "These things have I spoken unto you, that My joy may be in you, and that your joy may be fulfilled" (John 15: 11). *The words occasioned no surprise to the disciples; they knew that their Lord was the happiest man in Jerusalem, and they had often said one to another that the sentence of the Psalmist had been fulfilled in Him,* "God, Thy God, hath anointed Thee with the oil of gladness above Thy fellows." *And yet they might have had some questioning of mind as He said, "My joy," then.* For only a little while before the Saviour had revealed the distress of His spirit (John 13: 21); and in a few moments more He was to go out to His agony in Gethsemane. That anguish was to be followed by the shame of the arrest, the buffeting and evil-questioning of the High Priest's palace, the scourging and contumely of Gabbatha, and the lone darkness of the cross. But facing all this sea of sorrow, He calmly testified to His joy in God, and bequeathed that holy gladness to His friends. *Now, where a testament is, there must be of necessity the death of the testator. And it is by the action of His dying that our dear Lord is able to confer upon His followers the grace of gladness.* By His death and resurrection, by His ascension and reception of the promise of the Father, He conveys the spiritual energy of His own victorious life to all the children of faith. "Do not refuse joy from the Man of Sorrows," said one whose life bore eloquent testimony to his words, "for He gained it by His suffering." Joy is a grace; that is to say, it is a gift from the hand that was pierced. Gladness is ours, if we do but receive it. It is ours, as we say, "for the taking."

The joy which Christ confers upon His people is a gladness that has surmounted sorrow. It has passed through a darkness deeper than the midnight of our despair, and the darkness has changed to light. It has gone down into the bitterest water of our death, and has maintained its footing among the fierce floods, saying, "I feel the bottom, and it is good." It is victorious joy.

— *D. M. McIntyre*

November 7

"And of the rest of the oil that is in his hand shall the priest put upon the tip of the right ear of him that is to be cleansed, and upon the thumb of his right hand, and upon the great toe of his right foot, and upon the blood of the trespass offering" (Lev. 14: 17).

Having first put the blood of the trespass offering upon the ear of the cleansed leper, the priest was to put "upon the blood" the consecrated oil also. First came the blood of the atonement, then the oil of consecration.

The application of the blood upon the leper signifies that the whole body has been completely redeemed by the blood of Christ. The anointing of the leper signifies that the whole body must be fully sanctified for God's use alone.

1. The ear that was once charmed by the world is now charmed by the voice of the Beloved.

2. The hands once used in the service of Satan are now used in the service of the Lord.

3. The feet that ran in the way of unrighteusness now keep in step with Christ.

The saintly Andrew A. Bonar in his Commentary on Leviticus comments sweetly upon the anointing of the leper:

"The oil is put on the man's ear: 'Lord, I will hear for Thee.'

And on his right hand: — 'Lord, I will act for Thee.'

314

And on his right foot: — 'Lord, I will walk up and down for Thee.'

"The priest then pours all that remains of the oil upon his head that as it runs down in copious streams over all his person, *he might hear every drop saying, "Thou art His that saves thee'."*

Are you listening to the voice of the Spirit?

Are you working in the power of the Spirit?

Are you walking in the ways of the Spirit?

— *James A. Stewart*

November 8

ENTER INTO THY CLOSET. — Matt. 6: 6

Within "The Prayer of Silence" there is that secret and almost uninterrupted communion with the Father which may not improperly be described as "prayer without ceasing." When the human spirit persistently holds itself in the light of the divine countenance the thoughts and affections, whenever they are set at liberty, spontaneously centre on God. Every difficulty generates an appeal for help, every mercy excites an outburst of praise, every remembrance of the divine holiness awakens adoration. A stream of prayer, unmarked by those who stand by, and not clearly discerned even by the suppliant, lifts itself heavenward as an altar-flame. This continual engagement of the soul, while it re-acts upon the general direction of the mind towards God and gives to it stability, creates on the other hand an insistent demand for quiet spaces in the busiest life, spaces emptied of every secular task, that they may be occupied with the intercourse of prayer.

— *D. M. McIntyre*

315

November 9

TWO TRUMPETS OF SILVER. — Num. 10: 2

Two trumpets of silver we plead for this hour,
All beaten and fashioned in thy blessed power,
Oh Spirit divine from one piece make them all,
Endued with thy power to sound out thy call.

Oh Spirit sound out the alarm 'cross the land
Awaken, awaken our Lord's Holy Band,
So long they've not heard the sound of alarm,
Blow the Trump'ts clear to awaken from harm.

Send the 'larm sharply to hearts oh I pray,
Christ's people are sleeping, sleeping today,
Again I do plead my Heavenly Guide,
Two trumpets of silver to sound out for lives.

Burnished and molded in careful design,
Lest the call falter and Christ's people die,
Oh hear precious Spirit, two trumpets I plead,
Two trumpets of silver — This is our need.

— *Gail Horton*

November 10

EPAPHRODITUS ... FOR THE WORK OF CHRIST
HE WAS NIGH UNTO DEATH, NOT REGARDING
HIS LIFE. — Phil. 2: 25—30

The Scriptures tell us that Epaphroditus hazarded his life for Christ. All we know about him is derived from two passages in the letter he himself carried from Rome to Philippi. He is one of those brave souls who is brought from the depths of obscurity in connection with the imprisonment of Paul. He, for a fleeting moment, passes across the stage of apostolic history and leaves his name

316

forever enshrined in that mighty roll of men and women who risked their lives for the sake of the gospel.

The apostle uses one of his bold metaphors to express the service and spirit of his friend:

"He hazarded his life." (Weymouth)

"He set his own life at stake in his single-handed efforts." (Way)

The traveled veteran Roman soldier adopted the custom of the Greek soldiers who shouted when they won high stakes "by Aphrodite!" (Now Aphrodite was among the Greeks the goddess of gambling.) In Greek the expression would be *Epaphroditos*. Surely this expression was dinned into the ears of Paul day and night in connection with the gambling which went on around him. Now when he would write about his friend, he coins the expression from the barrack room and exclaims, "Epaphroditus, the gambler for the Lord. He risked his life and almost lost it for the sake of Christ and the gospel." Or, as in the more ancient Latin version the Greek is transliterated, *"He played desperado with his life."* Hallelujah, for such a spirit who staked his life and staked it recklessly in the service of his Master!

It is not difficult to imagine the ways in which this "desperado" risked his life. There was the long, tedious, dangerous journey from Philippi to Rome. There was the day and night ministering to Paul's needs as he became proxy for the whole assembly in Phillipi. In a thousand and one ways he eased the chafing of the aching wrists and made the apostle's chains less painful to bear. It may be he lost his health in his constant labors to win souls for Christ in the great metropolis. Possibly, he contracted that painful disease, malarial fever, from which many suffered in that day. Whatever it was, Paul says, "He was nigh unto death"; and it was because of his reckless devotion to Christ.

— *James A. Stewart*

317

Many sit at Jesus' table;
Few will fast with Him,
When the sorrow-cup of anguish
Trembles at the brim.
Few watch with Him in the garden
Who have sung the hymn.
But the souls who love supremely,
Let woe come, or bliss,
These will count their dearest heart's blood
Not their own but His.
Saviour, Thou Who thus hast loved me
Give me love like this!

November 11

A LITTLE LEAVEN LEAVENETH THE WHOLE LUMP. — 1 Cor. 5: 6

How small a temptation may cause a saint to have a great fall. The beginning of Peter's trial was nothing more than the simple remark of "a maid of the High Priest." "Thou also wert with Jesus of Nazareth." There is nothing to show that these words were spoken with any hostile purpose. For anything we can see, they might fairly mean that this maid remembered that Peter used to be a companion of our Lord. But this simple remark was enough to overthrow the faith of an eminent apostle, and to make him begin to deny his Master. The chiefest and foremost of our Lord's chosen disciples is cast down, not by the threats of armed men, but by the saying of one weak woman!

There is something deeply instructive in this fact. It ought to teach us that no temptation is too small and trifling to overcome us, except we watch and pray to be held up. If God be for us we may remove mountains and get the victory over a host of foes. "I can do all things," says Paul, "through Christ that strengtheneth me." (Phil. 4: 22.) If God withdraw His grace, and leave

318

us to ourselves, we are like a city without gates and walls, a prey to the first enemy, however weak and contemptible.

Let us beware of making light of temptations because they seem little and insignificant. There is nothing little that concerns our souls. A little leaven leaveneth the whole lump. A little spark may kindle a great fire. A little leak may sink a great ship. A little provocation may bring out from our hearts great corruption, and end in bringing our souls into great trouble.

— J. C. Ryle

November 12

TO KNOW THE LOVE OF CHRIST. — Eph. 3: 19

What the song of Solomon is to the Old Testament, that the Epistle to the Ephesians is to the New. It is the fragrant love letter of God to His children, and one of the key-words of the epistle is the word love. The apostle had not gone far into the epistle before, in the first chapter and the sixth verse, he speaks of "the beloved." That is the position in which our Savour stands to His Father. But in four other places he *discriminates* the various shades of the love of Christ to us, for we speak now of "the love of Christ that passeth knowledge." In the first chapter and in the fifth verse, adopting for a moment the possible rendering of the margin of the Revised Version, we have the love of Christ shown to us in foreordination. In the second chapter and in the fifth verse, the love of Christ is shown in His identification with us. In the fifth chapter and second verse the love of Christ is shown in His bloodshedding, and in that same fifth chapter and twentyfifth verse the love of Christ is shown as the Bridegroom and the Husband of the soul. The love that is deathless as His own love; the love that dared to stand together with us before the gaze of all worlds; the love that stooped to redeem us by the gift of blood; and the love of which the strongest, deepest love that ever man had to woman is as the glowworm torch compared to the sun in its meridian strength. *I want to focus my text. It will be of very little service to thee, and thee, and thee, oh! soul, shouldest thou leave this place with a vague intellectual knowledge of that love.* I would that thou shouldest hear the Bridegroom say to thee, "I love thee." That there may be a definite apprehension on the part of all. For there is as much love for each as though there were no other being in heaven or upon earth to share the love of Christ with thee. "Thou art as much His care as if beside no man nor angel lived in heaven or earth." It is not at all wonderful, therefore, to be told in the text that the love of Christ passeth knowledge, or, as I suppose the Greek might be rendered, passeth limit. It is illimitable. *The love of Christ to thee, and me, and each, is illimitable.* The whole wealth of Christ's heart, the infinite wealth of Christ's infinite heart, is thine to-night as though the sun should shine to light one firefly, or the Amazon flow to water the roots of one daisy. Jesus Christ, who combines the sympathy and tenderness of man with infinite capacity of God, loves the lowly, weary, sinning, worthless soul with all His force and gentleness and strength. *It passes knowledge, and yet we may know it.* That is the divine paradox.

— *F. B. Meyer*

November 13

BUT YE ARE KINGLY PRIESTS.

— 1 Pet. 2: 9, Darby

For the ministry we also need the unction of the Spirit. At the inauguration of Christ's official ministry, the Holy Spirit descended upon Him in a sacred anointing for His mediatorial work as Prophet, Priest and King. Basic passages taken up with this special ministry of the Spirit are Matt. 3: 16, 12: 18; Acts 4: 27—30 and 10: 38. *One* of the most profound mysteries of the New Testament is that Christ needed to be anointed by the Spirit. If our Redeemer could not begin His outward public ministry without this anointing, then how can we be so presumptuous as to think that we can accomplish anything that will stand the scrutiny of Christ's judgment seat if we ignore this anointing?

Imagine, if you can, a priest attempting to minister before the Lord and daring to touch the holy things of the sanctuary without having first of all been sprinkled with the holy anointing oil! God was so jealous for the sanctity of those who had been anointed for service that the penalty for failing to wash the hands and the feet when they ministered before the Lord was death! (Exodus 30: 19—21).

What then, think you, but death in its most awful form must have been the penalty of such presumption as that which we have suggested? *This anointing was the outward, visible sign of the impartation to the priests of those gifts and graces which qualified them as ministers of the Lord, the teachers, the guides and the intercessors of the Lord's people.*

— *James A. Stewart*

November 14

WHOM HAVING NOT SEEN, YE LOVE.

1 Pet. 1: 8

What is included? Surely first and foremost comes the joy of seeing Him. Where real love is, there is a desire to see the face of the loved one. I would not give you a "Thank you" for that love which does not make the person long to behold the countenance of the beloved. It is just because it is so natural a desire, that if people cannot see the face they try to get the best photograph possible. Well, you and I have not seen our beloved. At least, we have only seen Him through a glass darkly. We have seen some of His glory in His ordinances. We have sometimes caught a glimpse of Him as He has looked through the lattice work of some service. But up to this moment we have to sing —

> Jesus, these eyes have never seen
> That radiant form of Thine.

We know most of Christ now by testimony. We are very much in the position of Rebekah. You remember that Eleazar, Abraham's servant, had to go and find a bride for Isaac, and he was led by the Lord to go to Rebekah; and he told her about all the wealth of his master's son, and of his goodness and of his beauty of character; and in consequence of the testimony Rebekah accepted him. But I trow she anxiously waited for that moment when she should see him to whom she had given her heart. *Ah, the blessed Spirit is the true Eleazar, and He has talked to us about Christ, and said to some of us sixteen, eighteen, twenty years ago, "Wilt thou go with this man?" and our hearts replied "Yes"; and since then we have been walking to and fro, just waiting to see our Isaac. We are anxiously looking for that blessed hope. We want to feast our eyes on Him.* We have had plenty of letters from Him, and we love him well. The more often we read them, the better we love Him for having written them. We have had also many a message from Him, and "all His words are music"; but we want to see Him. I want to see those eyes that wept for me. I want to see that brow which was blood-bedewed for me. Do not you? If not, then drop the name of Christian. *If you do not really want to see Him, do not prate about loving Him.*

— *Archibald Brown*

Oh Come Lord Jesus, come!

AND WHEN THEY HAD LIFTED UP THEIR
EYES, THEY SAW NO MAN SAVE JESUS ONLY.
— Math. 17: 8

THYSELF

My Lord, I work for Thee from day to day,
And, serving Thee, I find a holy bliss:
But this I pray —
Let not the joy of service e'er replace
The heart's delight in Thy dear Self, Thy face
Be still before me, unbedimmed
By lesser view of nicely trimmed
Routine, mechanics of the task,
Success, or blessing I may ask
From Thee, and Thou bestow. For this,
O Lord, I pray.

I read Thy Word, O Lord, each passing day,
And in the sacred page find glad employ:
But this I pray —
Save from the killing letter. Teach my heart,
Set free from human forms, the holy art
Of reading Thee in every line,
In precept, prophecy, and sign,
Till, all my vision filled with Thee,
Thy likeness shall reflect in me.
Not knowledge, but Thyself my joy! —
For this I pray.

I come to Thee in prayer, O Lord, each day,
And good it is to seek Thy throne of grace:
But this I pray —
Let not the thousand needs I bring to Thee,
The sins, the cares, the burdens, hide from me
Thine own fair form: my whole desire
Be Thou, until all lesser fire

Consume in love's pure flame, and things
Once loved be dross. With eagle's wings
Upborne, I then shall see Thy face.
Thus, Lord, I pray.

— *J. C. Macauley*

Thyself! Dear Lord.

November 16

HE STAGGERED NOT ... — Rom. 4: 20

The Holy Spirit would never have recorded this incident in the life of Abraham if it were not fraught with great spiritual import. "For whatsoever things were written aforetime were written for our learning, that we through patience and comfort of the Scriptures might have hope" (Rom. 15: 4).

It was a human impossibility for him and Sarah to have a son at their age. Yet, under hopeless circumstances, he hopefully believed. He kept on believing in spite of all the Satanic assaults on his faith. "There was no wavering in his faith. He gave no thought to the want in his own body, though he was nearly a hundred years old at the time, nor to the deadness of Sarah's womb; he showed no hesitation nor doubt at God's promise, but drew strength from his faith, confessing God's power, fully convinced that God was able to perform what He had promised" (Rom. 4: 19—21, Knox).

His faith never quailed. There was no feebleness in his faith. *Under utterly hopeless circumstances he hopefully believed, being absolutely certain that whatever God had promised, He was bound by, and He was able also to make it good.* So mighty was his faith that "he gave glory to God". He gave glory to God before the promise was fulfilled. It would have been easy to give glory to God after the child was born; it is easy to give

324

the shout of faith after prayer is answered. We remember that the children of Israel had to give the triumphant shout of faith before the walls of Jericho would fall flat before them.

— *James A. Stewart*

Cry and shout thou resident of Zion!

November 17

BE SILENT UNTO THE LORD, AND LET HIM MOULD THEE. — Psalm 27:7, Luther

Let us cease from fleshly strivings and fleshly strugglings. Let us be silent before the Lord and with great joy let Him mould us into the vessel of His choosing.

— *James A. Stewart*

ETERNITY

There is nothing like a calm look into the eternal world to teach us the emptiness of human praise, the sinfulness of self-seeking, the preciousness of Christ.

— *Robert Murray McCheyne*

November 18

BELOVED, THINK IT NOT STRANGE CONCERNING THE FIERY TRIAL...BUT REJOICE.

— 1 Pet. 4:12—13

"Rejoice, inasmuch as ye are partakers of Christ's sufferings" is the key-word of this section — the Christian overcoming sorrow by the Cross. The beginning of this process is in ver. 12, where the beloved of the Lord are exhorted not to think it strange that fiery trials should come, for the purpose of it is, to adjust us. There is no such word as "unfortunate" in the Christian's vocabulary. God has planned his life, and any suffering he passes

325

through is in that plan — it is not mere haphazard. It is a real part of God's wonderful process. "Think it not strange," but rejoice in it. Paul says "joy in tribulation," and James, "count it all joy." Here it is called "the fiery trial," and that word *fiery* is from the same root as the word "pure." Trial is a purifying process, and we need it; it is sent to prove and test us.

— *Fidler*

November 19

WE SHALL SEE HIM AS HE IS. — 1 John 3: 2

God's way of making our walk correspond with our "holy calling," is to fill us with the blessed hope of Christ's coming, and to occupy us with His glory, so that "we beholding ... are changed." Man's way is to occupy us with ourselves: with *our* spiritual life, which is to be deepened; with *our* faith, which is to be increased; with *our* walk, that is to be perfected. God's way is to point us to Christ's glory in heaven; man's way is to point us to Christ's power in us. God says the hope of coming glory will purify us; man says it is the power of present faith that will do it.

Oh, dear brethren, beware of any presentation of any doctrine that takes the eye from Christ! Beware of any phase of it which puts anything, however minute, however plausible, however apparently good, between the heart and Christ. Beware of building on the promises, instead of on the Promiser; beware of being occupied with the blessing instead of with the Blesser. If the mere "blessing" be the object of our lives, we shall most certainly never attain it: but having the Blesser we have all He can give, and His richest blessing will be with us without an effort.

Hence, you will observe, here, that it is not the doc-

trine of Christ's second coming that will do anything for us, but it is Christ who is coming, on whom this, our purifying hope, is set.

— E. W. B.

Face to face! O blissful moment! Face to face — to see and know;
Face to face with my Redeemer, Jesus Christ who loves me so.

November 20

GOD IS A SPIRIT, AND THEY THAT WORSHIP HIM MUST WORSHIP HIM IN SPIRIT AND IN TRUTH. — John 4: 24

In considering the subject of Worship, the highest exercise of which the spirit of man is capable, it is important to remember that there is a great difference between the way it is presented in the two Testaments. In former dispensations God was hidden in large measure. His wisdom and His providence were displayed in creation. His love was seen in His care of those who confided in Him. His grace was declared by the prophets as something yet to be manifested. Consequently there was no immediate access into the presence of God. The veil was unrent. His Word to Israel was, "Draw not nigh hither" (Exod. 3: 5); "Worship ye afar off" (24: 1). *But since the advent of Christ, all is changed.* Grace and truth are now revealed. The veil is rent. The way into the holiest is now made manifest. In spirit every believer is invited to "draw near . . . in full assurance of faith" (Heb. 10: 19—22). The worship of the new creation is based upon the finished work of our blessed Lord. In spirit we enter the immediate presence of the Father in full consciousness of our sonship. *Worship is far more than prayer, or the enjoyment of helpful ministry.* It is the spirit's adoring occupation with God Himself, not merely in gratitude for His gifts, but because of what He is. It is this that the Father seeks. Worship is lowered as we become occupied with the externals even of Christianity. It reaches its highest point as our spirits are absorbed in contemplation of the matchless perfections of the eternal God, in the light of the cross and the empty tomb.

— *H. A. Ironside*

November 21

FROM SUCH TURN AWAY. — II Tim. 3: 5

The New Testament not only teaches the necessity of contending for the faith, but it also exhorts us to separate ourselves from those who deny the faith. There is no need for any child of God to be in ignorance as to his stand and his position before God and man. The Word of God is clear as to His instructions.

"Beloved, when I gave all diligence to write unto you of the common salvation, it was needful for me to write unto you and exhort you that ye should earnestly contend for the faith, which was once (for all) delivered unto the saints" (Jude 3). "I am compelled to send you this letter of warning; you have a battle to fight over the faith that was handed down once for all to the saints" (Knox).

"Whosoever transgresseth and abideth not in the doctrine of Christ, hath not God. He that abideth in the doctrine of Christ, he hath both the Father and the Son. If there come any unto you, and bring not this doctrine, receive him not into your house, neither bid him God's speed" (II John 9—11).

"Be ye not unequally yoked together with unbelievers; for what fellowship hath righteousness with unrighteousness? And what communion hath light with darkness? And what concord hath Christ with Belial? *Or what part hath he that believeth with an infidel?* And what agreement hath the Temple of God with idols? For ye are the temples of the living God. Wherefore, come out from among them and be separate, saith the Lord, and touch not the unclean thing, and I will receive you" (II Cor. 6: 14—17).

The Scriptures are implicit:

> "Try them" (I John 4: 1)
> "Mark them" (Rom. 16—17)
> "Rebuke them" (Titus 1: 13)
> "Receive them not" (II John 10)
> "From such turn away" (II Tim. 3: 5)

Our testimony regarding our position must not be like muffled bells, but clear and distinct as the Scriptures. Shall we obey God or man?

— *James A. Stewart*

November 22

GRIEVE NOT THE HOLY SPIRIT OF GOD AND BE YE KIND. — Eph. 4: 30—32

Speak Kindly

Speak kindly, for our days are all too few
    For angry strife;
There is deep meaning, if we only knew,
    In our brief life.
No nobler mission can be ours, if we
    A pang can stay;
Or, if amidst the rush of tears we see,
    Wipe one away.
Speak kindly. Gracious words, God-sent, God-given,
    Are never lost;
They come all fragrant with the breath of Heaven,
    Yet nothing cost.

Kind words are like kind acts: they steal along
    Life's hidden springs;
Then in the darkest storm some little song
    The sad heart sings.

Speak kindly, graciously, for all around
    Are pains and smarts;
The very air is full of moans and sound
    Of breaking hearts.

Seek, seek to bind them up, as once did Christ
    The gracious Lord;
So surely will His hand bestow on thee
    A bright reward.

                     — *S. Trevor Francis*

November 23

TO KNOW THE LOVE OF CHRIST. — Eph. 3:19
We should know the love of Christ experimentally; that is, we should sit down and ask for the Spirit of discernment to see the thread of love running through the beads of our life. "Whoso is wise will observe these things, even they shall understand the lovingkindness of the Lord." If you read that psalm you will find there is an account of storm, of a march through an arid waste, and of seven different episodes, many of them fraught with pain, and at the end of it the psalmist has what you may call the audacity to say, "If a man wants it he will find the lovingkindness of the Lord in the storm, in the wilderness, and even in the prison-house." *Let us therefore sit down and let that thought permeate the heart. Have your pencil, if you will, and begin to put down all the manifestations in your life of God's love to you, and methinks the more you write, like Bunyan's Pilgrim's Progress, the more it will grow on you, and you will fill one sheet of paper and want another, and then another and another.* I would like a man who is disappointed, whose heart is full of depres-

sion and desolateness, to try my recipe, to put down in order the manifestations of Christ's love, the sin which has been forgiven, the iniquity pardoned, the waywardness and wickedness with which He has borne. Oh, man, come sum it up, and I think you will throw down your pencil when you are half way through the enumeration, and say it passeth knowledge. *Also we should know by sympathy.* Kepler, the great astronomer, who laid the foundation of much of our knowledge of the stars, one day exclaimed, after spending hours in surveying the heavens, "I have been thinking over again the earliest thoughts of the Creator," and I think that every time a man or woman sacrifices himself or herself for another he is thinking over again the earliest, deepest thought of the love of Christ. *Have you not often felt as though God kept training you?* When you first loved that twin-soul, now your husband or your wife, did you not one day say to yourself, "I love?" I suppose this is what love is, and in that first attraction to another you woke up to a new realm and cried, "Why I suppose that Jesus Christ's love to me is something like this, only infinite." The quality is the same though not the quantity. Every time you do a gentle act for another who does not deserve it, every time you lay down your life to save others, every time you endure shame and spitting and scorn to rescue lost women and lost men, in the glow of your human interest, and amidst disappointment and rebuff you say, *"Well, thank God, I am seeing deeper than ever I saw before into what Jesus has been feeling for me."* Abraham learnt more of the love of God the day he was led up Mount Moriah than anything else could have taught him.

— *F. B. Meyer*

November 24

WILT THOU NOT REVIVE US AGAIN.
— Psalm 85: 6

We must be very careful to differentiate between revival in itself, and the spiritual state resulting from revival. REVIVAL is not God's standard for the Church but is the process through which the Church is restored to its former splendour and glory: "Wilt Thou not revive us again, that Thy people may rejoice in Thee?" (Ps. 85: 6). In days of revival there is a great time of heart-searching, when believers are smitten by the Holy Spirit as they realize afresh how far they have departed from the Lord. This spirit of brokenness results in deep humiliaton, repentance, confession and restitution. The pathway of humiliation is only the gateway to our receiving all God's fulness in His beloved Son. *It is not enough to be emptied and broken down before the Lord — the believer must be filled.* In order to be filled with all the fulness of God, and to live the normal, healthy, dynamic Christian life, the stricken believer must appropriate the risen, reigning life of Christ for his *practical daily walk.* "For I always beseech the God of our Lord Jesus Christ — the Father most glorious — to give you a spirit of wisdom and penetration through an intimate knowledge of Him, the eyes of your understanding being enlightened so that you may know what is the hope which His call to you inspires, what the wealth of the glory of His inheritance in God's people, and what the transcending greatness of His power in us believers, as seen in the working of His infinite might when He displayed it in Christ by raising Him from the dead and seating Him at His own right hand in the heavenly realms, high above all other governments and authority and power and dominion, and every title of sovereignty used in this age or in the age to come. God has put all things under His feet and has appointed Him universal and supreme Head of the Church, which is His body" (Eph. 1: 16—23).   — *James A. Stewart*

HE HAZARDED HIS LIFE. — Phil. 2: 30, Weymouth.

Oh, for a host of Epaphrodituses today! Unless we repent of our easy-going religious routine, this man will rise up against us in the Day of Judgment. The soft, flabby, hypocritical church, so far removed from the fellowship of the Lord's sufferings likes the dead-level of mediocracy in the things of God.

A disciple who is extravagant in his devotion to the things of Christ, and who recklessly stakes his all to evangelize a lost and dying world is counted dangerous and one to be severely avoided. When one breaks his alabaster box of precious ointment in allegiance to the dear Saviour, a cold calculating church rises up in protest: "To what purpose is this waste? It is all very romantic and sentimental, but is it really necessary?"

Our God has said, "One of you shall chase a thousand and two shall put ten thousand to flight!" That is heaven's arithmetic. He had rather have one utterly abandoned man or woman than a thousand who are half-hearted in service. Oh, for the spirit of a Henry Martyn! Oh, for the spirit of a David Brainerd!

Henry Martyn, with the honors of the Cambridge University at his feet, turned his back upon fame and fortune and all that was dear to him and blazed a trail for God in heathen lands. His was the cry, *"Now let me burn out for God."* At the age of thirty-one he was taken home a worn out old man, having contracted a fever during his last journey. Having laid all on the altar, he literally laid down his life for Christ.

— *James A. Stewart*

IF YE BE REPROACHED FOR THE NAME OF CHRIST, HAPPY ARE YE, FOR THE SPIRIT OF GLORY AND OF GOD RESTETH UPON YOU.

1 Pet. 4: 14

Do not overlook that saving clause — "for the Name of Christ." We glorify Him by accepting suffering at the hand of persecutors, "But," he adds, "let none of you suffer as a murderer, or as a thief, or as a busybody in other men's matters." There are two kinds of suffering, and it is no sign of grace if we suffer for our own misdoing, or as a busybody — that is the word "episcopos," bishop! Peter applies it to those who try to be overseers of other people's work! Someone runs a church in such a way — and they could do it so much better! Very well, if you can, try it — but put yourself into this verse, with the murderers and the thieves! *There is only one thing God has given us to do, and that is our calling. When we meddle with the calling of other people we suffer, and there is nothing to rejoice over in that.* There is no fellowship with Christ in that. So many tangles and clashes come through wanting someone else's job — jealousy, hatred! "Why was not I chosen for that?" That is just the expression of self. As you lay yourself on God's altar, He will put you into your right place, the place where you can best serve Him, and if you suffer *there*, "happy are ye." To suffer in the will of God is blessedness, to suffer out of His will is misery. "I am here," said Hudson Taylor, "by God's will, so that whatever difficulties overtake me, they are in God's will and I can rejoice in them." Can you say that? Can you look back to His calling you to that sphere of service and say, "God put me here and it is all right. He knows the difficulties and trials, and they are just working out His perfect plan and purpose."

— *Fidler*

November 27

HOLY! HOLY! HOLY! — Isa. 6: 3

Holiness as the consent and harmony of the divine attributes is the beauty of God, His essential glory. When the seraphim chant their antiphonal song around the throne, they veil their faces before the effulgence of that uncreated splendour. God dwells in light that is inaccessible. If we attempt to speak of the high and lofty One who inhabiteth eternity, whose name is Holy, we shall be constrained to cry with the prophet of vision, "Woe is me! for I am undone; because I am a man of unclean lips, and I dwell in the midst of a people of unclean lips." Remembering always that the thoughts of God rise above our thoughts as the heavens lift themselves above the earth, we may prepare our hearts for the contemplation of the divine holiness by elevating ourselves towards our highest aspirations.

— *D. M. Mc Intyre*

November 28

HE SHALL GIVE YOU ANOTHER COMFORTER. THAT HE MAY ABIDE WITH YOU FOREVER.
— John 14: 16

Theologians have for centuries discussed at great issue the meaning of this precious name of Paraclete. In our Authorized Version the Greek word "Paraclete" (Para-kletos) is translated "Comforter." John Wycliffe translates it as "Advocate." The word Paraclete comes from two Greek words meaning "alongside" and "I call." *The metaphor is derived from a law court trial.* A defendant is hard-pressed by the opposing barrister and, being unable to defend himself, espies across the court the familiar face of an influential friend, whom he beckons to him. His friend threads his way through the crowd until he stands beside him. From that moment on he is the Paraclete — standing beside, suggesting, enabling to withstand. Westcott says, "In defining this word the sense of advocate, counsellor, one who pleads, convinces, convicts in a great controversy; who strengthens on the one hand and defends on the other, meeting formidable attacks, is alone adequate."

The paraclete will comfort, strengthen and defend those purchased by the precious blood of Christ. It is only as we know the Person that we can fully interpret His name aright. In the Upper Room discourse we see the Holy Spirit as a Person Who teaches, reminds, testifies, comes, convinces, guides, speaks, prophesies, takes and brings. He is revealed, not only as a Person, but as a Divine Person:

1. Only a Divine Person could take the place of another Divine Person.

2. He that is able to teach the apostles all that is necessary for the execution of their ministry must know the "all things" of Christ.

3. He that is able to bring to the disciples' remembrance whatsoever Christ had said unto them must needs be God, because He must know their hearts and thoughts.

Into the blessed Name of "The Paraclete" we can write the answer to all our needs. The Spirit will see us right through to the "bitter end." This One, "called alongside to help," stands by us in the hour of sorrow.

— *James A. Stewart*

November 29

THOU SHALT REJOICE IN EVERY GOOD THING
WHICH THE LORD THY GOD HATH GIVEN
UNTO THEE. — Deut. 26: 11

REJOICE EVERMORE. IN EVERYTHING GIVE
THANKS. — 1 Thess. 5: 16, 18

Grave on thy heart each past "red-letter day"!
Forget not all the sunshine of the way
By which the Lord hath led thee; answered prayers,
And joys unasked, strange blessings, lifted cares,
Grand promise-echoes! Thus thy life shall be
One record of His love and faithfulness to thee.

— *F. R. Havergal*

Lord, I will sing and bless Thy name.

November 30

BOLDNESS TO ENTER INTO THE HOLIEST.
— Heb. 10: 19

Worker for God, minister of Christ, or in whatever
way you may be engaged in the Lord's vineyard, be
far more anxious about abiding within the veil. Leave
that restlessness and anxiety about your work with the
Lord. He will never fail to bless it if you yourself come
forth to it from the inner shrine.

In a world like this in which we are living, and
specially in our own day, in which the pressure from
without of demands and duties becomes increasingly
greater, we must have a central point of spiritual gra-
vitation. *That central point is only within the veil.* This
is the only thing that will prevent our life from becoming wasted. There will be a looseness — a frittering away
of all life's opportunities, and a sense of dissatisfaction
in everything. I know of nothing that will prevent a

man from defeating all the great aims and ends of life, but consciously and habitually abiding in the presence of God. The consciousness of a lost life, which sometimes comes back upon us with such force as to be almost overwhelming, has only one remedy — to live closer to God. Make *everything* of things unseen and eternal.

— *F. Whitfield*

December 1

ACCORDING TO YOUR FAITH BE IT UNTO YOU.
— Math. 9: 29

Receptivity is the word that describes the believer's true attitude, if he would daily "walk with God." Our faith will be the measure, not of Christ's fulness, or of His ability to give, but of our capacity to receive. "According to your faith be it unto you." The widow, in Elisha's time, brought her empty vessels. No matter how many or how large they were — the Lord filled them all. It was when the vessels failed that the oil ceased. The Lord Jesus prayed for Peter that his faith should fail not.

And so, whatever be the capacity of our faith, God will fill the vessel. This does not imply that when full we shall then cease to receive more. For it is the nature of real active faith to grow. The Apostle Paul was full of thankfulness on behalf of the Thessalonian Christians, because he could say of them, "your faith *groweth exceedingly.*" And so it will be true of the healthy Christian, — to-morrow's vessel will be larger than to-day's as to-day's was larger than yesterday's.

The more we learn of the character and grace of our infinitely precious Redeemer, the more we will be filled.
— *Evan Hopkins*

THAT GOOD, AND ACCEPTABLE, AND PERFECT, WILL OF GOD. — Rom. 12: 2

HOW I ASCERTAIN THE WILL OF GOD

1. — I seek at the beginning to get my heart into such a state that it has no will of its own in regard to a given matter.

Nine-tenths of the trouble with people is just here. Nine tenths of the difficulties are overcome when our hearts are ready to do the Lord's will, whatever it may be. When one is truly in this state, it is usually but a little way to the knowledge of what His will is.

2. — Having done this, I do not leave the result to feeling or simple impression. If I do so, I make myself liable to great delusions.

3. — I seek the will of the Spirit of God through, or in connection with, the Word of God.

The Spirit and the Word must be combined. If I look to the Spirit alone without the Word I lay myself open to great delusions also. If the Holy Ghost guides us at all, He will do it according to the Scriptures and never contrary to them.

4. — Next I take into account providential circumstances. These often plainly indicate God's will in connection with His Word and Spirit.

5. — I ask God in prayer to reveal His will to me aright.

6. — Thus, through prayer to God, the study of the Word, and reflection, I come to a deliberate judgment according to the best of my ability and knowledge, and if my mind is thus at peace, and continues so after two or three more petitions, I proceed accordingly.

— *George Muller*

December 3

THAT CHRIST MAY DWELL IN YOUR HEARTS BY FAITH. — Eph. 3: 17

What have we here then? A spiritual fact. Some people think that real things are in the sphere of the visible, and the things that are in the sphere of the invisible are not real. It is just the very opposite. "The things which are seen are temporal; but the things which are not seen are eternal." Now, here we have a great fact in the spiritual sphere. You say, "I do not see it." Then there is a blessing in reserve for you — it is for you. Of course, we are not speaking now of Jesus in His glorified body; in that sense He is in heaven. But we are speaking of His spiritual presence, as when He said, "Lo! I am with you always." I believe the Word of God means just what it says, when I read "Christ in you," and "that Christ may dwell in your hearts by faith," believe it! You say, "Ah! yes, you see it is *by faith.*" Well, and what do you mean by *faith?* Analyse that thought. Does it mean that you have to imagine it, and if you imagine it, it will be true? *No! Faith must have a fact to rest upon, and the fact is antecedent to the faith.* It is not your believing that makes it true; you have to believe it because it is true. But Christ will be to you practically what He is to your faith. *This is the great object of the Spirit's working in the inner man in order that Christ may dwell in your hearts by faith.* Oh, grand reality! It comes to some of us, beloved, as a marvellous revelation; it gives a wonderful lift to the spiritual life. Is it really true that I have the risen Christ, the real spiritual presence of the Lord Jesus Christ indwelling — that He is to look out of my eyes, that He is to speak with my lips, that He is to walk with my feet, that He is to work with my hands? Is that true? In closing, let me tell you what that good man, Dr. Alexander Maclaren, says upon this very passage of Scripture. There is a sermon of his upon this very text. One sentence only let me give you. On this passage, "that Christ may dwell in your hearts by faith," he observes, "Let me say, in the plainest, simplest, strongest way that I can, that that dwelling of Christ in the believing heart is to be regarded as being a *plain, literal fact.*" Directly you grasp that, you will find a power. Don't puzzle your brain about it. We want God — nothing short of God; and where God is, we have the Father and the Son and the Spirit. Nothing short of God can satisfy our hearts, or meet the necessities of our being. *Wonderful truth! That He should not only be for us, but in His infinite condescension and love should come to dwell in our hearts by faith.*

— *Evan Hopkins*

December 4

WHEN HE IS COME... — John 16: 8

The entire life of a believer in Christ may be revolutionized by accepting in simple faith the scriptural doctrine of the ministry of the Paraclete. I believe that in John, chapters fourteen, fifteen and sixteen, we have the deepest and highest teaching concerning the ministry of the Holy Spirit. The words of our Lord concerning the Person and doctrine of the Spirit should be read prayerfully and carefully day after day on our knees, until the very glory of these precious truths floods and fills our souls.

I make bold to say that no one can have a clear conception of the person and ministry of the Spirit of Pentecost, if he ignores the teaching set forth in these chapters. Here are the real vital facts concerning His blessed person and work. If I go to the Acts and the Epistles and ignore these chapters, I will only have an imperfect and incomplete view of the subject. Here is a reservoir of Scripture doctrine. A preacher could easily preach many sermons on one single utterance of Christ as it fell from His gracious lips in the Upper Room. These words were not spoken in cold technical language to theologians, but from a tender, overflowing heart to sorrowing disciples.

The Lord wanted to prepare His disciples for the future. He must make known to them His death on Calvary's Cross, and also the incarnation of the Holy Spirit. In the middle of His discourse, He drops, as it were, a bombshell in their midst, by announcing to them His departure. The disciples were startled, perplexed, even dazed, and they cried in effect: "Lord Jesus, we cannot live without Thee! As the ivy clings to the wall, we cling to Thee. Lord, Thou art our life! Lord, Thou must not go away! Lord, Thou canst not go away! Lord, we would be failures; Thou must not leave us; We cannot live without Thee!"

To these perplexed disciples the Lord Jesus gave the most wonderful news about the coming and the ministry of the Paraclete. He said in effect: "Yes, because I have told you I go away, sorrow has filled your hearts. Now do not let your hearts be troubled; do not let them be afraid. Listen! I have some wonderful news for you" (John 16: 6 and 14: 1).

— *James A. Stewart*

December 5

THE COMFORTER, THE HOLY GUEST.
— John 14: 26 Lit.

Let us put ourselves in the place of these disciples. Suppose we had lost a loved one, say on the battlefield, as so many of us have. What we desire most today is to see that lovely face and hear that tender voice. *The disciples were like that.* They wanted no substitute; they wanted to see Christ alone with them, and to hear His voice. Yes! all the disciples wanted was the Lord Jesus Christ, Himself, and herein lies the significance of His

342

words. He says that the coming of the Holy Spirit is to be as though He Himself were coming.

Our Lord did not say that He would request of the Father a Comforter. The key to His message was that the Father would send in His name ANOTHER Comforter. Why another? Because He Himself was the first Comforter, and the Holy Spirit would be the second Comforter. He would be another Person just like the Lord Jesus. As you know, there are two Greek words for "another:" HETEROS, meaning another of a different kind, from which we get our English word, Heterodoxy. Paul uses this word in his letter to the Galatians, when he says, "another Gospel" (Gal. 1: 6). The other word for "another" is ALLOS, meaning another of the same kind or quality. Hallelujah! this is the word the Lord uses here! *The word "another" does not connote one who is instead of someone else, but rather a second person who is in addition to the first.* As one has said, "The absence of one is the presence of the other; or let me rather say, that there is no absence, no distance, no departure, no separation! Christ, Himself, is one with His Holy Spirit, and with Him, temples in the heart of His mystical body." Thus, our Lord makes the same even to be at once His coming, and His sending; and He speaks of the Spirit now, as His own Presence, and now as His Substitute during His absence." *In other words, one of the vital truths of the Upper Room is this, that in the Person of the Holy Spirit, the Lord Jesus, as the risen, exalted, glorified Redeemer would come to His disciples.* Though henceforth they will not know Him "after the flesh," they will know Him in a more intimate, dynamic way (II Cor. 5).

— *James A. Stewart*

December 6

AND WHEN THEY HAD PRAYED, THE PLACE WAS SHAKEN ... AND THEY WERE ALL FILLED.
— Acts 4: 31

Our Heavenly Father, we come to wait on Thee for the gift of Thy Holy Spirit for service. Oh God, give us the Spirit. Empty us of self and self-seeking. Oh God, bring us down in the dust before Thee, so that we may be filled with the Holy Ghost, so that we may have power with God and with man! Oh Thou God of Elijah, we pray that a double portion of Thy Spirit may come upon us today, that we may be anointed for the work Thou hast for us to do; we know that we have but a little while to stay here!

Oh, God, help us to bear fruit while we live! May we no longer be toiling day after day and month after month, and seeing no fruit. Oh Jesus, Master, Thou hast gone up on high; Thou hast led captivity captive; Thou art at the right hand of God, and Thou hast power.

O, give us power; Thou canst give us a fresh anointing. We pray that Thou wilt do it to-day. We pray that Thou wilt breathe upon us as a breath from heaven. Grant that we may know what it is to have the Holy Ghost resting upon us for service ... We ask it all in the Name and for the sake of Thy beloved Son. Amen!
— D. L. Moody

December 7

A BRUISED REED SHALL HE NOT BREAK, AND THE SMOKING FLAX SHALL HE NOT QUENCH.
— Isa. 42: 3

The reed was bruised, no music sweet
Could from the lute the player make,
It seemed as if it were more meet
To break it and another take.

But One in pity saw the bruise
    And smoothed it out and made it straight;
Fit for Himself again to use,
    Of His grand harmony partake.

O God, I am that bruised reed,
    Thy songs of grace must almost cease;
Refit me for The Service need,
    Bring from me hymns of joy and peace.

The oil was spent within the lamp,
    The flickering wick though still alight
With moistening oil was scarcely damp
    And every moment grew less bright.

But One stood by and saw the spark
    Who would not quench it, but He came
Lest it should fade into the dark
    He poured in oil, renewed the flame.

O God, I am that smoking flax,
    Thy feeble flame is burning low,
Breathe on me, Spirit of the Lord,
    And cause the light once more to glow.

— George Goodman

These poignant almost pathetic words were written
by this blessed Bible teacher during great days of pain
before his translation.

December 8

WE HAVE SUCH AN HIGH PRIEST, WHO IS
ABLE TO SAVE THEM TO THE UTTERMOST
THAT COME UNTO GOD BY HIM SEEING HE
EVER LIVETH TO MAKE INTERCESSION FOR
THEM. — Heb. 7: 25, 26, 8: 1.

Oh that God would open our hearts to know and
prove what our royal priesthood is — what the real
meaning is of our living and praying in the name of
Jesus, that what we ask shall indeed be given us! O
Lord Jesus, our Holy High Priest, breathe the spirit
of Thine own holy priesthood into our hearts. Amen.

— *Andrew Murray*

December 9

FORASMUCH THEN AS CHRIST HATH SUF-
FERED FOR US IN THE FLESH, ARM YOUR-
SELVES . . . WITH THE SAME MIND, FOR HE
THAT HATH SUFFERED IN THE FLESH HATH
CEASED FROM SIN . . . — Pet. 4: 1—2

*Since Christ suffered in the flesh and died, arm your-
selves with the same mind. The mind of Christ is an
armour against going under in days of trial. Suffering
is a means of adjustment to God's will, and everything
depends upon how you interpret it; upon right, sane,
sober thinking; the renewed mind thinking out the whole
position in the light of God.* "Arm yourselves" — it is
a weapon, a shield, which will guard you from the
suggestions of the evil one — "the same mind" — the
mind of Christ. Conformity to Christ is the goal. He
suffered in His sinless flesh in order that our sinful
flesh might go to the Cross: *only there* is it incapable
of sin: "he that hath suffered in the flesh hath ceased
from sin." The flesh wants this world's goods; but "ye

took joyfully the spoiling of your goods" — the loss of "goods" may be God's way of deliverance. The flesh leans on the arm of flesh. Then, it may be, the Lord takes away our best friends, or turns them into enemies. So we lean on God alone, and the loss of friends becomes a blessing. The flesh may lean on successful service, on big congregations, on popularity. Then the Lord lays us aside, and sickness cuts us off from everybody, and we discover that it is not *our* ministry or service, but the Lord's! and the suffering is a blessing. Whatever He sends into our lives it is that we should "no longer live the rest of our time... to the desires of men, but to the will of God." *God is trying to cut us off from human desires that we may fall back upon Him and rest there, finding all we want in Him.*

— *Fidler*

December 10

ABIDE IN ME. — John 15: 4

Life is built a day at a time; and the Scriptures keep this constantly in view in their promises. So, Christian, tired and somewhat disheartened, take the Lord a day at a time. Let the life-time you deal with be just for today; and for *today* you possess nothing less than THE WHOLE CHRIST OF GOD!

Handley Moule

The Second Coming of Christ is the one event, the one doctrine bound up with and fulfilling every fundamental doctrine, every sublime promise, every radiant hope, giving inspiration to every practical exhortation, and furnishing the basis of Apostolic appeal to the highest type of Christian living.

— *I. M. Halderman*

347

Lord, her watch Thy Church is keeping
When shall earth Thy rule obey?
When shall end the night of weeping,
When shall break the promised day?
See the whitening harvest languish,
Waiting still the laborer's toil;
Was it vain, Thy Son's deep anguish?
Shall the strong retain the spoil?

December 11

YE ARE SONS . . . Gal. 4: 6

*Sonship being founded on resurrection, stands con-
nected with perfect justification — perfect righteousness — perfect freedom from everything that could in
anywise be against us.* God could not have us in His
presence with sin upon us. The father could not have
the prodigal at his table with the rags of the far country
upon him. He could fall on his neck and kiss him in
those rags. It was worthy and beautifully characteristic
of his *grace* to do; but then to seat him at the table in
rags would never do. The grace that brought the father
out to the prodigal reigns through the righteousness which
brought the prodigal in to his father. It would not have
been grace, had the father waited for the son to deck
himself in robes of his own providing; it would not have
been righteousness to bring him in in his rags; but both
grace and righteousness shone forth in all their respec-
tive brightness and beauty when the father went out
and fell on the prodigal's neck, and yet did not give
him a seat at the table until he was clad and decked
in a manner suited to that happy position. God in Christ
has stopped to the very lowest point of man's moral
condition, that by stooping He might raise man to the
very highest point of blessedness in fellowship with Himself.

— *C. H. McIntosh*

December 12

THE KING HATH BROUGHT ME INTO HIS CHAMBERS — Song of songs 1:4

A MISSIONARY'S JOY

The holiest hour that comes in the day
Is the trysting time when I kneel to pray,
Soon is forgotten each weight and care,
I walk with my Father in a world so fair.

O great is the joy in this silence sweet,
I pray in his presence and fall at his feet
And long for the fulness of love and power,
To live on forever in the strength of this hour.

The sense of his nearness can never be told,
It fills with new peace all the space of my soul,
In visions of rapture I look on his face
And feel all about me the gifts of his grace.

An hour alone at his altar bright
When the soul is swept on to greater height,
Makes the day sacred before his throne.
And lifts all life to a loftier tone.

His voice I hear through the silence deep,
Like dreams that come on holy feet,
It wings my spirit to rest and repose,
And gives a joy that earth never knows.

— *Rosalee Appleby*
(Brazil)

December 13

SOW THY SEED . . . Eccl. 11:6

WHEN THE REAPING TIME COMES

Our Heavenly Father in the plainest, simplest way condescends to speak to us.

"In the morning sow thy seed, and in the evening withold not thine hand." That is, "Use any and every opportunity which the Lord is pleased to give thee; seek to redeem the time, for thou hast but one life here on earth, and that a *brief* life — a very brief one as compared with Eternity; therefore make good use of it." Oh, the blessing that results from attending to this! On every occasion, under all circumstances, after we have sought the Lord's blessing and are in a proper state of heart, let us drop a word for Christ here and there and everywhere, and after we have spoken it, bring it before God again, and again, and again in prayer.

When the reaping time comes, and we find ourselves in glory, that child for whom we prayed will be found there! That aged cripple whom we met incidentally on the road, and to whom we spoke, will be in Heaven. That person in consumption whom we visited every day for a long time, and who gave little or no heed at all to what we had to say, will be found in glory, having at last laid to heart what we spoke so many times to him, and though we had no information about it, God blessed our word. Oh, the multitude of instances we shall find at last, when our work, labour, or service has, contrary to natural expectation, been blessed!

I was once standing here about sixty-two years ago, preaching the Word of Life, and after I had done I was cast down because my words seemed to me so cold, so dull, so lifeless. And not till three months after did I hear that through that very address abundant blessing had been brought to

Nineteen Different Persons.

And precisely thus we shall find it in our labour and service in the end. Often and often it appears to us that the many opportunities made use of have been lost. Yet it will be seen that all was owned of God, all put down in His book of remembrance, our labour, after all, was not in vain, and the reaping time has come.

But let us carefully see to it that when the reaping time comes there will be something to reap because we have been *labouring*. If there be no labour, if there be a careless, thoughtless walk, without prayer and crying to God mightily, then let us not be surprised if when the harvest time comes there is no reaping as far as we are concerned. But as assuredly as there has been the sowing, as there has been the laying out of ourselves for God, most assuredly we shall reap.

"For thou knowest not whether shall prosper, either this or that." We are ignorant of what God is about to do, because He does not tell us if at this particular time He will own our labour and service or not. Therefore, our business is at all times to seek to lay out ourselves for God, for, as I have stated before, *we have but one life, and this*

One life is a brief life.

"Or whether they both shall be alike good." God may bless, not merely at one time, but both times. In the morning the work may be commenced, in the evening the Holy Ghost may deepen it, and God may bring double blessing out of our poor, feeble service.

Oh, let us seek to attend to this precious exhortation!

— *George Muller*
(in his 92nd year)

351

December 14

WE WERE EXCEEDINGLY OVERWHELMED AND CRUSHED SO THAT IT WAS BEYOND BEARING.

II Cor. 1: 8, free translation.

Pressed out of measure and pressed to all length;
Pressed so intensely, it seems beyond strength;
Pressed in the body and pressed in the soul,
Pressed in the mind till the dark surges roll;
Pressed by my foes, sorely pressed by my friends;
Pressure on pressure, till life nearly ends.

Pressed into knowing no helper but God;
Pressed into loving the staff and the rod.
Pressed into liberty where nothing clings;
Pressed into faith for impossible things.
Pressed into living a life in the Lord,
Pressed into living a Christ-life outpoured.

— *L. S. P.*

Hallelujah for the pressing!

December 15

THOU ART MY BELOVED SON. — Luke 3: 22

THE FATHER'S DELIGHT IN HIS INCARNATE SON

Christ being God as well as Man, the divine and human natures being ineffably united in Him, He was capable of meriting both in what He did and suffered. If He had been Man only, He might have obeyed and also have suffered, but He could not have merited either in obeying or suffering. A mere man might have been upheld by infinite power, in obedience and suffering; but no proper merit could possibly attend either his obedience or his sufferings, how great soever. Infinite power resident in the divine Person of Christ sustained His human nature in His obedience and sufferings, but the union of His human nature with His divine Person renders His obedience and sufferings properly meritorious. If He had not been Man He would not have been a meet subject to obey the law on account of men, nor to suffer a penal death for the sins of man. And if He had not been God and Man, and both united, He could not have merited by His obedience or sufferings. *For it is the infinite dignity of His Person which gives infinite worth to His obedience, and from that aries the immense value of His sufferings.* Thus the constitution of the Person of Christ fits Him for carrying into execution all the wise and glorious purposes of the Father concerning the objects of His everlasting love. And because the Father from everlasting foresaw how He Himself would be infinitely glorified and the Church be effectually secured by the obedience and sufferings of Christ, therefore He eternally had the highest complacency and delight in Him (Isaiah 42: 1).

— *John Brine,* 1760

Blessed Spirit enable me this day and every day to delight in the Darling of the Father's bosom!

December 16

PUT ON THE WHOLE ARMOUR OF GOD, THAT YE MAY BE ABLE TO STAND AGAINST THE WILES OF THE DEVIL — (The stratagems)

— Eph. 6: 11

Speaking strictly within the Scriptures, the Church is not even on the earth. It is viewed by God as seated with Christ in the heavenlies. Positionally it is there, conditionally it is here, but spiritually it must reckon itself dead, buried, raised and seated with Christ in heavenly places. If the conflict of the Church is not against "flesh and blood," against who is it?

"Against principalities, against powers, against the rulers of the darkness of the world, against spiritual wickedness in heavenly places."

Four times "against." Four things "against," — "principalities," "powers," "rules of darkness," and "spiritual wickedness."

Let us ponder and consider these persons and powers of the underworld now holding possession and position in the upper world. Who are they? Where are they? Why are they?

They are wicked spiritual hosts in military organization camped and entrenched in the heavenlies. They are invisible agents of wickedness in an organized spirit world. They are the rulers of the darkness of this age. They actually exercise rule over this world in this age time of darkness and delusion. They direct the energy of the age. They are unquesionably organized in military order. Militarism not only prevails on the earth, but maintains in the heavenlies. Intimations and allusions to this organization may be found in Ephesians 1: 21 and Colossians 2: 15. The Book of Revelation seems to open unto this very sphere and describes a future struggle (see Rev. 12: 7—9). The leaders of these hosts alone are mentioned.

When Christ was raised up from the dead and exalted to the highest point in the universe, He passed through these organized ranks who were powerless to prevent Him passing through and up. Says Ephesians 1: 20: "Far above all principalities and power and might and dominion." Christ has been raised infinitely above them and they wait beneath His feet for their future humiliation and casting down.

Having failed to defeat Christ, the Head of the Church, they now turn their attention to the Church, the Body of Christ. God has purposed that the "heavenlies" will be the sphere of the future service of the

354

Church (see Eph. 3:10). Its calling is heavenly, its ministry will be heavenly, therefore its conflict is "heavenly." The place now occupied by "wicked hosts" will be then occupied by the Church. The Church must realize the character of this conflict and be properly armored. "Put on the whole armour of God," says the Apostle, "that ye may be able to stand against the wiles of the devil." The word wile is "stratagem," cunning art of a spiritual foe. Not a flesh and blood conflict where human wit must meet human wit, but a warfare issuing for the secret counsels of a world of darkness and demons. This is the one and only sphere of the conflict and contest of the Church. All other enmity to the Church is created and promoted from this seat of antagonism.

— *Leon Tucker*

December 17

PUT UP ... THY SWORD. — Math. 26:52

THE SHEATHED SWORD

The natural man is a fighter. It is the law of his carnal nature. He fights with his fist and sword, tongue and wit. His kingdom is of this world, and he fights for it with such weapons as this world furnishes.

The Christian is a citizen of heaven, and is subject to it's law, which is universal, whole-hearted love.

In his kingdom he conquers not by fighting, but by submitting. When an enemy takes his coat, he overcomes him, not by going to law, but by generously giving him his cloak also. When his enemy compels him to go a mile with him, he vanquishes the enemy by cheerfully going two miles with him. When he is smitten on one cheek, he wins his foe by meekly turning the other cheek. This is the law of the new life from Heaven, and only by recognising and obeying it can that new life be sustained and passed on to others.

This was the spirit of Paul. He says, "Being reviled, we bless; being persecuted, we suffer it; being defamed, we intreat" (1 Cor. 4: 12, 13). "The servant of the Lord must not strive," wrote Paul to Timothy, "but be gentle unto all men." This is the spirit of our King, this is the law of His Kingdom.

Is this your spirit? When you are reviled, bemeaned and slandered, and are tempted to retort, He says to you, *"Put up thy sword into the sheath."* When you are wronged and illtreated, and men ride rough shod over you, and you feel it but just to smite back, He says, "Put up thy sword into the sheath." "Live peaceably with all men." Your weapons are not carnal, but spiritual, now that you belong to Him, and have your citizenship in Heaven. *If you fight with the sword; if you retort and smite back when you are wronged, you quench the Spirit.*

— *Samuel Logan Brengle*

December 18

HE BROUGHT ME TO THE BANQUETINGHOUSE.

— Song of songs 2: 4

> *Jesus! I am resting, resting*
> *In the joy of what Thou art;*
> *I am finding out the greatness*
> *Of Thy loving heart*
>
> *Thou hast bid me gaze upon Thee,*
> *And Thy beauty fills my soul,*
> *For, by Thy transforming power,*
> *Thou hast made me whole.*
>
> *Jesus! I am resting, resting*
> *In the joy of what Thou art;*
> *I am finding out the greatness*
> *Of Thy loving heart.*

356

Oh, how great Thy loving kindness,
Vaster, broader than the sea:
Oh, how marvellous Thy goodness,
Lavished all on me!
Yes, I rest in Thee, Beloved,
Know what wealth of grace is Thine,
Know Thy certainty of promise,
And have made it mine.

Simply trusting Thee, Lord Jesus,
I behold Thee as Thou art,
And Thy love, so pure, so changeless,
Satisfies my heart;
Satisfies its deepest longings,
Meets, supplies its every need,
Compasseth me round with blessings:
Thine is love indeed.

Ever lift Thy face upon me,
As I work and wait for Thee;
Resting 'neath Thy smile, Lord Jesus,
Earth's dark shadows flee.
Brightness of my Father's glory,
Sunshine of my Father's face,
Keep me ever trusting, resting,
Fill me with Thy grace.

— *J. S. Pigott*

December 19

I FEAR LEST, BY ANY MEANS, AS THE SERPENT
BEGUILED EVE THROUGH .HIS SUBTLETY, SO
YOUR MINDS SHOULD BE CORRUPTED FROM
THE SIMPLICITY THAT IS IN CHRIST.
— 2 Cor. 11; 31 A. V.

*There is a great battle to-day over the use and control
of the mind, not only in the world, but among the children of God.* The Apostle Paul writing in 2 Cor. 10: 3—5
says: "For though living in the flesh, my warfare is not
waged according to the flesh. For the weapons which I
wield are not of fleshly weakness, but mighty in the
strength of God to overthrow the strongholds of the
Adversaries. Thereby can I overthrow the *reasonings* of
the disputer and *pull down all lofty bulwarks* that raise
themselves against the knowledge of God, and bring
every *rebellious thought* into capitivity and subjection to
Christ" *(Conybeare).*

The *mind of the Christian* is also the strategic centre
of the "war on the saints" which Satan wages with
ceaseless and fiendish skill. And for this reason. The *mind
is the vehicle for the Spirit of God,* dwelling in the spirit
of the believer, to transmit to others the truth of God,
which alone can remove the deceptions of Satan which
fill the minds of all who are in the darkness of nature.
If the Holy Spirit is dwelling in the regenerate spirit
have you considered the question of His *outlet?* If it were
only by speech you would be an oracle! But there are no
"oracles" on earth now. The *"oracles of God" are the
Scriptures.* The Word of God is being displaced not only
by the Higher Critics, but by many of God's own people
by their taking supernatural "revelations" as being of
equal authority with the written Scriptures. There are
wrecked lives because they have turned from the Word
of God to what they call direct revelation. There is a
direct revelation by God the Holy Ghost illuminating

the Word of God, and putting it into the spirit, but not apart from the Scriptures.

The Holy Spirit and the mind of the believer.

If the *mind is the vehicle of the Spirit* it is absolutely necessary that the Spirit of God should have full possession of it, with every "rebellious thought" brought into captivity to Christ. The Holy Spirit, dwelling in the spirit, needs the mind as a channel for expression, but it may be so blocked up, and filled with other things, that He is unable to transmit all He desires to do. A "blocked" mind means the spirit unexpressed, and a spirit unexpressed is a stoppage of the outflow of the Spirit of God to others.

— *J. Penn-Lewis*

December 20

LET THIS MIND BE IN YOU. — Phil. 2: 5

In Ephes. 1: 18, we read, "The eyes of your understanding" being "filled with light". *Here is the mind illumined by the Spirit.* It is the vehicle of light. You *see* with the mind, you *feel* with the spirit. David said, "My *spirit* made diligent search". The mind is filled with light from God in the spirit, illuminating the mind. This brings into action the perceptive faculty of the mind, whereby the believer is able to spiritually discern spiritual things. The various marginal readings of 1 Cor. 2: 13, show the new mind in use. It is able to "discriminate," "examine," "combine," "compare" and "explain" spiritual things which the "natural" man knows nothing about. The perceptive faculty of the mind renewed by the Spirit of God enables us more clearly to know how to prove the good and acceptable will of God. "If a man walketh in the day he stumbleth not," said the Lord. In broad daylight a man does not need to fall over stones in his path before he sees them. *And so it is spiritually. With a new mind filled with light by the Spirit, the believer sees the path wherein he should walk, and discerns the will of God clearly without the confusion and perplexities of the partially renewed mind.*

— J. Penn-Lewis

Blessed Spirit deliver me this day from carnal reasonings!

December 21

I WILL NEVER LEAVE THEE NOR FORSAKE THEE. — Heb. 13: 5

What a strong negation is here! Literally the words are: "I will not not leave thee, neither will I not not forsake thee." *The revised Version has it thus:* "I will in no wise fail thee, neither will I in any wise forsake thee." Says Weymouth: "I will never let you go; I will never forsake you." He will not merely *see* us through; He will *accompany* us through. For the Christ who exhorts His servants, saying: "Go," encourages them, saying, "Lo, I am with you alway." This promise, moreover, is for *all ways*. When our way is rosy, and life is a sweet thing, He joyfully says: "I will never leave thee, nor forsake thee." And when our way is gloomy, and life has lost its zest, then into the topsy-turvy of our troubled hearts He comes, and sweetly whispers: "Thee forsake, nor thee leave, never will I." A bright boy, who had often heard his father use these words, lay dying. By his bed knelt a sorrowful parent, and prayed: "Lord, in Thy great mercy, make good now to our laddie Thine own promise, 'I will never leave thee, nor forsake thee.'" Quickly from the sick-bed that prayer was interrupted by these words, in gasping tones: "Never will I." "What is it, my boy?" gently asked the father. "Never will I," repeated the lad, with great effort. Then, understanding, the boy's father said: "Thee forsake nor thee leave never will I." And from the pale, parched lips came this: "That's it, daddy." For in those hushed moments when two worlds were meeting, the heart of that boy was realizing the fact of Christ's unfailing presence. *His assertion is our assurance, His statement our security;* and since He has said: "I will never leave thee, nor forsake thee," therefore we may say: "I will not fear."

— *R. D. Johnson*

I will not fear!

December 22

DO ALL THINGS WITHOUT MURMURING AND DISPUTINGS. — Phil 2: 14

One of the first requisites in the homelife is politeness. Why should a man cease to treat his wife as a lady because she is always at his side? Is she not as sensitive to notice a slight, as quick to appreciate a tiny attention, as ever she was? Are the trifling courtesies of life robbed of their fragrance, because yielded by her husband? Still, if she drops her handkerchief, he must pick it up, but she must not drop it simply to test him. Still, if she rises to leave the diningroom, he must open the door. Still, if he does not catch what she says, he must say, I beg your pardon. Still, he must save her needless exertion. Let him always act as a Knight in the Order of Christian gentleness, of Christ's highbred nobility. *Noblesse oblige toujours.* And she must always be the true-born gentlewoman, because she is one of the King's daughters.

There must be, also, the willingness to ask pardon and to forgive. Sometimes it has happened that the one has been nervously overwrought, and the other unduly sensitive, and a word has flashed like a rapier from its sheath, causing a smart for many an hour afterward, hurting the one who inflicted it even more than the one who suffered. *How well would it be if the unkindness were instantly followed by the frank confession and restoration, like God's, to the old blessed place of sunlight.* This were better far than to leave the matter to right itself, or to act as though it had never happened, whereas each surely knows that it has left a scar. It is not enough to bring a present from the city, thus, to salve over the sin. Let the poison be pressed out of the wound, so only can it be properly healed. Let there be the frank confession.

— *F. B. Meyer*

December 23

BE KINDHEARTED, FORGIVING EACH OTHER, EVEN AS GOD ALSO IN CHRIST FORGAVE YOU.
— Eph. 4: 32, R. V.; Math. 18: 15—20

My forgiveness is to be brave. I am not to wait for the offender to confess his fault; at once I should seek to end the quarrel. Even if he resents my approach to him, and is once more angry with me, I am to go. GOD strengthen me for what is so delicate and hard.

My forgiveness is to be quiet. Alone I must seek out the brother who has wronged me; and, if that is not sufficient, there must be as little publicity as there can be. How much I aggravate matters, if I make my griefs common property and talk of them everywhere!

My forgiveness is to be potent and permanent. GOD adds mighty sanctions to it, when it is gone about in the right spirit. If the wrongdoer will not repent, the sin I bind on his conscience GOD binds too. If I win him to sorrow, GOD forgives as certainly as I do. Ah, what solemnities are here!

My forgiveness is to be prayerful. When I carry it to the Throne in company with a friend as full of yearning and love as I, Our Lord hears and grants our petition. Selfishness gains no boon from Him; but pure affection does rise to His ear and win His response.

My forgiveness is to be Christly. This is my encouragement that, when I practise it in the true fashion, He is with me and with those whose spirit is akin to mine. He never forgets His little flock. Where its members kneel, He bends over them. — *Alexander Smellie*

362

AND THE WORD WAS MADE FLESH. — John 1: 14

THE ROYAL BIRTH

A thousand lamps within the palace burn,
Soft carpets for the tread;
All rich and costly are the broider'd wraps
That deck a royal bed.
But when the Prince of Life on earth was born,
'Twas not in stately room;
The lantern's feeble flame of light revealed
A stable lost in gloom;
And in a manger-bed our Lord was laid,
By Whose almighty pow'r were all things made.

With bated breath the courtiers waiting stand
To greet a royal birth,
And loudly is the news proclaimed abroad
That all may know on earth.
But when He came, the Promised One of old,
To dwell with Adam's race,
Within the crowded haunts of busy men
For Him was found no place.
So in the beasts' abode He oped His eyes,
Whose shining glance had held all Paradise.

This earth's proud empires fade and pass away,
Its kingdoms rise and fall,
Their rulers great, who once held fullest sway,
Death covers with his pall.
But that fair Babe, so still in Mary's arms,
As "Lullabye" she sings,
No pow'r in earth or hell can ever crush,
He is the King of kings!
Yet Jesus is to us His sweetest name,
For as our Saviour first of all He came.

— *J. Fryer*

December 25

FOR GOD SO LOVED THE WORLD. — John 3: 16

In Genesis 3: 15 we have the Protoevangelion. That is, in this verse we have the fountainhead of all prophecies concerning God's glorious plan of salvation. The verse reads as follows: "And I will put enmity between thee and the woman, and between thy seed and her seed; it shall bruise thy head, and thou shalt bruise his heel." God promised that from the seed of the woman He would raise up the Emancipator and Deliverer to destroy the works of Satan. John 3: 16, therefore, is the fulfillment of Genesis 3: 15. "For God so loved the world, that he gave his only begotten Son, that whosoever believeth in Him should not perish, but have everlasting life." (See also Heb. 2: 14; 1 John 4: 14; Acts 3: 26; Gal. 4: 4).

— *James A. Stewart*

> *FOR GOD, the Lord of earth and Heaven,*
> *SO LOVED, and longed to see forgiven,*
> *THE WORLD in sin and pleasure mad,*
> *THAT HE GAVE the greatest gift He had*
> *HIS ONLY SON — to take our place,*
> *THAT WHOSOEVER — Oh, what grace!*
> *BELIEVETH, placing simple trust*
> *IN HIM, the righteous and the just,*
> *SHOULD NOT PERISH, lost in sin,*
> *BUT HAVE ETERNAL LIFE in Him.*

— *Barbara C. Ryberg*

Oh dear unsaved reader, receive God's beloved Son today and you will be saved!

December 26

HIS SPEECH IS THE VERY PERFECTION OF
SWEETNESS; YEA, IN HIMSELF IS THE CON-
CENTRATION OF LOVELINESS.

— Song of songs 5: 16, Spurrell

Blessed adorable Lord, I bless Thee that Thou art the
concentration of loveliness. Oh, to be transported to lofty
heights as I contemplate the glory and majesty of Thy
Person.

— James A. Stewart

December 27

APPLES OF GOLD. — Proverbs 25: 11

GOLDEN SAYINGS

I used to ask God if He would come and help me, then
I asked God if I might come and help Him; then I ended
by asking God to do His own work through me.

— Hudson Taylor

There is only one holy life; there is one victorious life
and that is the risen life of Christ lived in you.

— James A. Stewart

Let every sigh be changed into a hallelujah.

— Stockmeyer

Bend us, Oh God! Oh make us completely submissive
to Thee.

— Evan Roberts

It is not the rank of the messenger that counts, but the
ring of the message.

— Edward Last

December 28

GRACE IS POURED INTO THY LIPS.
— Psalm 45: 2

AN INVITATION TO PREACH
To James Hamilton

My dear Friend, will you excuse lack of ceremony and come down tomorrow to preach to us the unsearchable riches of Christ? Come, my dear sir, if you can, and refresh us with your company. Bring the fragrance of 'the bundle of Myrrh' (S o S 1: 13) along with you, and may grace be poured into your lips.

Your brother in Christ

— *Murray McCheyne*

December 29

SO SEND I YOU. — John 20: 21

So send I you, to labor unrewarded,
To serve unpaid, unloved, unsought, unknown,
To bear rebuke, to suffer scorn and scoffing,
So send I you, to toil for me alone.

So send I you, to bind the bruised and broken,
O'er wand'ring souls to work, to weep, to wake,
To bear the burdens of a world a-weary,
So send I you, to suffer for my sake.

So send I you, to loneliness and longing,
With heart a-hungering for the loved and known,
Forsaking home and kindred, friend and dear one,
So send I you, to know My love alone.

So send I you, to leave your life's ambition,
To die to dear desire, self-will resign,
To labor long and love where men revile you,
So send I you, to lose your life in Mine.

So send I you, to hearts made hard by hatred,
To eyes made blind because they will not see,
To spend, tho' it be blood — to spend and spare not,
So send I you, to taste of Calvary.
                              — *John W. Peterson*

What a blessing these lines have been to me!
Read them until the Spirit burns them into your heart.
                              — *James A. Stewart*

December 30

AND THE DEVIL SAID UNTO HIM. — Luke 4: 3

THE TEMPTATIONS OF THE SANCTIFIED

Sanctification does not place the soul beyond temptation. On the contrary, it brings it to exceptional exposure.
The experience furnishes a new basis for attack. *Our
Lord's temptation followed His baptism, not only as a
matter of time, but of consequence.* The temptation was
the outcome of the experience. It was upon the testimony of the baptism the attack was made. If He was
tempted like as we are it follows that, as we become like
Him, we shall be tempted as He was. The wilderness is
never far from the Jordan. The relations of the natural
and the spiritual have to be adjusted, and Satan will seek
to win us back through the demands of the flesh, the
problem of bread, and the obligations of common toil. If
he fails there, he will test along the avenue of courageous faith, and tempt to presumption and vain glory. The
second often succeeds where the first fails. Grace is made
the occasion of sin, when we disobey God under cover
of faith. The final temptation of Spirit-filled people is to
use carnal weapons in spiritual aims. The world is accepted under plea of its service to the kingdom. The peril
of these temptations is in their subtlety. To the saints
Satan comes as an angel of light. The beast is transformed

into the likeness of a lamb. The very elect are deceived, if they cease to live in the Spirit through whom comes discernment as well as power. God is able to keep us from stumbling, and to set us before the presence of His glory without blemish, in exceeding joy, but we need to watch and pray lest we enter into temptation.

— *Samuel Chadwick*

December 31

THE WATCHWORD OF THE NIGHT

Christ is coming! Ringing heavenward
Voices through the night —
Waiting with uplifted foreheads
Stand the sons of light.
Heaven-lit eyes and hearts all burning,
Eager feet earth's wild flowers spurning;
Lip to lip the cry repeating.
Heart to heart the answer beating,
Christ is coming! — Come, Lord, come!

Christ is coming! In a moment,
Shall the shout resound;
And the voice of heaven's archangel,
And God's trumpet sound.
Then the sleeping saints arisen,
Bursting from their earthly prison,
With the living upward soaring,
See their Lord with eyes adoring,
Christ is coming! — Come, Lord, come!

Christ is coming! Speed the message
Writ on heart and brain,
'Till, from all the courts of heaven,
Sounds the last Amen.
'Till the watchmen of the dawning

Shall call out the blessed morning; —
And the glad cry shall be given,
As the earth-born rise to heaven,
Christ is coming! — Come, Lord, come!

Christ is coming! We are waiting
'Mid the shadows dim:
Longing 'till the night's dark pinions
Fold their plumes to Him.
Waiting by each gate of sorrow,
Thinking of the glad to-morrow;
Standing 'neath His banner, keeping
Watch, while all the world is sleeping.
Christ is coming! — Come, Lord, come!

Christ is coming! Christ is coming! —
We have waited long;
Eager for the first glad rapture
Of the endless song.
Eager to bow down before Thee;
Longing, Saviour to adore Thee;
Waiting 'till our lips forgiven,
Shall repeat Thy praise in heaven,
THOU ART COMING! — Come, Lord, COME!

— Heyman Wreford

Dear Reader, are you ready for His coming?